SONDHEIM

Martin Gottfried

PHOTOGRAPHS BY MARTHA SWOPE
AND OTHERS

HARRY N. ABRAMS, INC., PUBLISHERS

Editor: Robert Morton
Designer: Dirk Luykx
Photo Editor: John K. Crowley

Library of Congress Cataloging-in-Publication Data
Gottfried, Martin.
  Stephen Sondheim / Martin Gottfried.
    p.   cm.
  Includes index.
  ISBN 0–8109–3844–8
  1. Sondheim, Stephen.   2. Composers—United States—Biography.
I. Title.
ML410.S6872G8   1993
782.1'4'092—dc20
[B]   93–6931

Illustrations copyright © 1993 Harry N. Abrams, Inc.
Text copyright © 1993 Martin Gottfried

Published in 1993 by Harry N. Abrams, Incorporated, New York
A Times Mirror Company

Printed and bound in Japan

Above:
*The London company in the 1992 anthology
show,* Putting It Together, *featured Diana
Rigg (second from left), better known as a
stage and television dramatic actress.*

Endpapers:
*Sondheim took a bow amid applauding
friends, performers, and musicians (Lee
Remick is on his right) at the 1985 Carnegie
Hall tribute.*

Back of endpaper:
*Sondheim's movie music has ranged from the
richly atmospheric orchestral score for the 1974
film* Stavisky, *directed by Alain Resnais, to the
sultry "Sooner or Later," from* Dick Tracy,
*which won the Academy Award for the Best
Song of 1991. Here Madonna sings it at the
award ceremonies as she had sung it in the film.*

Previous pages:
*The first anthology of the composer-lyricist's
work was* Side By Side By Sondheim,
*introduced in London and moved to New
York in 1977.*

CONTENTS

Dedication

This book is dedicated to Burt Shevelove, who proved that brains and humor are the keys to quality.

ACKNOWLEDGMENTS

Stephen Sondheim on the set of Sunday in the Park with George.

In the course of writing *Sondheim*, I sought background information and advice from, first of all, one of his early teachers, Professor Milton Babbitt who, along with Paul Gemignani and Jonathan Tunick, helped describe Stephen Sondheim's training and musical processes. Directors Harold Prince, James Lapine, and Jerry Zaks provided production background on the various shows, and Angela Lansbury remembered what it was like to work with Sondheim from an actor's point of view. As for the biographical chapter, Susan Blanchard, Katharine Hepburn, Mary Rodgers, and Jimmy Hammerstein had the memories and the anecdotal instincts that make a writer's life easier.

I am grateful to all of them for having been so generous with their time and such fun to talk to. I am also lucky to have spoken about Sondheim and his shows over the years with Arthur Laurents, Jule Styne, Dean Jones, Elaine Stritch, Barbara Barrie, John McMartin, Harvey Evans, Patricia Birch, Len Cariou, Dorothy Loudon, Larry Gelbart, and Jerome Robbins; lucky as well and very glad to have talked—before they died—with Burt Shevelove, Jack Gilford, Leonard Bernstein, Zero Mostel, Larry Kert, Boris Aronson, Michael Bennett, and the incomparable Dorothy Hammerstein.

This book reflects Sondheim's work in its reasonable organization and overall beauty, and that is the doing of designer Dirk Luykx. The copy editor, Peter Simon, cleaned up my misspelled articles and misplaced semi-colons. Paul McKibbins of Rilting Music all but relieved me of the tedious task of rounding up lyrics permissions, for which I am almost religiously grateful. Two old friends helped me with the rest—John Crowley, who always chooses the photographs for my Abrams books with acute sensitivity; and of course my editor Robert Morton, who as usual was heartless in his demands for first reducing my text, then shortening it and after that, making a few final slashes—all and always in the pursuit of the best possible book. I do thank them here and now.

I am grateful, most of all, to Stephen Sondheim for the letter he wrote in 1964, not (as I presumed when opening it) in thanks for my early support of his work, but to criticize my praise for Lorenz Hart. That letter was my first insight into his cranky, hypercritical and dazzling mind. It was also the beginning of conversations over the years, leading up to the many hours of interviews he provided for the purposes of this book.

Finally, I appreciate Sondheim for his talent, which has remained astonishing; for his truly formidable intelligence; and for his integrity and values, which are inspiring in the brittle world of show business and the larger, actually more cynical world that surrounds it. He is probably the only subject I would have trusted to read a manuscript about himself and restrict his comments to the facts. Whenever there is any talk of personal honor, he could well serve as the reference point. Without his endlessly aggravating and nitpicking notes, this book could not begin to accurately reflect the preciseness of his splendid mind or the beauty of his art.

Martin Gottfried

INTRODUCTION

"It's going to be terrific," Harold Prince said. "We're going to be able to do anything we want to do!"

"Oh, God," Sondheim thought, "he's crazy. What a fool! We're going to be dead and starving in the gutter in two years. What is he talking about?"

Stephen Sondheim is the giant of the modern musical stage. He is to today's Broadway what Kern and Gershwin, Hammerstein and Hart were to yesterday's. Those great composers and lyricists and their merely mortal colleagues created our vast library of American popular song. Their music is catchy and endearing and often lovely. Their lyrics are tender or clever or touching. We know these songs, to use the apt phrase, *by heart*, and they have become a beloved part of our culture.

Stephen Sondheim has written only a few such songs. "Send in the Clowns," is the best known. Rather than composing songs that are enjoyed outside of their shows, he has set his sights on different objectives. He has developed a kind of music that transcends song to serve broader theatrical purposes. It is as a composer of theater music, and as a writer of words sung to that music, that he has achieved greatness. It is a unique greatness.

Because each of his shows is different, so is its music. There is a startling difference between the scores for *Follies*, *Sweeney Todd*, and *Sunday in the Park with George*, and yet Sondheim's unique musical voice sings through each. Indeed, once the ear is attuned to it, there is scarcely a more beautiful, intriguing, and engaging music in the modern theater.

The words he writes to suit his music are not merely graceful, smart, and technically correct as lyrics; they do not only serve to make dialogue and even entire scenes musical. They express some of the feelings and anxieties that are at the center of our lives in our time.

In a field notorious for early burnout, as Sondheim approached his mid-sixties he was the same theatrical adventurer he had been as a youth. And if despite his best intentions, adventure was still unwelcome on the commercial stage, he stubbornly and resolutely continued to dare it. For four decades, a Stephen Sondheim show promised sophistication, originality, artistry, and substance. By setting so high a standard for himself, he has been the conscience of all Broadway musicals. The question is, how important are Broadway musicals?

It would be wonderful if all the world were overtures and glitter, but sorry to say there are more important things than show business. It is even possible that without musicals, life as we know it might still continue. That is why, more important than the shows Stephen Sondheim has helped create, more important than his powerful and transporting scores or his dramatic and stimulating lyrics is his artistic idealism and its underlying tenet: the belief that our best lies in our intelligence. For him the creative act is a knowledgeable one. Art is not something that simply arrives with a brainstorm; it is the product of art-making, a composition of training, competence, craftsmanship, technique, and *thinking*. That is the theme of *Sunday in the Park with George*. The painting, the poem, the music are the *result* of this process and come at its *end,* not at the start.

It is to such a linking of art with intelligence and productivity that this book is dedicated.

Beginning with *West Side Story*, and with but one exception (*Do I Hear a Waltz?*) that proved he could survive adverse conditions, every show with which Stephen Sondheim has been involved has been a work of serious artistic intention. Every musical for which he has written both the music and the lyrics has been of uncompromised integrity—and each one unique, each attempting the dangerous or, as he says, the "unexpected." Their subjects have included marriage and divorce (*Company*), age and life choices (*Follies*), love and sex (*A Little Night Music*), betrayal and revenge (*Sweeney Todd, The Demon Barber of Fleet Street*). He has written shows about culture shock (*Pacific Overtures*), lost innocence (*Into the Woods*), even the mind of the murderous outsider (*Assassins*). There is not another writer in the American theater, no composer or playwright, present or past, who has been more unswervingly and productively high-minded.

This book intends to explain, illustrate, criticize, and celebrate Sondheim's work. It means to champion, in the process, his uncompromised values on a Broadway whose producers and audiences have grown intellectually lazy and artistically timid. He seems afraid only of the clichéd, the banal, the careless, and the unintelligent.

He is in this way a hero.

PORTRAIT OF THE ARTIST AS A YOUNG MAN

The opening night of *West Side Story* should have made Stephen Sondheim happier. On that evening, September 26, 1957, he began to fulfill an ambition that had consumed him since childhood—to have a musical on Broadway—and he was only twenty-seven years old.

But he was not happy that evening. The first review ignored him, the second was bad, and thirty-five years later, as the reigning giant of the Broadway musical theater, with wealth, recognition, acclaim, a close circle of friends, and all the perquisites of success bestowed upon him, he still remembered, "Atkinson [of *The New York Times*] totally ignored me. . . . When it's your first show, it's really upsetting."

Stephen Sondheim seems to find for himself the darkest view, the one that envelops him in a shadow that he cannot escape. Even his sense of humor is mordant. It is a gloom that can make him seem arrogant, remote, and even forbidding.

His body language can be best described as "uncomfortable." When seated he scrunches, and when standing he tries to scrunch. He is usually either squinting or closing his eyes or covering his face with his hands. It is as if he is turning his body, his mind, his entire self inward, so as to concentrate all the more on thinking and talking.

He speaks in a low and soft voice, with plenty of "ums" for thinking. Every thought and word seems mulled over and chewed on until it is right. Indeed, the way some people are athletes, Sondheim appears to enjoy the exercise of *thinking*—of literal thoughtfulness and of regular thoughtfulness too, for although he can be frank to the point of cruelty, he can also be the most sensitive of people.

All of this thinking seems to be articulated, as if intelligence doesn't count until it is put into words. He *loves* words; he loves to talk and does so in complex, qualified, and subclaused sentences, editing himself as he goes along. And his favorite social thing seems to be explaining: It almost doesn't matter whether the subject is an antique puzzle, the source of a word, or the nature of a chord progression. It makes for intense, focused, and challenging dialogues that demand as much of a conversational partner as he demands of himself.

But beneath the verbal superstructure, behind the facade of arrogance, and inside the exterior of cool logic—there in the dark is a "neurotic" in his own sense of the word: an uncommon, unclichéd, and unpredictable human being. Likewise, beyond the brilliance of his mind, his insistence on logical precision and the exactitude of language, lies the humanity of his music.

Indeed, this person is not unlike song, in which words lend coherence, explanation, and justification to abstract, pure, and defenseless music.

Stephen Joshua Sondheim spent the first ten years of his life in a way typical of New York's Jewish upper middle class in the 1930s. His parents lived in a rather elegant apartment building, the San Remo on handsome Central Park West, and they sent him to progressive private schools like Ethical Culture and Fieldston.

His father was a successful Seventh Avenue dress manufacturer (Herbert Sondheim, Inc.) whose chief designer was the former Janet Fox, nicknamed "Foxy." She was also Mrs. Herbert Sondheim, and Stephen, their only child, was born on March 22, 1930.

Sondheim's mother, Janet Fox, always called "Foxy."

There was a connection between the garment industry and the theater. Broadway shows were where most Seventh Avenue manufacturers entertained the store buyers who came to New York twice a year to look over the new lines. Herbert Sondheim took his visiting buyers to the musicals and then brought the musicals home with him, picking out their hit tunes on his grand piano in the living room. He would also play for his young son, who years later would "remember when I was a kid sitting on the piano bench and my father putting my small hand on his little finger—because he always played the melody with the top note. He played essentially chords, with the pinky making the melody. So he was a natural musician," and, Sondheim adds, "a terrific fellow—wonderful, wonderful."

The youngster was soon taking piano lessons ("like any nice upper-class Jewish boy"). His mother would later tell *Newsweek*, "When Steve was only four, he was picking out tunes on the piano. Aaron Copland said that he obviously had tremendous talent." Whether or not that was true, he did begin taking lessons at six, and, Sondheim remembers, his mother would call him out to play for her cocktail parties. But as any youngster would, he "got tired of being dragged out for company" and, because of it, quit lessons entirely.

When he was ten, his father left Foxy for Alicia Babé. The divorce agreement allowed weekly visits, and father and son would often spend those days at the big presentation theaters in Times Square—the Paramount, the Strand, the Capitol, the Roxy, Radio City Music Hall—where stage shows alternated with movies. Herbert also continued taking Stephen to the theater, as he had been doing since the boy's childhood. The first show Sondheim remembers seeing was *White Horse Inn*, with Kitty Carlisle. He also went with his dad to see Rodgers and Hart's *The Boys from Syracuse* and Jerome Kern and Oscar Hammerstein's *Very Warm for May*. There had been the occasional play (*Arsenic and Old Lace*, for instance), but musicals were the great love of Herbert Sondheim.

Although the youngster had thus far been sent to progressive schools, Foxy transferred him to the New York Military Academy in Cornwall-on-Hudson after the divorce. It seems a startling change, but in response to suggestions that such schools might be considered disciplinarian, he insists that, in fact, he enjoyed the academy. There was something in its organization, its very strictness, that appealed to the orderliness of his developing mind, and there was something else he liked there: "They had the second largest manual organ in the state. I just loved all the buttons and gadgets."

In 1941, a year into the academy and already two grades ahead for his age (eleven), he was at home one afternoon, between school's end and the start of summer camp, when his mother's friend Dorothy Hammerstein arrived for a visit. In tow was Mrs. Hammerstein's ten-year-old son, Jimmy. Youngsters detest such forced meetings, but this one made for an instant friendship.

The afternoon began, as so many childhood afternoons still do, with a game of Monopoly, and at the end of that first visit the boys informed their mothers that Steve was coming the next weekend to the Hammersteins' summer place in Doylestown, Pennsylvania. Within a week, camp was canceled so that Steve and Jimmy could spend the entire summer together with the Hammersteins. After that, as Jimmy says, "Emotionally, Steve never left."

Jimmy's father was Oscar Hammerstein II, the lyricist of such songs as "All the Things You Are," "The Last Time I Saw Paris," and the wonderful score for *Show Boat*. He was then forty-six years old and a very big man, six feet, four inches and solid. His clothes were always rumpled, his hair was clipped frizzy, crew-cut style, and his complexion was landscaped with acne. Oscar Greeley Clendenning Hammerstein II was also the most urbane and courtly of men, having once been advised by Mae West, no less, that "the theater ain't for you kid. You got too much class!"

Everyone seemed to agree, none more than his beautiful wife, Dorothy, who remembered, "Maybe he would use swear words and things but I never heard him do it because he was not that kind of a man around the house. He was a *gent,*" and in fact, as a couple, Oscar and Dorothy Hammerstein seemed to be class itself.

Sondheim with his mother.

"Ockie," as he liked to call himself (in college it had been "Ock"), had suffered many flops since *Show Boat* in 1927. It was a measure of his character that he could still be optimistic, productive, and cheerful. Late each afternoon, he would emerge from his study after a full day's writing (he was probably working on *Carmen Jones*, his Southern black adaptation of the Bizet opera, for he had begun to despair of ever reemerging on Broadway). "We were not allowed to disturb him," Jimmy remembered, "but once Dad was finished, he would forget whatever mood work had got him into. Then the games would begin."

Besides Jimmy, the Hammerstein family included children from previous marriages, among them Dorothy's daughter, Susan, and Oscar's son, Billy, and they all played games. Steve and Jimmy might spend a rainy day digging obscure card games out of a book of Hoyle's rules, but games of all kinds were a way of life for the entire household: croquet and tennis in the late afternoon, then crosswords, anagrams, and spelling competitions after dinner. And all of this family fun seemed exactly what the young Stephen Sondheim had been waiting for, especially the word games played with Oscar—this affectionate, cultured, sagacious, towering, and perfectly perfect father figure.

A few years later, the youngster would be submitting his own puns and anagrams puzzle to the *New York Times* ("They rejected it," he'd remember, "but they said I was perspicacious . . . which I had to look up").

He "osmosed," as he put it, into the Hammerstein household. "They were my surrogate family. My mother was a difficult lady and I had a difficult time with her."

"Difficult" was hardly the word for Foxy Sondheim. "She was too dangerous a mother to call even 'decent,'" Jimmy Hammerstein would later say. "She had to be the worst mother I've ever seen. [Steve] adopted us and if you prized your mental health it was a sensible emotional position to take. And Dad always had time to talk to him." Jimmy's half-sister, Susan, was perhaps even more sensitive to young Sondheim's inner suffering. "As a child he was full of rage and pain and anger," she remembered. "Ockie seemed able to bypass that and get to some other place in him."

Indeed, the relationship with Oscar Hammerstein would come to shape and inspire Sondheim's life. "I wrote for the theater," he would frankly say, "in order to be like Oscar. I have no doubt that if he'd been a geologist, I would have become a geologist."

Doylestown is in Bucks County, a fashionable section of Pennsylvania. (Foxy Sondheim bought a farm there, too, but while she rented her land to farmers, the Hammerstein place, Highland Farm, which everyone called "The Farm," was their own working farm, even winning its share of cattle-breeding ribbons. There Stephen Sondheim was to become a Broadway musicals wolf boy, raised in a show business world far from conventional society. He would live not with ordinary citizens but among creatures who dwelt in theaters and spoke a language of opening numbers, ensemble turns, and comedy routines. In this alien land, blockbuster hits and showstoppers were life's important things, rather than partnerships and tax write-offs. Thus Sondheim would be ill equipped for a career in pursuit of acquisition, unfit for a world where creativity and laughter were not matters of everyday life.

As the unhappy, traditional side of his boyhood receded, he left the military academy in 1942 and went off to George School in Newtown, Pennsylvania. In the prep school hierarchy, George may not have been as fancy as Andover, Exeter, or Groton, even though at $1,400 a year it was just as expensive. More important, as a Friends Society school, it provided an excellent and progressive education.

As a Friends Society school, it also made certain religious demands—attendance, for instance, at twice-weekly Quaker meetings—but that could hardly have bothered Foxy Sondheim, who, to say the least, had a detached relationship with her Judaism (Sondheim frankly considered her to be anti-Semitic). As for himself, he was not given a bar mitzvah and in fact does not recall ever having been in a synagogue during his youth. He did, however, inherit a sense of Jewishness from his father, along with an affection for the Yiddish expressions that were part of everyday conversation in the garment industry.

A very young Stephen Sondheim with his father, Herbert, on the lawn of a vacation house in Larchmont, New York.

If a Quaker school appealed to Foxy Sondheim's interest in progressive education and "gentileness," George School had other attractions for her son: It was a mere fourteen miles from The Farm, and Jimmy was scheduled to enroll two years later. By then Stephen was spending so much time with the Hammersteins that they gave him his own bed, and, Jimmy remembered, "He was enmeshed in the web, the fabric of my family." Indeed, the next Christmas vacation he would go to The Farm straight from school, skipping Foxy entirely, and the Hammersteins seemed to like it that way. "We had a very traditional kind of Christmas around the house," Jimmy would recall, "and Steve was part of that tradition."

Sondheim always talked freely about Oscar Hammerstein's importance in his life, personally and professionally, but he was more circumspect about his relationship with Dorothy Hammerstein. If, as Jimmy Hammerstein felt, "Steve had no positive ties to his mother," he developed a profound love for this handsome, elegant, wise, and entirely wonderful woman. And the feelings were mutual. "In a peculiar way," Dorothy said, "he was my child."

Things had actually worsened between Foxy and him. Jimmy once found himself at her farm for lunch, sitting between mother and son and cringing in the cross fire. "It was all sarcasm and innuendo with them facing each other. He was just a kid but he dished it as well as she did. They were like two adults only he wasn't grown up yet and so it was just weird—something out of a play you didn't want to see. I'd be mute, sitting there between them. I'd never heard stuff like that before. 'Really!' And 'What about so-and-so you screwed out of the business?' The only thing that kept [Steve's] psyche from becoming weird was his alternative home with us."

Of course no adolescent can entirely escape the affront of an emotionally abusive mother. Doubtless this teenager had to expend some of his brilliance on defense systems, the most immediately effective of which was escape on a bicycle to the Hammersteins.

By the time Jimmy caught up with him at George School, Sondheim had developed a coterie of friends, girls as well as boys (he would always have a circle of female friends). "He was both standoffish and social," Hammerstein recalls. "He was a driven kid with early ambition. He wanted to get on with life. Do everything." And he was all of fourteen years old.

At George he resumed piano lessons and even gave recitals. "My right hand was terrific," he would later remember, "but I'm extremely right-handed and the amount of work I would have had to do to make my left hand viable was insane." Nevertheless he considered the possibility of a concert career until, during a school recital, he forgot the middle part of a Chopin Polonaise-Fantasie. Thinking quickly, he replayed the first section. The audience didn't seem to notice, but he renounced performing ever after. He never would be a facile pianist, although he would be able to play his own scores very well. (His singing of them, which is close to terrible, is the one area in which he is a typical songwriter.)

As a youngster, then, he was productive and focused, as if concentrating on work and turning outward to avoid contact with an inner unhappiness. Certainly the stabilizing presence of Oscar Hammerstein—his patience, his love, and his combination of intellectualism and idealism—lent the youngster support and direction. In later years Sondheim would say, "He saved my life." He would also say that Oscar was probably a better father to him than to Jimmy, Billy, or Susan. Perhaps, in some curious way, Hammerstein needed a surrogate son as much as Sondheim needed a surrogate father. His stepdaughter Susan said, "Ockie was able to give something to Stevie that he couldn't give to his own sons. The relationship was good for both of them."

During sophomore year at prep school, he began writing his first show—"I'm sure," he says, "just to imitate Oscar." Meantime Hammerstein had just scored a tremendous comeback in his first collaboration with Richard Rodgers. Their musical, *Oklahoma!*, was a hit of hits, and taking a personal advertisement in *Variety*, he listed his recent string of flops, scrawling beneath, "I've Done It Before and I Can Do It Again!"

The George School show, the first-ever Stephen Sondheim musical, was called *By George!*, and like so many school shows, it was a satire of campus life with the teachers' names changed for laughs. He collaborated on the script with a couple of classmates and wrote the score. He still has it—"all imitation commercial theater songs."

By George!, he thought, "was pretty terrific," and he asked Oscar to read it "as if it were just a musical that crossed your desk as a producer." Then he conjured up "visions of being the first fifteen-year-old to have a show on Broadway."

Next morning Hammerstein telephoned and suggested that the youngster come over for the review.

"Now you really want me to treat this as if it were by somebody I don't know?"

"Yes, please," the boy urged.

"Well, in that case," Oscar said, "it's the worst thing I ever read in my life."

That could bring tears to an adolescent's eyes and nearly did.

"I didn't say it wasn't talented," Hammerstein hastily added. "I said it was terrible and if you want to know why it's terrible I'll tell you."

With that the famous Broadway librettist-lyricist who had written *Show Boat* and *Oklahoma!* combed over *By George!*, beginning with the first stage direction. From afternoon until dusk he turned pages, showing, as Sondheim remembered, "how to structure songs, how to build them with a beginning and a development and an ending . . . how to introduce character, what relates a song to character . . . four hours of the most *packed* information. I dare say, at the risk of hyperbole, that I learned more that afternoon than most people learn about songwriting in a lifetime."

Sondheim has related the story of that afternoon in countless interviews over the years, not only describing the genesis of his career but, in the process, paying homage to his mentor. It was of course an extraordinary stroke of luck for him, both professionally and personally.

Indeed, if this were a story about the Horatio Alger of songwriters, it could not seem more contrived: a young man growing up in love with Broadway musicals, being foster-fathered and now tutored by the theater's most significant librettist-lyricist, Oscar Hammerstein II, whose career spanned operetta (*The Student Prince* with Sigmund Romberg), the landmark *Show Boat* written with the founding father of American popular music, Jerome Kern, and now *Oklahoma!*, another trailblazing show and the newest and biggest hit of all; an Oscar Hammerstein who was dedicated to two basics in all of life, progress and teaching. And his one and only student was Stephen Sondheim.

It was this teenager upon whom Hammerstein was lavishing his dedication; Sondheim, whom he had chosen as his spiritual son, the beneficiary and repository for his most dearly held convictions. It was as if the man had decided to bequeath the best in himself—his theatrical standards, his social idealism, and his personal morality—to this boy. Teachers seek immortality through their students, and perhaps Oscar Hammerstein sought his in Stephen Sondheim.

Hammerstein outlined a future course of study. As the first assignment, the youth was to write a show (all of it—book, music, and lyrics) that was based on a good play. Next would come a musical made from a flawed play. The third assignment would be to base a show on a work that was not written for the stage at all, such as a short story or a novel. Finally he was to write an original musical.

The relationship with his mother continued to be very painful, and in an effort to escape it, the precocious, stagestruck, worldly yet naive youngster informed her that he would rather not live with her anymore. He moved into his father's house, which Herbert had been renting in Stamford, Connecticut. Not that young Stephen would often be there or that he considered anywhere preferable to The Farm, but whenever he did come home from school, home was now with Herbert and Alicia. They'd married and had two sons, Herbert, Jr., and Walter, and it seemed to Jimmy Hammerstein that "Steve liked having kid brothers." But his heart was in Doylestown with Oscar and Dorothy, Jimmy, Billy, and Susan, and it was there, in 1945, that he met Mary Rodgers. She was fourteen years old, and her parents had brought her along for a weekend visit.

In public Richard Rodgers and Oscar Hammerstein were as close as the stars and stripes, but in private their relationship was less intimate. Oscar, according to his wife, was not nearly as content as when he had worked with Jerome Kern. They had shared temperament, humor, values, and a joy in life. He and Dick Rodgers were simply different. Hammerstein was intellectually curious and absorbed by social and political issues; he was concerned with principles and integrity. As Sondheim says, "He was a moral man."

Richard Rodgers was of lighter weight, interested in writing songs, show business, drinks with his pals, and the occasional girlfriend. Hammerstein told Sondheim that he had "conflicted feelings" about his partner, and his stepdaughter, Susan, felt, "If they had not been in business together, I don't think they would have been particularly close." Perhaps the wives—the two Dorothys—were closer than the men, but even their friendship was business-related. At least that was how Dorothy Hammerstein perceived it. She was certainly the warmer of the two. Dorothy Rodgers was not quite as nasty as Foxy Sondheim, but she was bad enough for Mary to say, "It was my fantasy that my parents would die and I would be adopted by the Hammersteins."

So besides their brightness and their love of Broadway musicals, Mary and Steve had in common the need for surrogate parents. In a saddening reference to such privileged children of parents who are not parents, he describes The Farm as "virtually an orphanage" for the likes of Mary and himself. And it was there that these two orphans with parents met.

"There was this boy hanging around," Mary would remember. Like her mother she was willowy and good-looking. Steve was not tall (and never would be, eventually stopping at five feet, eight and a half inches). He was also pudgy as well as being, as Mary put it, "a real slob." Nevertheless she found him immensely attractive.

When she first saw him at The Farm that weekend, she wasn't quite sure who he was, and he certainly didn't bother to introduce himself. "He was obviously not a Hammerstein but he was there all the time and he was perfectly fascinating. I had no idea what I was dealing with but there was a chess set there and we played and of course he beat me three times in a row, very handily and a little snottily, and I thought, 'Oooooh, I'm dealing with heavy-duty brains here.' "

Dorothy Hammerstein was a successful interior decorator, and she had carpeted and furnished the 150-year-old farm house with style. Sondheim once described this house as a place of "extraordinary serenity. The living room was dark and cool and chic." There was also a Steinway concert grand piano in it and Mary Rodgers was very impressed when this arrogant little fifteen-year-old Stephen Sondheim "sat down and played a great deal of Gershwin and I fell madly in love with him."

She went home thinking, "I've never met a mind like that in my entire life," and hoped, "maybe he'll write me a letter in Connecticut," where her parents had a country place, but "of course he never did."

The next year Sondheim was graduated from George School, and in the autumn of 1946, he entered Williams, the intimate (then 1,100 men), exclusive, and excellent college in Williamstown, Massachusetts. Although its music department was small, he decided—after a momentary consideration of mathematics—to major in composition and piano.

If Oscar Hammerstein was his first theater mentor, his first musical one was Robert Barrow, who was head of Williams's two-man music department. "He just turned my head," Sondheim remembered. "He was like a male Mary Poppins, snip-snap, no nonsense, a totally unromantic view of music and not music appreciation. His whole attitude toward music was that you make it like you make a table. It was all about craft. It was a totally disciplined, very clear-eyed view . . . what an F sharp is; very basic harmony and theory. I always thought that music was composed by sitting at the piano and the muse visits you. Barrow taught us . . . that art is hard work. [Sondheim would paraphrase that as "art isn't easy" in *Sunday in the Park with George*.] You learn the technique and then you put the notes down on paper and that's what music is."

Sondheim (far right) with the Hammersteins—Oscar, Dorothy, their son Jimmy— and Nedda Logan, wife of Joshua Logan. When Dorothy died, on August 3, 1987, Sondheim was devastated. At the funeral, he twice burst into tears.

Literally, "composing" does mean organizing, being orderly, and keeping under control. It is almost a description of Sondheim and a prescription for anyone's security. Perhaps it was comforting, or at least not risky, to deal with such dependables as composition and the mathematics of music (and in his spare time, the precision of lyrics). This is artistry within reason.

At school he composed a piano sonata and a piano suite. His influences, he says, were Gershwin, Stravinsky, Prokofiev, and his beloved Ravel, whom he "woke up to. But," he would add, when it came to songs, "most of my musical influences were from the theater: Porter, Jerome Kern."

At the end of freshman year he headed for Doylestown and the Hammersteins. That summer, the summer of 1947, Oscar was preparing for the production of *Allegro*, a Rodgers and Hammerstein musical in the modernist style of *Our Town*.

When rehearsals began in New York, Ockie got him a job as a gofer with the show. The seventeen-year-old typed scripts, ran out for coffee, hung around rehearsals, and even traveled to New Haven for the show's first tryout. "I got as far as the Boston opening before going back to college. That was my official baptism."

The first show he wrote at college was *Phinney's Rainbow*, so called because the president of Williams was James Phinney Baxter and there was a current Broadway hit named *Finian's Rainbow*. The musical was produced during Sondheim's sophomore year, and some of its material remains amusing, for instance, "How Do I Know?", a satire of "How Deep Is the Ocean?"

That song of Irving Berlin's was a series of questions (How much do I love you?/I'll tell you no lie,/How deep is the ocean?/How high is the sky?). Young Sondheim's satire has its sophomoric qualities—he was, after all, a sophomore—but it certainly is precocious.

> Why do I feel just the way I always feel,
> When my feelings will never show?
> You said good-bye when I said hello,

And I asked you when
And you said I would know!

But how will I know when I know
That you said no?
I just don't know!

He acted too, in school productions ranging from Greek tragedy to such contemporary dramas as Emlyn Williams's *Night Must Fall* and Clifford Odets's *Waiting for Lefty*.

During the summer between sophomore and junior years, he finished the first of Oscar's assignments, *All That Glitters*. It was a musical adaptation of the George S. Kaufman and Marc Connelly comedy *Beggar on Horseback*. Word began filtering back to New York about the gifted young songwriter, and ultimately the first Stephen Sondheim song that would ever be played for the world to hear was a song from this show, performed live on a New York radio station.

By junior year he had abandoned not only acting but playing the piano in public in order to concentrate on writing the musicals that Oscar had assigned him. Ultimately *All That Glitters* would be produced at school, although Hammerstein couldn't see it because *South Pacific* was in rehearsal. "That," Sondheim says, "was the only time I remember being disappointed about Oscar not seeing a youthful show of mine." And, indeed, with this song for the bourgeois Cady family in *All That Glitters*, his lyric writing was already improving markedly.

The Cadys plan, the Cadys plan
To make as much money as we can.
We use all our money to make the time pass;
We don't mix with "people," the common mass.

Just small-town society, big town brass—
But most of the time we just sit on our
Middle class.

If Oscar was a father figure, he did not replace Herbert Sondheim, either symbolically, emotionally, or in fact. Stephen still visited his dad and still enjoyed his company. Together they went to see *Kiss Me, Kate*, a show whose lyrics impressed the young man tremendously, and afterward he watched with pleasure as Herbert banged out the Cole Porter score. "My father couldn't read [music]," Sondheim says. "He played entirely by feel. He played show tunes and pop tunes, not terribly well, but he and his best friend—another clothing manufacturer—would raise money for charity by playing parodies of show tunes, like 'Some Enchanted Buyer.' "

Sondheim would never be as deft as his father at playing "by feel" (or, as some say, "by ear"). The perfectionist in him cannot allow for instinctual harmonization. "Harmony," he says, "is too important to me," and there is something about his character to be grasped in this. Harmony is the rational element in music, just as melody is the emotional element and rhythm the physical or sexual element. Harmony, it is tempting to think, *would* be that important to him. (When he heard about that notion he responded, "Harmony is the *most* important element in music. That is its character.")

He plunged into the second assignment, adapting a flawed play, and the one he chose was Maxwell Anderson's *High Tor*. "It taught me something about playwriting, about structure, about how to take out fat and how to make points." This show was never produced because Anderson was himself hoping to musicalize *High Tor* with Kurt Weill, and so the rights were unavailable.

Sondheim's choice for Hammerstein's third assignment (musicalizing a novel or story) was *Mary Poppins*, and once more he wrote the libretto as well as the music and lyrics. "It was very difficult," he remembered about this project, "to structure a play out of a group of short stories and I wasn't able to accomplish it." By the time he finished the show, he was being graduated (magna cum laude) with the class of 1950, taking the Hutchinson Prize, the school's highest honor in music.

The Hutchinson was a working prize, a $3,000 fellowship that could be renewed for a second year. The award could have been applied to conservatory study or graduate work in musicology, but Sondheim "didn't want anything else except composition and theory. *Just to understand how music works.*"

So there it is again, the notion of composing as work of reason rather than as sheer artistic inspiration. Indeed, understanding how things work is a recurring motif in his conversation, an absorption by, almost a need for, order and orderliness. Sondheim's fascination with the right words, whether in puzzles or conversation; his demands for precision in lyric writing, exact rhymes, proper punctuation, flawless prosody (the matching of word accentuation to musical meter); the meticulous organization of his files, papers, recordings; his sometimes nit-picking insistence on factual accuracy: The pattern hints at obsession.

He decided to use his prize money to study composition and theory with Milton Babbitt, the pioneering electronics composer. With that to look forward to in the fall, he spent the summer of 1950 as an apprentice at the Westport Country Playhouse in Connecticut. The head of the apprentices was Frank Perry, who would later become a movie director. The apprentices were stagestruck youngsters with theater connections; in fact one of them turned out to be Mary Rodgers, and Steve, leaning through a backstage window of the barnlike theater, called out a big hello as she arrived.

Mary, now between junior and senior years at Wellesley College, wasn't at all sure that she was going to like him. Following their Gershwin and chessboard introduction, she had seen him only once: at the opening night of *Carousel*. The show had left both teenagers so weepy they'd avoided eye contact for fear of eternal humiliation. Mary's feelings were bruised by his unawareness of her schoolgirl crush. But, she later said, "Of course I instantly adored him," and side by side they would paint scenery or run errands. When they'd first met, she had found him "smart-serious." Now he was "smart-funny. There was a lot of silly humor," Mary would recall. "It was wonderful. We had a very good time."

They were doing whatever needed to be done at a busy summer-stock theater. "The plum job was stage-managing," she remembered. "The crappy job was props. Then you had to get into your car and drive all over the county collecting antiques to be ruined on stage."

As a graduation present, Herbert had given Stephen a secondhand Chevrolet, and while Mary stayed in her parents' nearby summer home, he commuted to his father and Alicia's place in Stamford. It was now their country home, as they had taken an apartment at Fifth Avenue and 82nd Street.

The summer-stock summer of 1950 was "a great summer" for this bright and lively group of apprentices, Mary remembered. "We ran our own after-hours bar, we were all crazed and wanted to stay up all night. We hung out a lot and at the end of every evening Steve would play his stuff." The high point of his stuff, at that point, was the *Mary Poppins* score.

"We knew somehow," Mary said, "that he was going to have to do this. He was going to have to get there because there was a desperation.

"He just . . . it was all he wanted to do in the world."

That fall Stephen moved in with his father, sleeping on a cot in the dining room. Once a week he headed downtown by subway to Milton Babbitt's apartment-studio on East 19th Street for a four-hour work session.

Babbitt, a compact man with twinkly eyes, had a comfortable warmth about him. Then in his thirties, he was an associate professor of music at Princeton. He had also earned a reputation as an eccentric in a music world that was slightly off its axis to begin with. He was one of the first composers to work with electronic sound synthesizers. "He had already turned

his back on serial music," Sondheim remembers. "He was always the avant-garde of the avant-garde."

But there was another musical side to Milton Babbitt, and it was endearing. The avant-garde of the avant-garde yearned to be a Broadway songwriter; in fact he had Mary Martin in mind for a show he was writing about Helen of Troy. Milton Babbitt, then, was smart yet quirky, esoteric but earthy—not at all unlike Sondheim, and their shared interest in the great old songwriters was but an extension of the kinship. The "avuncular"—Sondheim's adjective—Babbitt ("everybody's Jewish Uncle Milton") and the budding show writer would begin each workday with an hour of popular song study, analyzing, for instance, Kern and Hammerstein's "All the Things You Are," a song the members of ASCAP would later vote the best popular song ever written. (Sondheim would one day quote Babbitt's analysis of this song to a class in musical theater that he taught at Oxford.) Only after discussing Kern would Sondheim and Babbitt be braced for a Mozart symphony or a Beethoven string quartet.

If Milton Babbitt never would write a Broadway show, if he was not a gifted songwriter, he certainly was a gifted teacher and enjoyed exercising the gift. So he taught this eager young student the fundamentals of good popular music, such as the opening statement of melody in the first chorus of a standard thirty-two-measure, or "AABA," song; its restatement for the second eight measures (in the case of "All the Things You Are," continuing to drop in tone.). Babbitt would demonstrate how the next part, the middle (the release, or bridge, of a song—its "B" part), should not be an utterly new melody but, rather, should be an outgrowth from the first melody. And Sondheim would pass all of this along to Mary Rodgers, enjoying teaching as he enjoyed being taught.

He also studied serious musical composition with Babbitt and, during this time, wrote a two-piano concerto. In years to come, despite his formal training and notwithstanding the richness of his theater and movie music, he would never again, sorry to say, pursue serious musical composition.

Studying musical composition does not mean learning how to come up with a melody. It means studying how thematic material can be organized and developed, what overall schemes are possible, how and why keys are chosen and when they might be changed. It is the study of harmonic theory and modulation; the uses of dissonance (unresolved, "unharmonious" combinations); rhythm and the variety of time signatures; the application of dynamics and tempo. But first and last, composition is the study of musical organization, structure, and development.

The "how" of composing also includes the orchestration of pieces. For unlike the person who writes songs, the composer of classical music must first decide what he is going to write, what form he intends. A symphony? A piano study? A chamber work? That immediately leads to the question of instruments. Is it going to be a sonata for violin and piano? A harp concerto? A woodwind quintet? One day Babbitt assigned Sondheim the task of taking a Beethoven piano piece and orchestrating it for string quartet. Beethoven himself had done that. Babbitt then compared the composer's version with Sondheim's. "What it taught you to do," Sondheim says, "is analyze what Beethoven had in mind in terms of the *lines* instead of the chords. When we analyzed Mozart we were concerned with orchestration not in terms of coloration but in terms of what Mozart considered an important *line*."

At home, meanwhile, he worked on the last of Oscar Hammerstein's assignments ("my fourth oeuvre"), an original musical. For relaxation he went to parties, the theater, and most of all, the movies. They had always been his passion; he and Jimmy Hammerstein used to come into New York from Doylestown on a Saturday afternoon just for two sets of double features. He also maintained college friends like Dominick (Nick) Dunne—later to be a successful novelist—as well as newer ones, the writer-director Burt Shevelove, for instance, and Harold Prince, whom he'd met as Mary Rodgers's date on the opening night of *South Pacific* (Sondheim was only eighteen at the time, but Prince had already heard about the whiz at Williams).

He read newspapers but, surprisingly, not books—never would, he says, "irritated by poor writing styles and besides, a slow reader." And so that was his life, along with sleeping on the cot in the dining room of his father's Fifth Avenue apartment.

Herbert was urging him to move out and get a job. It was not a matter of middle-class values; he was concerned about how his son would support himself when the fellowship ended. For young Sondheim, though, the life of composing was all he wanted. He loved studying with Babbitt, who would remain a lifetime mentor, friend, and uncle. In fact, forty years later, they would still be discussing the structure of Kern's "All the Things You Are." He liked Herbert's Knabe grand piano and as he himself says, "Composing was my indulgence." Anyway, he would always be prone to inertia.

He was also progressing with the final Hammerstein assignment. Might not this, the completely original musical, be the one for his Broadway debut?

He called the show *Climb High* and based it on the experiences of a classmate, telling

*Aristophanes' * The Frogs * had been adapted for production in the Yale University swimming pool by Burt Shevelove, when he was teaching at the School of Drama. In 1974 Shevelove got Sondheim to provide new songs for a revival sponsored by the Yale Repertory Theater.*

the story of "somebody in college coming to New York to be an actor." Once again he wrote the libretto as well as the music and lyrics. It is interesting—no, charming—no, endearing—to listen to the Sondheim mind at work as he searches for just the right words while describing the source of that title:

That title *Climb High* was taken from a slogan—no,
not a slogan—*apothegm*—that was published—no,
not published—*cut*—on the stone pillars that led to—*flank*—
a walk leading to the dormitory I was living in. It read:

Climb high,
Climb far,
Your goal the sky,
Your aim the star.

At last, tired of being nagged by Herbert (who was now asking him to pay for his laundry), he took a small apartment, sharing the rent with a roommate who went off to a job every day. That left him alone with the first piano he ever owned. It was the cheapest Steinway, the "GI" model, so-called because it was an upright built squared-off so that it could be easily stowed on wartime troop ships. It was secondhand but it was his.

The summer of 1952, Mary Rodgers and Steve collaborated on a musical for television, *The Lady or the Tiger?*, based on the Frank Stockton story. She was herself a composer, and each wrote complete songs, words and music, but the show went unsold. Steve also gave Mary a song for a present, "Mommy on the Telephone," because her line was always busy and he could never get through. And he wrote a song called "The Two of You" for the popular television puppet show "Kukla, Fran and Ollie." It was performed many years later in one edition of *Side by Side by Sondheim*.

That summer too, he came up lucky at a dinner party when he was introduced by Oscar to George Oppenheimer, who was then a screenwriter and playwright and later a critic. Oppenheimer said that he was looking for an assistant to help write a television series, and Hammerstein said, "Steve needs a job. Why don't you show him some of your stuff, Steve?"

He got the job and within weeks moved to Los Angeles. He had never written a professional script and considered himself a composer first, a lyricist by knack, and a librettist only by necessity. Yet his first professional work was as a writer of television scripts, for a series based on the *Topper* movies.

The Los Angeles collaboration with Oppenheimer continued for six months and some thirty episodes, of which they wrote ten together. "Topper" starred Robert Sterling and Anne Jeffreys as a couple who die in an avalanche and come back as ghosts. The show was first broadcast on October 9, 1953, and the series ran for some four years. It still can be seen on late-night reruns. There is nothing in it to suggest Sondheim's future, but the experience did provide him with a way to earn a living. A couple of years later, during a six-month break in the writing of *West Side Story*, he would be able to earn needed money by writing scripts for an erudite television show called "The Last Word."

He thinks that writing television scripts was excellent experience. "It teaches you a lot in terms of economy. With the 'Topper' series, you had to tell your story in four chapters: the 'teaser' before the first commercial, the first act before the middle commercial, the second act before the last commercial, and finally the 'coda.' You had to tell it all in twenty-two-and-a-half minutes."

Yet he has never wanted to write his own librettos. "When I'm restricted to music and lyrics," he says, "it imposes a kind of economy and a clarity of thought on me that may not be suitable for dialogue." That is not the clearest of statements. What he seems to mean is that the formality and preciseness that are so appealing to him in music and lyrics are lacking in librettos. Why, then, does he not himself create an elegantly structured form for a libretto?

Sondheim's lifelong friend Mary Rodgers, here with him and Prince at the Company *recording. She co-produced the documentary film of the session. Sondheim had helped her when she needed an extra song for her revue,* The Mad Show. *Under the pseudonym, Esteban Ria Nido he wrote "The Boy From . . . ," a hilarious parody of the bossa nova hit, "The Girl From Ipanema."*

The answer may be either that he himself does not know what that form would be or, as he says, that he enjoys the collaborative process and would not want to work alone.

While in California he finished *Climb High* and mailed it to Oscar, believing that it had commercial possibilities. "I was already developing my own musical style. There were vamps [introductory rhythmic setups] that you'd think were from *Merrily We Roll Along* or *Company*. It was more sophisticated than what was on Broadway at the time but it wasn't all *that* sophisticated. You could hear my [musical] voice just beginning to sound." (This may sound like, and even be, arrogance, but it is a self-belief that seems to come to gifted young composers who have grown accustomed to enthusiastic responses. George Gershwin would play his youthful songs, turn to a listener, and grin, "Isn't that great?")

"At that point," Sondheim later mused, "I was much better trained in music. [Lyrically] I was still imitating Oscar in terms of emotion. At that age, considering the hothouse existence I'd led, just getting out in the world—I didn't have a lot of insight into lives that weren't like mine. There's very little in the lyrics that I would stand by these days but there's stuff in the music that's not too bad."

Climb High was like a regular Broadway show in at least one respect: it had book problems. A strong book—besides being interesting, funny, dramatic, and rhythmic—should also be a lean book. It *must* be lean, because half of a musical's time is occupied with musical numbers, which leaves only an hour or so for dialogue. More book than that will make a musical seem talky—"booky." The first act alone of *Climb High* was ninety-nine pages— longer than the entire script of *South Pacific*. When Oscar returned it, he circled the "99" and wrote, "Wow!"

Later, in a detailed letter, he stressed the importance of economy in writing musical scripts. The letter was mailed to the New York studio apartment to which Sondheim returned. He had saved enough of his "Topper" earnings to support himself for six months, although he continued submitting television scripts (and sold one, an adaptation of a Roger Angell story in *The New Yorker*). He also played his scores for anyone who would listen.

One of the listeners was the Broadway producer Lemuel Ayers (co-producer of *Kiss Me, Kate*), and while Ayers was not eager to produce *Climb High*, he was impressed enough to commission a three-song tryout (at $100 apiece) for a musical he *was* planning to produce. The show was based on a play (*Front Porch in Flatbush*) by Philip and Jules J. Epstein, authors of the movie *Casablanca*. It was to be called *Saturday Night*, and Sondheim would be given the assignment: He was to write the words and music for his first Broadway show.

THE CRAFTS OF LYRICS AND MUSIC

A song is made up of music and lyrics. Without words there is no song and that is simple enough. Lyrics at the least provide the vocalist with something to say while singing. For the listener they usually offer up an idea, something to occupy the mind while the spirit is being moved. But sometimes they are the most interesting thing about a song, conveying a thought or a feeling in a few well-chosen words. And at their best lyrics can unite with the music to create something greater than the separate parts, something that is more than either melody or light verse.

For instance, Richard Rodgers's music becomes inspiring when set with Oscar Hammerstein's "You'll Never Walk Alone." Irving Berlin's words for "There's No Business Like Show Business" make his own catchy melody an exhilarating one. An ordinary tune by Jay Gorney becomes chilling, ironic, and tragic when sung to E. Y. Harburg's "Brother, Can You Spare a Dime?"

Sondheim wrote "The Two of You" during the 1950s for the children's television program, "Kukla, Fran and Ollie," but it was never performed until being added to Side By Side By Sondheim *during the run.*

Above:
Sondheim was being celebrated by sophisticates before he was popular with the general public. A compendium of his music called Side By Side By Sondheim *was first produced at London's Mermaid Theatre on May 4, 1976, by Cameron Mackintosh, who became the era's dominant entrepreneur, presenting* Cats, Les Miserables, *and* Miss Saigon. *The show was transferred to Broadway in the spring of 1977. Hermione Gingold (left), who had costarred in* A Little Night Music, *and Larry Kert, once of* West Side Story, *joined the cast of* Side By Side By Sondheim *in New York.*

Above, right:
The original company of Side By Side By Sondheim *brought over from London included (left to right) Julia McKenzie, David Kernan, and Millicent Martin.*

In short, lyrics complete the song, and yet because music is so mysterious, because it seems *magical,* composers are held in awe while lyricists are considered their junior partners.

Is writing lyrics an equal half of what Sondheim does? He says, "I've always thought of lyric writing as a craft rather than art. . . . It's largely a matter of sweat and time consumption. Once the basic idea for a lyric has been set, it's like working out a crossword puzzle."

He is being modest. Lyrics can be airy, enchanting, even eloquent. In the theater lyrics make the music useful. A song can transcend entertainment to become part of the dramatic fabric. Lyrics are also the crucial link between music and dialogue. The linkage point—when an actor stops talking and starts singing—can be one of the most awkward in a show. Deft lyrics make this transition graceful.

The kind of lyric writing that Sondheim really seems to be minimizing is for standard or formula kinds of songs, which he rarely writes. He is not a *songwriter.*

He claims that he fell into lyric writing out of convenience, that it was easier to write them than to find a collaborator. He considers himself foremost a musician and has always found composing the more challenging, the more interesting, and the more rewarding task. Nor is he alone in denigrating lyric writing. Alan Jay Lerner liked to tell of a dream about his family which, concerned with his disappearance, traced him to a hotel room where he'd been working on *My Fair Lady.* When they asked what he had been writing, he proudly read:

> I could have danced all night,
> I could have danced all night,
> And still have begged for more.

The relatives stared at each other and then "took me off to a madhouse."

That is how absurd and trivial lyricists fear their work appears. They do seem to have the easiest of musical theater tasks, merely setting one syllable to each note in a song, and there are so few of those notes. Sondheim himself points out that "the average lyric has maybe sixty to eighty words."

But those are not just any sixty to eighty words. A song's notes have irregular time values. They are set to varying rhythmic patterns. Word accents are also irregular. Thus setting words to music is not merely a matter of placing so many syllables on so many notes. The accents of the words must match the accents of the notes.

That is the aspect of lyric writing that Sondheim compares with working out a crossword puzzle, but, as with a puzzle, doing it correctly is not always easy. Even Oscar Hammerstein admitted, "It is difficult to fit words into the rigid framework of a composer's meter." Yet he added, "This very confinement might also force an author into the concise eloquence which is the very essence of poetry."

The *craft* of lyric writing, then, demands a keen ear for musical meter, note value, and word pronunciation as well as a knowledge of prosody, rhyme, rhyming patterns, and singing requirements. But the *art* of writing lyrics—the "concise eloquence" of which Hammerstein spoke—requires grace, wit, composition, and the ability to wrap up an idea in a phrase; it needs a sense of compact drama. Theater lyrics make still greater demands.

It is through the artistic exercise of the craft that great lyricists achieve what Hammerstein called the "very essence of poetry" and Sondheim, with only his second Broadway production, *Gypsy* in 1958, vaulted into their ranks. This work demonstrates a complete mastery of traditional (or "book") musical lyrics: lyrics that dovetail with and then continue the drama; lyrics that sit neatly on the music and reflect its spirit; lyrics that capture the flavor of the production; lyrics that express character in a way that dialogue could not, yet do so in language consistent with the character's speaking style and personality; and finally, lyrics that crystallize a notion, express a feeling, make a song.

Natalie Wood played Louise to Rosalind Russell's Rose in the bland movie version of Gypsy, *which Sondheim and Arthur Laurents loathed. In 1992 they approved a new television version to star Bette Midler.*

Funny, you're a stranger who's come here,
Come from another town.
Funny, I'm a stranger myself here.
Small world, isn't it?

Funny, you're a man who goes traveling,
Rather then settling down.
Funny, 'cause I'd love to go traveling.
Small world, isn't it?

We have so much in common,
It's a phenomenon.
We could pool our resources
By joining forces
From now on.

Lucky, you're a man who likes children,
That's an important sign.
Lucky, I'm a woman with children.
Small world, isn't it?
Funny, isn't it?
Small and funny and fine.

This song, "Small World," is sung in *Gypsy* by the hard-boiled stage mother, Rose, in an effort to romance Herbie, the easygoing manager-to-be of her kiddie act. In her sledgehammer way she points out their similarities, expanding on the colloquialism, "small world, isn't it?" That is the idea that Sondheim is seeking to exploit in the song, at the same time letting this neediness unmask a vulnerability beneath Rose's brash exterior.

Her idea of what they have in common is of course contrived to sell Herbie on her, yet the ingenuousness is appealing: They are both strangers (first chorus), they both enjoy traveling (second chorus), and finally, as a bit of a stretch in the coincidence department, he likes children and she has two (last chorus). (The composer of its music, Jule Styne, a child of Tin Pan Alley, fretted that a male pop vocalist could never sing Sondheim's line "I'm a woman with children." Many Broadway songwriters of Styne's generation could not understand that serving a show's purposes is reason enough for a song.)

Sondheim uses everyday language in this piece for Rose, beginning with "Small world, isn't it?" and building on its idea of coincidence. Keeping his rhymes simple (town/down, sign/fine) he applies the Hammerstein device of repeats. There are repetitions of "funny," "lucky," "stranger . . . here," "traveling," "children," "isn't it?" In addition to their sonic value, repetitions accentuate the song's theme of coincidence. Just as with his rhymes,

Sondheim makes certain that the repetitions fall in exactly the same place in each chorus: the first and last words of the first and third lines.

Appropriate to Rose, the rhymes are not only simple; there are hardly any of them. They sometimes come in unexpected places, because predictable rhyme schemes condition listeners to anticipate rhymes—to *hear* them when it is preferable that they be *felt*.

"Small World" does have some wily rhymes in the release—"common," "phenomenon," and "now on"—so quiet and easy that the ear can skip them by, which the smart lyricist does not mind. He is not in business to remind everyone of his ingenuity. He prefers to create the illusion of monologue so that his rhymes are felt but not noticed and function for rhythm's sake. Sondheim ends the song softly with similar-sounding words rather than rhymed ones ("lucky," "funny") and a sweet, recapitulating coda, "small and funny and fine."

It is a perfect lyric, slipping into Styne's lovely melody without a wrinkle.

Yet Sondheim is not being just modest when he compares writing lyrics to working crossword puzzles; there is a wordplay in matching a specific number of syllables to a specific number of notes and in working those words into metric and rhyming schemes. But beyond the wordplay there is art to be done in lyrics. Perhaps it was more flamboyantly done when lyricists like Lorenz Hart and Cole Porter were writing from their own points of view rather than a character's. Poetry or wit that might be dazzling when sung in a supper club may not be appropriate to a character like Rose in *Gypsy*. The art in such a case is more subtle and the only eloquence Sondheim allows her in "Small World" is "small and funny and fine." It is rewarding nevertheless.

Sondheim may have gotten his lyric-writing foundation from Oscar Hammerstein, but he was also listening to the other American songwriters. While classmates were studying batting averages or reading pulp fiction, this youngster was devouring the song catalogs of Dorothy Fields, Jerome Kern, Lorenz Hart and Richard Rodgers, Cole Porter, and Irving Berlin; the songs of the Gershwins, E. Y. Harburg or Johnny Mercer and Harold Arlen, Howard Dietz and Arthur Schwartz, and the team of Buddy DeSylva, Lew Brown, and Ray Henderson. His own favorite lyricists include Cole Porter ("for playfulness"), E. Y. Harburg ("for antic imagination"), Dorothy Fields, and Frank Loesser ("for their command of conversational, colloquial language").

Dorothy Fields had been a familiar face in lucky young Sondheim's life. A woman of his parents' age, "Aunt Dorothy" was beautiful, dark-haired, chain-smoking, hard-drinking, sophisticated right out of a movie, and generally, in Sondheim's word, "sensational." She was also his audience and enthusiast. Her presence in his young life was almost as fortuitous as Hammerstein's, and even as a young professional he would bask in her compliments. She was the author of such model lyrics as "On the Sunny Side of the Street," "A Fine Romance," "I Can't Give You Anything but Love," and the later "Hey, Big Spender." Her clean work, her interest in character lyrics, and her ear for conversational English were not lost on the young Sondheim.

The genesis of his longer songs lay in Oscar Hammerstein's "Bench Scene" for *Carousel*, which changed the direction of Broadway musicals. It might be well to pause and study the piece, for so much of Stephen Sondheim's work has followed in the direction it pointed out.

Like *Liliom*, which is its Ferenc Molnár source, *Carousel* is about a brash ladies' man, Billy Bigelow (Liliom), who is a barker for a carnival merry-go-round. His customary bravado falters when he woos the quiet and tentative Julie Jordan, for he senses that she is accustomed to gentler men. The musical culmination of this wooing scene will be the beautiful "If I Loved You," but librettist-lyricist Hammerstein had bigger things in mind than a traditional book scene leading into a traditional ballad.

To begin with, even though "If I Loved You" will be sung by Billy and Julie, Hammerstein set the verse with lyrics for Julie and her friend Carrie to sing in an introductory scene.

These words were drawn from his research into the language of textile mill workers in turn-of-the-century New England.

> When you work in the mill, weavin' at the loom,
> Y'gaze absent minded at the roof,
> And half the time yer shuttle gets twisted in the threads
> Till y'can't tell the warp from the woof—

The words have nothing to do with the song "If I Loved You" that is to come; as a concession to commercial popularity, that song will have lyrics that make sense outside of the show. But these words are dialogue relating to *Carousel*, and Richard Rodgers's music follows their rhythm, Hammerstein writing *lyric theater*. So moments later, as Billy and Julie pause near the bench at center stage, Hammerstein abandons "If I Loved You" entirely, hearkening back to "You're a Queer One, Julie Jordan," which Julie and Carrie had sung earlier. He now gives Billy lyrics for that melody (which, like "If I Loved You" and opera, uses dialogue for a title).

As this landmark "Bench Scene" proceeds, some lines are sung alternately by Julie and Billy, or a line is sung and the response spoken. There are fresh musical themes introduced for just four lines of verse (a quatrain), followed by brief exchanges of dialogue. In the midst, too, musical themes and portions of the lyric are recapitulated and slightly altered, while the theme music of "You're a Queer One, Julie Jordan" is woven throughout.

Only this late, and only in the lyric, is there a hint of the song to come, the first hint of love for this unlikely couple.

> And half the time the shuttl'd tangle in the threads
> And the warp'd get mixed with the woof.
> If I loved you—

BILLY

(Spoken) But you don't.

JULIE

(Spoken) No, I don't. (She sings)

> But somehow I can see
> Jest exactly how I'd be . . .

And at last the beautiful melody:

> If I loved you,
> Words wouldn't come in an easy way.

But this beloved song is not going to be sung quite yet. The romance blossoms first, with lyrics that, in Irving Berlin's opinion, "make Oscar Hammerstein a poet and everyone else just a lyricist."

BILLY

(Spoken) Ain't much of a tide tonight. Hardly any.

(Singing an entirely new musical theme)

> You can't hear a sound—not the turn of a leaf,
> Nor the fall of a wave hittin' the sand,
> The tide's creepin' up on the beach like a thief,
> Afraid to be caught stealin' the land.
> On a night like this I start to wonder
> What life is all about.

And I always say two heads are better than one
To figger it out.

(Spoken) I don't need you or anyone else to help me. I got it figgered out
for myself. We ain't important. What are we? A couple of specks of *nothin'*.
Look up there.

(Singing)

There's a helluva lot o' stars in the sky,
And the sky's so big the sea looks small.
And two little people,
You and I,
We don't count at all.

Billy tries to shake free of this foolish reverie. Then he can only wonder.

If I loved you,
Time and again I would try to say
All I'd want you to know.

So at last this most gorgeous of songs. And only now does Hammerstein write a popular song lyric.

The "Bench Scene" is lyric theater, a way to make a musical continuously musical. It is
what Hammerstein had worked toward since *Show Boat*. It is the direction that Sondheim
would follow.

As a composer who writes his own lyrics, Stephen Sondheim belongs in a special cate-
gory that includes Stephen Foster, Irving Berlin, Cole Porter, and Frank Loesser. Like those
masters, he is more than good at two different creative acts; he is his own perfect partner and
this gives him an advantage over a team.

A composer-lyricist brings the same sensibility to the words as to the music. The
composer-lyricist makes a single entity of what, for partners, is a collaboration, an approxi-
mation of each other's voice. Because of that, there is something about the composer-lyricist's
songs that surpasses even the best of teamwork: the words sound like the music.

In speaking of the writing in a lyric, Sondheim can seem casual till it hurts, dismissing
as "all of that" such rarefied qualities as "grace, affinity for words, a feeling for the weight of
words, resonances, tone." One would guess that he seems cavalier only in modesty. He is a
natural poet, and that isn't part of the "craft." That is the gift.

Lyric writing certainly involves the gift, but beautifully chosen and phrased words are
only part of the job, just as dramatic purpose and character style are only part of the job. An
underpinning of craftsmanship is necessary, the tailoring of words to music, for if that is not
fittingly done then beauty and eloquence are beside the point. And it is the technical part, the
craft, that can be learned.

In a traditional popular song, the first thing we notice is the title, and that is usually the
first thing the lyricist writes. He has to know what the song is going to be about. Before Oscar
Hammerstein began writing theater lyrics as dialogue, song titles stated the themes: "Always,"
"Dancing in the Dark," "Two Sleepy People," and so on. These titles were to be repeated, at
the very least, at either the start or the end of each chorus. Irving Berlin said, "You have to
repeat the title as often as possible so they'll know what to ask for when they buy the record,"
and sometimes, as in the case of "Always," he had no shame about it. Because most theater
music still comes in the form of a free-standing number or song, lyricists tend to repeat their
titles, if only as ways of establishing the subjects on which they are elaborating.

Next noticed is rhyming. Rhymes are not necessary, but they are traditional in light verse and lyrics, and they do lend words a musical quality; they make the words *lyrical*. For Sondheim, "the function of a rhyme is to point up the word that rhymes—if you don't want that word to be the most important in the line, don't rhyme it. Also," he says, "rhyme helps shape the music, it helps the listener hear what the shape of the music is."

Like most lyricists, he especially enjoys inner (or internal) rhymes, which occur in the middle of a sentence, for instance, "Here's to the ladies who lunch/Aren't they too much/Keeping house but *clutching* a copy of LIFE/Just to keep in touch." Sondheim believes such rhymes "speed the line along . . . give it a shine. . . . Inner rhymes can also be used for strength."

In these same lines from *Company*'s "The Ladies Who Lunch," "much" and "touch" are outer rhymes, falling at the end of lines. These particular ones are also "masculine" because they rhyme on the final syllable. A "feminine" rhyme is made before the last syllable, for instance, "tumblers, grumblers, fumblers, bumblers" ("Comedy Tonight" from *A Funny Thing Happened on the Way to the Forum*). Feminine rhymes are softer than masculine ones and are useful to emphasize transitional, rather than conclusive, notes or chords.

It is hardly surprising that such devices appeal to people who enjoy wordplay. During a speech on lyric writing that Sondheim delivered at New York's 92nd Street "Y" in 1971, he almost lovingly described the exactitude of true rhymes. (Untrue rhymes are bad rhymes, incorrect rhymes, or "near" rhymes such as "Siberia" and "superior," which was used by Cole Porter, no less, in *Silk Stockings*). He explained the difference between a rhyme and an identity, noting that "in a rhyme, the vowel sound is the same but the initial consonant is different, as in 'way' and 'day.' In identity, both the vowel and the consonant that precedes the vowel are exactly alike, as in 'consternation' and 'procrastination.' " Identity, in other words, is repetition rather than rhyme.

On the other hand the same word or phrase sometimes will be repeated intentionally. It was a favorite device of Oscar Hammerstein. In "A Wonderful Guy," he established an opening pattern of repetition ("I'm as corny . . . I'm as normal"), did it again in his second chorus ("I am in a conventional dither/With a conventional star in my eye"), and concluded with *thirteen* consecutive repetitions of "I'm in love." The device was very effective in communicating exhilaration.

Sondheim likewise uses massive repetition, such as to communicate madness when he starts *eighteen* consecutive lines with "Momma" in *Gypsy*'s "Rose's Turn." The purpose of the device is similar: to communicate emotional extremity, a loss of self-control. The repeating word or phrase creates a rhythm, a drive, and a build toward outburst.

A technical companion to rhyme in lyric writing is prosody, the correct stressing of syllables so that they sit on the music without being mispronounced (fitting words, as Hammerstein said, "into the rigid framework of a composer's meter"). Sometimes a lyricist is so eager to use a word for purposes of rhyme or imagery that he will bend it—mispronounce it—or stress the wrong word in a sentence to fit the musical beats. Sondheim ranks among the most meticulous in his attention to correct prosody. This discipline, dealing as it does with language, words, and precision, goes to the heart of his mind. Yet he would seem to have fudged the stresses in these lines from the title song in *Do I Hear a Waltz?*

> Such lovely Blue Danubey
> Music, how can you be
> Still?

The lyrics do not seem to scan correctly when sung to the song's waltz rhythm: "how CAN you be STILL?" Then again, perhaps the words could, after all, be read with those stresses. Sondheim, of course, insists that they could. It would seem that a debatable lapse is as careless as he gets.

With Tyne Daly's rendition of the musical nervous breakdown, "Rose's Turn," at the climax of the 1989 Gypsy revival, director/librettist Arthur Laurents had finally rid it of all Broadway sentimentality.

A lyricist should also be aware that the words are sung, not spoken, and that they must be intelligible when sung. Sondheim has correctly criticized Lorenz Hart's "make two lovers of friends" (from "I Could Write a Book") for sounding like "make two lovers a friend" because of the closeness of the "a" and "eff" sounds. When, as an "all-knowing" adolescent, he had expressed his low opinion of Hart to Hammerstein, his mentor reminded him of Lorenz Hart's gifts. "He freed the rest of us," young Sondheim was reminded, "to use colloquial English in our lyrics."

Sondheim's persistent and public criticisms of Hart's lyrics have been curious, unseemly, and have sometimes even appeared perverse, since no other lyricist seems so closely related to him in approach, sensibility, or ability. The mistakes that exist in Lorenz Hart's work are far outweighed by his elegance, wit, tenderness, precision, and ingenuity in such songs as "It Never Entered My Mind," "I Wish I Were in Love Again," and "My Funny Valentine." There are lyricists Sondheim admires who have made their mistakes as well. Oscar Hammerstein's "where has last July gone?" (in "Many a New Day") sounds like "where has last you lie gone" because of the close sibilants in "last" and "July." But Hammerstein, Hart, and their contemporaries were the pioneer lyricists, and Sondheim's technique is based on their mistakes as well as on their achievements.

Perhaps it's that Hart is the competition: Before Sondheim came along, he was the popular choice for state-of-the-art lyric writing. Perhaps it's that Sondheim generally tends to disparage established figures—Ira Gershwin is another. There might also be a loyalty to Oscar Hammerstein implicit in his sniping at Hart, since Hammerstein regularly placed second to Hart in any comparisons of Richard Rodgers's collaborators.

Another aspect of rhyme is its dependence on pronunciation. What is correct? Academic linguists take the attitude that any regional accent is correct *in its region,* but most lyricists seek "correct" pronunciations. They consult rhyming dictionaries, check the preferred pronunciations in standard dictionaries, and respect "mid-Atlantic" English: the unaccented language as it would be spoken in an imaginary spot halfway down the East Coast between Maine and Florida. That is radio announcer's English, sounding accentless to most Americans.

Even the best of lyricists can innocently slip into regionalisms. In "Little Tin Box," Sheldon Harnick wrote:

> There is faith, hope and charity,
> Hard won prosperity,

which rhymes "charity" with "prosperity." A sheepish Harnick said with a chuckle, "They rhyme in Chicago," and an unchuckling linguistics professor concurred. "I'm from Chicago too," he said, "and they sound the same to me." That wasn't good enough for Harnick, though, who regrets the mis-rhyme.

Sondheim is meticulous on this subject (he pointed out the mistake to Harnick). Combing through his hundreds of songs, it is all but impossible to find a careless or incorrect rhyme. When a mistake appears—the French "liaisons," for instance, being rhymed with "raisins" in "Liaisons" from *A Little Night Music*—he typically refuses to concede any error. He insists that a joke was intended in the mispronunciation of "liaisons." Not that he does not claim to be perfect. He even offers to find his own mispronunciation—but cannot find any.

As for regionalisms, although his personal speech is New York–inflected, his rhymes are not. The trueness of his ear might well be traced to being a musician.

Sondheim himself says, "The lyrics come at you and you hear them once. Quite often [you feel], 'I didn't get the lyric until I heard the record.' " Indeed, lyrics are often lost in the barrage of entertainment information exploding from the stage: a story, singing, orchestral accompaniment, dance, musical staging, nowadays even choreographed scenery. These have greater impact than lyrics.

Cleanness, minimalism, neatness: His lyric writing has been a journey toward precise simplicity. By the time he wrote the score for *Assassins* in 1991, he could control his lyrics with such delicacy, such subtlety, and such finesse that a bone-chilling kind of pathos could be communicated within a harrowing selection of cheerful clichés to buck up the show's cast of murderers.

> Everybody's
> Got the right
> To be happy.
> Don't be mad,
> Life's not as bad
> As it seems.
>
> If you keep your goal in sight,
> You can climb to any height—
>
> Everybody's
> Got the right
> To their dreams.

MUSIC

Music seems to be the magical art. Heard but not seen, it exists in the air, untouchable yet capable of deeply touching our feelings, even our senses. Being wordless, it eases the mind, and that leaves the listener vulnerable to its engaging melodies, its powerful rhythms, and its transporting harmonies.

The effects of those elements can be emotionally—and sometimes almost physically—overwhelming. Pity those who have never experienced a wave of musical passion, the shiver down the spine; who have not felt the need to tap a foot, clap hands, or snap fingers; to sing and dance. For unlike any other art form, music can stimulate us to physical action. It can literally *move* us.

Zan Charisse was Louise in the 1974 revival of Gypsy. *Jerome Robbins's original concept was to make the show a cavalcade of vaudeville acts.*

Magical as it may seem, however, formal or composed music is not plucked from the air. Like any art form, it is made. It is conceived, organized, written down, and then performed. The only reason music seems to be magical is that we cannot imagine composing it ourselves, the way we can imagine drawing a picture or writing a story. After all, most of us have drawn and written, if not as adults then certainly as children. But most of us have never composed music and cannot imagine how in the world it is done.

Stephen Sondheim, with only his second show, *Gypsy*, was appreciated and esteemed as a lyricist. It has taken much longer for him to be recognized as a composer. For a long time he was advised by observers in and out of show business to stick to writing lyrics, and in many quarters even today, his music is admired rather than loved. That is because the theater audience (critics included) is not nearly as educated in its musical taste as in its literary taste. Theatergoers can appreciate the wit of Cole Porter's lyrics, the poetry of Lorenz Hart's, the ingenuity of E. Y. Harburg's, but their musical taste is generally simpler, with outer limits set by the high-class show tunes of Gershwin, Rodgers, Berlin, or Loesser. That is why, for example, it took so long for Kurt Weill and Leonard Bernstein to win the hearts of Broadway audiences.

Like Weill's or Bernstein's music, Sondheim's does not instantly register on the untutored ear. Listeners cannot immediately hum it the way they can hum a familiar type of tune. For although they appreciate surprise and challenge in lyrics, they deplore it in music.

Even today, in a rock-and-roll era that has no place for what was once called "popular" music, Broadway composers are still often measured by their hits, and a simple tunesmith who can write a catchy melody is likelier to be appreciated than the composer with loftier ambitions. It is easier to whistle "Doin' What Comes Natur'lly" (Berlin, *Annie Get Your Gun*) than "My Man's Gone Now" (Gershwin, *Porgy and Bess*). Indeed, Broadway's music has generally been written not by composers but by songwriters.

Some of them could not even read or write the musical language of lines, dots, and wiggly flags. There have been a few who could barely pick out a tune on a piano, and some who could not even manage that.

As musical comedy thrived—and it was popular from the start—some *composers* emerged from the pack of *songwriters*. They recognized the potential for a musical theater more ambitious than musical comedy. Gershwin wrote longer songs and stretches of recitative for *Of Thee I Sing*. Its sequel, *Let 'em Eat Cake*, was almost entirely sung. These developments culminated in his opera in the Broadway vernacular, *Porgy and Bess*.

Kurt Weill, in shows like *Lady in the Dark* and *Street Scene*, pursued "a special brand of musical theater which would completely integrate drama and music, spoken word, song and movement." Weill hoped that out of musical comedy could develop "a musical theater which could eventually grow into something like an American opera" only on Broadway, "because Broadway represents the living theater in this country."

As in Weill's case, classical training led Leonard Bernstein to think in terms of opera too. He was convinced that *West Side Story* "would lead to some form of American opera," for it was "a show where so much was conveyed in music, including the enormous reliance upon dance to tell plot."

Stephen Sondheim is fulfilling those hopes with a sense not of opera but theater. Although some of his shows have been produced in opera houses, *A Little Night Music* and *Sweeney Todd*, for instance, the musical theater that he develops is not conceived in operatic terms. In fact he has refused operatic commissions, explaining that opera companies do not offer enough previews to polish the work at the start nor, later, enough performances *period*. His main reason for resisting operatic lures, it would seem, is that he favors the Broadway style, the Broadway flavor, the Broadway tradition, and the Broadway taste of the Broadway theatergoer.

There are some aspects of opera that he finds tempting, and they are related to its artistic purity, its freedom from commerce. "You can write about anything you want," he says, "and have it played by a fifty-piece orchestra." That means a lot to him as a composer. He was not thrilled that *Sunday in the Park with George* and *Into the Woods* were served by small orchestras, or that *Assassins* (presented in an off-Broadway theater) was played by three musicians. He feels that his theatrical adventurousness and sophistication are unwelcome in a commercial theater that has become mindlessly spectacular and spectacularly expensive.

Yet it was Broadway musicals that inspired his career, and they are still his chosen medium. His notions may be lofty and even esoteric, but his roots are in the sounds, the rhythms, the colorations, and the traditions of Broadway.

"I'm 'Mr. Show Business.' " he says. "I'm from Broadway and I'm proud of it, too."

WRITING THE MUSIC

Sondheim's approach to composing music is, in at least one respect, like Oscar Hammerstein's approach to writing lyrics: the first step is thinking.

Before a single note is set down on paper or struck on a piano, he considers what kind of music is going to be composed for the new show. What is to be its tone? Its style? Its sound? This tone or style, Sondheim says, "includes harmonic language, rhythmic language and melodic language." Deciding it determines the musical style of the entire score, and that can take weeks of thought. It is the root decision from which all the songs will flow, because they are related to, and integrated with, each other. Thus the score of a Sondheim show can be thought of as a forty-five-minute (or longer) fabric of words and music rather than as twelve or fourteen songs.

In first contemplating a show's musical language, he seeks out an overall tone for the composition ahead. All the components of the music—melody, harmony, rhythm—will be expressed in that language. As for melody itself, which is the most noticeable component of stage music (it is what the average person hums, and songs are, after all, called "tunes"), even the methodical Sondheim has to admit that a little artistic creativity is involved—"a tap on the shoulder from the muse."

That melodic idea, though, which might be just four or six notes in a row, is but raw material. Movies about composers notwithstanding, songs do not arrive—complete with lyrics—as the inspired creator sits singing at the keyboard. Just as a goldsmith will use his precious metal as but the medium for his artistry, the composer's ultimate song will result from working with those four or six notes, developing and structuring them into a larger form that comes around to the desired effect and conclusion. Even the most instinctual songwriter creates in this way.

For Sondheim the music will be created in a deliberate "melodic language." Melodic language is the style and way the melody is expressed. The same series of notes can be made to have different effects. For instance the songs "Cabaret" by John Kander and "Put on a Happy Face" by Charles Strouse begin with the same five notes, but they sound completely different. And Leonard Bernstein was proud of using the same four notes to start the otherwise different "Maria" and "Cool," both in *West Side Story*. As Sondheim points out, "A melody can be harmonized in sixty-five different ways. You can make the same set of six notes anything from sixteenth-century to George Gershwin. Melody does not define anything; harmony and rhythm define tone, style." Thus the same melody has the potential to become different songs.

In order to make music, Sondheim deliberately strips it of mystique. This does not deny musical ardor but puts it in its place, which is a private place. An ardent craftsman is a handicapped one. Understanding music makes it manageable, makes it something that can be dealt with in a rational way, the better to control it. This is the way most any serious artist, popular or fine, approaches creation.

Other decisions concern the form to be used. Will this be a song of standard length and organization or will it be developed at length? Will additional themes be introduced, and how will they relate to each other? Will the piece be sung by one person or a group? Will the singer be a man or a woman? (The singing voice of the actual actor will also be taken into account if the piece is being written after the role has been cast.)

The musical style and language for a particular project rarely come to him at the outset. In seeking a style for *Pacific Overtures*, the 1976 Kabuki musical about the westernization of Japan, the only thing that he knew was what he *didn't* want. He didn't want a traditional Broadway version of Oriental music like *The King and I* or *Flower Drum Song*. Neither did he want the opposite, an actually Japanese score. He made jottings on paper, putting down notes in small groupings, speculating about chord structures, sketching the occasional melodic idea and seeing how he could play with it; how he could elaborate on it and develop it from four measures to eight or twelve; seeing if it could go anywhere.

He experimented with harmonic combinations and considered the use of wood blocks, gongs, and other Oriental instruments. Then, while casually listening to music by the contemporary Spanish composer Manuel de Falla, he found himself inspired.

How could music written by a twentieth-century Spanish composer serve as the model for a show set in historical Japan? Perhaps de Falla's "Nights in the Gardens of Spain" suggested to Sondheim an approach he might take to Japanese music without actually writing on the Eastern scale. Perhaps he felt an exotic tension and a spare orchestral shimmer that could be applied to the particular style and story of *Pacific Overtures*. De Falla's music was not the model but the stimulation that inspired a musical language, a musical character. "It took me a month to arrive at that style," Sondheim would recall about the search for an Oriental musical language that would be accessible to Western ears. "And by arriving at the style, making lots of notes, notations, chords, chord structures, melodic ideas, I finally could put down eight or twelve bars or something slightly developed and say, 'Yep, that's the sound!' "

In this we can grasp how a composer first "hears" his music. It arrives as an approach

The stage pictures on which director Harold Prince collaborated with the master scenic designer Boris Aronson made Pacific Overtures *look like a Japanese watercolor.*

to composition, a style, and perhaps a sequence of a few notes with a harmonic change. When Sondheim understood what de Falla was doing, he came upon his own idea and his composing could begin. Indeed, it had begun.

Sondheim likes to compare composing to writing. Composing, he says, also involves syntax and a vocabulary. "Music," he says, "is worked out, whether it's for a show or a symphony. This is an F sharp. It's a leading tone to G in the key of G major. And the way you have differences in writing, between singular and plural, you have differences in music between major and minor or between a leading tone and a suspended fourth. But it's a language you learn—it's logical—and once you learn it you apply it to the work."

Theater music is, of course, sung music, and any composer of vocal music must take into account the possibilities and limitations of the human voice. Thus it is not enough for songs to be good; they must also be singable, which Sondheim was able to observe while writing lyrics for the intuitive musician Jule Styne, who was composing *Gypsy* for Ethel Merman. He likewise observed as the more schooled Leonard Bernstein sometimes wrote beyond a singer's capabilities. For instance, Bernstein refused to change any notes in *West Side Story*'s "I Have a Love," even though Carol Lawrence had to strain to reach them. Perhaps that was because, in the concert world, a performer is expected to be able to sing anything that is written. Broadway singers are generally not quite that proficient.

Sondheim had noticed a more realistic attitude among the great songwriters like Kern,

Rodgers, and Gershwin, who instinctually understood tessitura, the range of the human voice, and generally confined themselves to a span of an octave and a half. "That's a range that virtually anybody can sing," Sondheim says. "When you start pushing one or two notes beyond that, the voice begins to get strained."

Yet his songs have ranged as wide as an octave and a seventh, or fifteen notes. Some of his higher notes in *Anyone Can Whistle* had Angela Lansbury's voice breaking under the strain to reach them. Thirty years later he was still working at keeping his music within manageable limits.

Each of his shows has been musically different, each score designed to serve the particular production. He took a vaudeville approach to *A Funny Thing Happened on the Way to the Forum*, put a middle-European burnish on *A Little Night Music*, and assumed traditional musical comedy forms for *Merrily We Roll Along*. His first responsibility is to suit the show's intentions, and yet he still has a musical identity. There is a Sondheim sound, whether in the sophisticated *Company*, the fanciful *Into the Woods*, the sardonic *Assassins*, or the pastiches of *Dick Tracy*.

This musical voice is melodious but dry and often bittersweet. Its tone is underlined by harmonies that are frequently soft, subtle, transparent, and occasionally unsettling or disarming—and evocative of the harmonies of the French "Impressionist" composers, Debussy, Poulenc, Satie, and most especially Ravel. The dissonant accompanying lines that so often can be heard in his music are not jarring but more like barbed modifiers of the melodies, as if to fend off shallow sentimentality. And even when the mood is lively or the singing is in chorus, there is a muted quality to his music. He prefers the subtler qualities, such as pensiveness, piquancy, amusement, insinuation, poignance, irony, and bitterness, rather than the declamatory, effusive, boisterous, hilarious, sentimental, or enraged. Schooled musician that he is, he will not choose the obvious sequence, preferring the unexpected route, and yet, Broadway composer that he is, he will find a way to resolve a complex progression in a conclusively theatrical way.

All of this seems to reflect not only his dichotomous musical background (classical and theatrical) but his thoughtfulness and rationalism. And so his music's dynamics tend toward crescendos rather than fortissimos, and his rhythms are lively or deliberate instead of being breathless or languorous. His melodies tend to move across small intervals, at least in the middle, even when rangy in overall shape. These small steps, set with mild dissonances and delicate harmonies (rather than broad strokes), are why it takes a little time and musical discretion before some listeners can appreciate the delicately distracting music in such songs as "Lovely" (*Forum*), "I Remember" (*Evening Primrose*), "Someone Is Waiting" (*Company*), "Every Day a Little Death" (*A Little Night Music*), "Good Thing Going" (*Merrily We Roll Along*), or "Not While I'm Around" (*Sweeney Todd*). But such musical patience is not beyond the general public, as Sondheim's biggest hit, "Send in the Clowns," proves.

He has composed bigger, heart-on-the-sleeve songs, too (the kind that songwriters call "soaring"), such as "With So Little to Be Sure Of" (*Anyone Can Whistle*), "Losing My Mind" (*Follies*), and "Not a Day Goes By" (*Merrily We Roll Along*), but for Sondheim, they are the exceptions.

The musical influences to which he admits are Harold Arlen and Jerome Kern from the theater and, from classical music, Ravel and Prokofiev. He also puts Puccini and Gershwin on the list, but the former is hard to hear in his work, and George Gershwin seems, rather, to have simply drawn on the same sources as Sondheim, namely, Ravel and Prokofiev. Audible, too, in Sondheim's music are Stravinsky's dry transparency and, in unexpected apposition, the colors and chord progressions of Rachmaninoff—all within the pervasive French influence, all susceptible to a nagging and bittersweet dissonance.

Musical dissonance does not mean a clashing or harsh sound, as is sometimes thought. That, Sondheim points out, is *discordance*. Dissonance refers to two or more tones played at the same time that do not at first sound charming because they don't make the "sweet" sound of familiar harmony. We call that pleasant musical quality "harmoniousness" because the combination is consonant, it feels whole, natural, and complete, therefore pleasant or nice. On the other hand an unexpected combination of notes can at first be jarring because it is unresolved, it feels unfinished—hence, dissonant. A simple example might be Gershwin's taxi horns in "An American in Paris." While "pleasant" or "harmonious" sounds are subjective, varying from the trained to the untrained ear, this definition of dissonance should serve.

In song a dissonant combination, while unexpected, can, with familiarity, become very pleasing. Sondheim points out that this usually occurs when it is promptly "resolved" (in the musical sense)—rounded off, the way a final "amen" rounds off a hymn. Leonard Bernstein's music for "Maria," which is repeatedly dissonant, has become a very popular song. Indeed, the dryer music of Stravinsky, Ravel, Prokofiev, or Copland can be as "harmonious" as the sweeter music of Tchaikovsky, Rachmaninoff, Verdi, Puccini, or Chopin.

THE WORK PROCESS

Early in 1992, Sondheim and librettist-director James Lapine agreed to begin a new project, a pair of one-act musicals. Usually a show starts with the script. When that is finished, the composer and lyricist choose the spots for their songs. As they incorporate parts of the script into their songs, the librettist rewrites. Later the director may suggest that songs be put elsewhere.

Sondheim and Lapine do not collaborate in this traditional way because, as the composer-lyricist and writer-director, they eliminate several middlemen. They also do not write traditional musicals. For the new show, as with their previous *Sunday in the Park with George* and *Into the Woods*, they were working toward a synthesis of music and dialogue. Thus it made more sense for the two to work concurrently.

They agreed that the show should start with a long musical/dramatic sequence like the opening of *Into the Woods*. After Lapine finished the first eight pages of script, Sondheim went to work. He wanted to weave music through the scene, leaving Lapine's dialogue intact except when lyrics were necessary. Even in those cases, he meant to try, when possible, to set Lapine's actual words to music ("he's a rhythmic writer and relates to music").

Beginning with a blank sheet of music paper, he set down a series of vertical lines to indicate beats, because Lapine's opening scene involves a certain amount of walking. He knew that a conversational rhythm would have to be established, because there was going to be speaking within the music. So he penciled in different beats to indicate those points—where characters speak and where they sing.

He drew a light line to indicate an overall shape for the as-yet-uninvented melody and marked off a series of Xes for vocal inflections and then musical notes to indicate approximate pitches he had in mind. As for the "invention" of melody, he says, "I might know I want the phrase to go in a certain general way but I don't know whether it's going to go C-G-E-F or C-G-E-F Sharp.

"After that," he blithely adds, "all I have to do is fill in the notes."

Those notes, the melody, will not be developed into a formal song at once. Perhaps Sondheim will decide to do that later in the scene. Meantime there will be several musical themes or phrases to create. He has already marked off three lines of Lapine dialogue to be set to music. He has also scanned the script for other lines to set, intending to musicalize the dialogue in "fragments and then the fragments may grow and you get a two-line phrase and then the next time he speaks it may be [singing] a four-line quatrain and the next time he speaks it will be five lines."

At another point in the eight-page scene, there is a stage direction for two characters to kiss. Sondheim marked his music paper for a musical theme to come at that moment. Elsewhere he has jotted down actual notes for the girl in the scene to sing. Taking the paper to the piano he tries it out. (Musicians tend to give status points for composing away from the piano.)

"Sounds fine," he said, "but when I start to harmonize, I may change it. The point is, I know it's the inflection I want for her."

On another sheet of music paper, he has jotted down brief runs of notes, musical ideas, and worked out different ways for them to go—"a half dozen different variations with different kinds of notes, different harmonies." He is also beginning to think about the instrumental sound. "There's a percussion thing I want to go through this whole thing and I haven't figured out exactly what that is. I'm thinking of going over to Michael Starobin [the orchestrator] and playing around with some electronic sound because I know nothing about how you make electronic sound. I know the kind of thing I want. I want to find the right kind of percussive sound because I have my rhythms written out percussively."

"But I'm not sure that I have the tone of this piece yet."

And so his composing began.

THE PRODUCTION PROCESS

When the music is finished, it is not finished. In the theater even a schooled musician like Sondheim turns in music that is for piano and voice only. Certainly his scores are more detailed than those written by the average Broadway composer. Even Richard Rodgers, who had some musical training, wrote his songs on just two staffs (rows of music lines), the upper for the melody and the lower for simple harmony and counterpoint (what musicians call a "basic bass and afterbeats accompaniment").

Sondheim writes detailed piano arrangements on three staffs, the top one for the melody and the lower two for the accompaniment, including exact rhythmic patterns, harmonies, inner voices, and counterpoint (while uncommon, notating on three-staff paper is not astounding; there are other Broadway composers schooled enough to do this). In his later scores, he even marks metronome settings to indicate exact tempi.

As for the sophistication of his piano arrangements, even as late as *Evening Primrose* (1966), in the opinion of orchestrator Jonathan Tunick, they were still "written in the established format of popular songs. The right hand always doubles the melody. It's pretty much of a formalized accompaniment." However, three years later, when Tunick first heard *Company* played by its composer, he was struck by the notable growth. Listening to Sondheim sing and play, the orchestrator thought, "These are art songs. These are like Debussy songs. This isn't just oom-pah, oom-pah show music."

ORCHESTRATION

One of the most common criticisms of Broadway composers by trained musicians is that they do not and cannot orchestrate their own music. In serious music, orchestration is part of composition.

Sondheim is not trained in orchestration, but being a musician, he is particular about those who do it for him. His first orchestrators, Sid Ramin and Irwin Kostal, were good enough to have worked with Bernstein on *West Side Story*; they orchestrated *A Funny Thing Happened on the Way to the Forum*. Don Walker, one of Broadway's best from the 1930s through the 1960s, orchestrated *Anyone Can Whistle*. Jonathan Tunick became Sondheim's alter ego in orchestrating the historic series of shows with Harold Prince as well as *Into the Woods*. These may be the finest orchestrations in Broadway history. When Tunick was unavailable to do *Sunday in the Park with George*, Sondheim asked Michael Starobin to do it, and Starobin did the job on *Assassins* as well, being particularly knowledgeable about the synthesizers that this little musical needed. Tunick and Starobin remain the composer's regular orchestrators.

The orchestrator's job, in Tunick's view, is "to orchestrally interpret Steve's dramatic intentions . . . interpret the piano idiom that he writes in his accompaniments. Because you don't just take the same notes and write them on an orchestra score. The pianistic color devices are very different and must be interpreted."

The piano is a unique instrument, and it can achieve unique effects. For one thing it simply sounds different from other instruments. As Tunick says, "The piano will play notes that aren't there because the low note—let's say it is a C—vibrating will make upper strings vibrate also (overtones)—an E. In an orchestra, if there are loud instruments, horns, playing the C, I might write in that E for a muted horn to play."

The composer's playing of the score usually is the orchestrator's first experience of the music, and in the case of Sondheim, it is a thorough, if not exactly virtuosic, piano performance. His singing of the songs is even less suave. "Steve grumbles them out an octave below pitch," Tunick says with a laugh, and because he is "diffident about his own voice, he tends to glorify the abilities of the imaginary singers who are going to sing the songs." That is why his songs can, on occasion, be more difficult to sing than he imagines.

Ordinarily a composer simply hands over sheet music with the notes scribbled in pencil, replete with erasures and cross outs. It is perhaps inelegant, but it is for the orchestrator's eyes only—except in Sondheim's case. His manuscripts are reproduced by music copyists. These printed versions are typical of his perfectionism (or else an obsession with neatness). He has even had his college songs professionally recopied.

Nevertheless Tunick usually asks for the original manuscript "because it helps me to see how the piece is constructed, with his shorthand and his abbreviations."

The song "It's a Hit!" celebrates composer Jim Walton's triumph in Merrily We Roll Along. *Omitted from the original cast album, it forms an added treat on the longer compact disc version of the show. Complex and witty, the song looks at Broadway success from past pain as well as present exhilaration.*

MUSICAL DIRECTION

There is little choreography in Sondheim's musicals because there is so much book and music. However, choreographer Patricia Birch provided effectively atmospheric musical staging for A Little Night Music.

Above, right:
In A Little Night Music, *Mark Lambert played Henrik, the frustrated divinity student who urgently sings "Now."*

At the same time as the orchestrator is engaged, so is the musical director. This is a job with two distinct responsibilities. Before the show opens, the musical director is charged with transforming written music into staged music, almost exactly as the dramatic director transforms a script into a play. The musical director takes a hand in the casting so that the actors are capable of singing the songs; then he teaches them the songs. After the show opens, the musical director is the conductor in the pit. He is the chief supervisor of the day-to-day performances, the representative of the choreographer and director as well as the composer.

Beginning with *Company* and the other Harold Prince collaborations, Sondheim has worked with only two musical directors, Harold Hastings and, after Hastings died, Paul Gemignani, who took over *A Little Night Music* and has done all the shows since.

The musical director's job begins when the composer first plays the score. "I love that," Gemignani says. "Steve's [performance] is terrible but I pay attention to what he's talking about and what he thinks about the score and where it comes from and what it means." With the start of rehearsals, Sondheim leaves Gemignani to teach the songs to the company. However, the score is not treated as inviolate. If a key must be changed to accommodate an actor, for instance, Gemignani goes ahead and changes it. "Steve never says, 'Don't touch my work,' but he doesn't like surprises either. He'd be angrier if I added a bar of music and didn't tell him about it than if I took something out that didn't work. At this [rehearsal] stage of the game I'll go ahead and try it and if it works I'll call him and say, 'Look, this is what we tried this afternoon. Do you mind it?' And he'll either say, 'Let me see it,' or, 'No, I don't mind that.' "

Toward the end of rehearsals, the orchestrator returns with his finished work, and the company is assembled for one of the most exciting moments in the production process: when the show's music is played by the full orchestra for the first time. This is so special a time that it is usually restricted to the immediate family of the show.

Until then the company has been performing with the rehearsal pianist. A certain excitement has already set in with rehearsing on the actual sets and the appearance of costumes. Each of these steps in realization has raised the company's morale.

When the thin and solitary banging of the rehearsal piano, so associated with hard, repetitious work, becomes what Tunick describes as "this big burst of color," there is a stunning epiphany. But it is not merely sound that has been added. There is also, as Tunick says, "the human energy from a whole new group of people—twenty-five new people in the show and they are all contributing something.

"And," he sardonically adds, "it's all downhill from there because the orchestra gets buried in the pit and you only hear them through speakers and it's never the same again."

OPENING DOORS

In theatrical jargon, writing "on spec" means writing for a producer on the speculation that he might produce the work. This is the way many writers get their start, but it was not "on spec" that twenty-four-year-old Sondheim was writing three songs for Lemuel Ayers's planned production of *Saturday Night*. He was being paid a paltry $300, but he was being paid. He was a professional at last, and not only because he was being paid. In his own opinion, he was writing songs for the first time on the professional level. After hearing the songs, the producer agreed and invited Sondheim to join him and Mrs. Ayers in their California home to work on the score for, at long last, The Broadway Debut.

Structurally *Saturday Night* is like other librettos of the 1950s, each scene concluding with a musical number of one kind (love ballad) or another (ensemble). The common wisdom at the time was that a musical's script should be a complete play, coherent without the songs, and that was probably the best that could be said about this one.

It is set in 1929 Brooklyn among a group of middle-class bachelors, restless on two consecutive, dateless Saturday nights. Gene, the central character, is a runner for a Wall Street brokerage house. His friends are content to spend their Saturday nights looking for girls to take to the movies, but he has fantasies about a more exciting life across the bridge in Manhattan and prefers to crash society events there. The guys advise him to "Be yourself kid/Be yourself," but Gene sings:

> The beautiful people
> Who live in grace
> On Sutton Place
> Have robes and peignoirs
> And purchase Renoirs.

Sondheim's music for this song ("Class") is very Fred Astaire, which is appropriate, but it is also anonymous and could have been written by, were there such a thing, a generic Broadway songwriter. He has not yet found his musical voice and the search would not be helped by the penchant for pastiche that this and the next song betray. The lyric for "Class" is also in period style, written and rhymed in the kind of sophisticated way that this character would be emulating.

When Gene is foiled in an attempt to crash a debutante ball, he lingers outside the ballroom and hears the society band playing. The song for this moment, "Love's a Bond," is in the style of a period fox-trot. Sondheim's lyrics are neat and witty, playing on Wall Street jargon, because stocks and bonds relate to the plot (the market crash, Gene's get-rich-quick ideas, money consciousness) and because a society band of the period might have played such a song.

Sondheim filled the lyrics of West Side Story's "Tonight" with heavenly imagery for the balcony scene between the star-crossed lovers, played by Larry Kert and Carol Lawrence.

> Love's a bond that's pure,
> Its dividends are sure.
> This bond, if you get it,
> Is stable and yet it
> Will grow if you let it mature.

That is also a nice triple rhyme, "get it," "yet it," and the interior rhyme, "let it mature."

Also lingering outside the ballroom is Helen, another social-climbing gate-crasher. She is pretending to be a Southerner, but her accent is not very convincing. That is why Sondheim writes dialect into the lyric. As Gene dances with her, she sings:

> This is nice, isn't it?
> Ah mean, the music.
> This is nice, isn't it?
> Ah mean, the band.
> Don't you think
> We make natural partners?
> Ah mean, like food and drink,
> Or supply and demand?

Young Sondheim's waltz is enchanting, ballroomy, and slightly suggestive of Richard Rodgers's "Falling in Love with Love" in its stirring bass line, its sweep, and its melodiousness (what some musicians call "a waltz in one," meaning that the conductor can sweep across the three waltz beats with one swing of the baton). That is not such a bad musical neighborhood to be in.

The plot is the drama of Gene's seeking to reach the society life by speculating on Wall Street. When his stock fails to go up with the rest of the market, he borrows money on a car he is watching for a relative, hoping to redeem it before the owner returns. Nearly jailed for the crime, he is saved by a plot contrivance and then realizes (as Helen already does) that happiness lies in being himself; that is, living the life into which he was born.

Aside from this being a rationalization for the unaspiring, it runs contrary to everything that makes Sondheim's career an adventure in artistic originality, risk-taking, and idealism. Too, the script's philosophy of justifiable mediocrity is reflected in its unimaginative narrative style, its dreary story with drab characters, lumpy flow, and cheerless humor. Had *Saturday Night* ever been produced, it surely would have flopped.

Sondheim's score, however, shows him ready for Broadway. It demonstrates his talent for theater song, his craftsmanship as both a composer and lyricist, and his Hammerstein-influenced theatrical notions. One number ("In the Movies") is a full-blown musical-dramatic sequence covering four pages of script in lyrics and dialogue. It promises the Sondheim ahead, and he proudly remembers that Dorothy Fields liked it especially.

And then, in the spring of 1955, Lemuel Ayers died.

There was little hope of finding another producer. So many shows were around and so many were being presented, that nobody needed anyone else's to produce. Sondheim had proudly given a copy of the *Saturday Night* score to his father as a birthday present. "To Dad on his 60th," he had inscribed it. "Hope I can give you one of these every year for the next forty years at least."

Perhaps the next one would be for a show that was actually produced. This one was dead, and as Mary Rodgers saw it, that was a "crushing disappointment for Steve."

Disappointment or no, Sondheim was on his way. He had been introduced to the Broadway community, and his sociability would lead him to new opportunities. In a far away future, this would be known as "networking."

The first opportunity was of the once-in-a-lifetime variety. It happened at a Broadway opening-night party where the playwright Arthur Laurents mentioned that he was working with Jerome Robbins and Leonard Bernstein on a musical version of *Romeo and Juliet*. When Sondheim asked who the lyricist was, Laurents replied that Betty Comden and Adolph Green might have a conflicting movie commitment, and then he clapped a hand to his forehead and cried, "My God! We never thought of you!"

A week after auditioning for Bernstein (playing the *Saturday Night* score), Sondheim was offered the assignment. He told Oscar Hammerstein, "I really don't want to do this," and he meant it. His impulses, his training, his ambitions, and most important of all, his sense of identity were tied up with being a composer. But Oscar convinced him that *West Side Story* would offer the chance to get started on Broadway with top professionals, and Sondheim accepted the job (supporting himself, in the meantime, by writing for the television program "The Last Word").

Sondheim would ultimately write lyrics only for three shows, and they would all have music by first-class composers—Bernstein, Jule Styne (*Gypsy*), and Richard Rodgers (*Do I Hear a Waltz?*)—in the cases of Bernstein and Styne, the best theater scores of their careers. And not merely that. *West Side Story* is arguably the best music that Leonard Bernstein ever composed for *any* medium, and *Gypsy* may well be the greatest traditional Broadway score ever written.

Sondheim would seem to have had much to do with those achievements. It is not by coincidence that Jule Styne never wrote another show in a class with *Gypsy*. As for Leonard Bernstein, he was, of course, Leonard Bernstein, and had already written wonderful theater songs for *On the Town*, *Wonderful Town*, and *Candide*. Yet *West Side Story* is more than just wonderful theater songs. It is an extraordinary synthesis of classical technique and the Broadway flavor, and Sondheim already had a feeling for that synthesis. In turn his own music would be profoundly influenced by Bernstein's. Add to Sondheim's uncanny luck, then, this youthful collaboration with one of the most important musicians of his time.

What made *West Side Story* innovative was not its subject matter of prejudice and gang wars. Daring as that was for a musical, it could have been dealt with in traditional musical and choreographic language. The script itself is a conventionally constructed melodrama, leading in the traditional way from scene to song, scene to song. What made this show innovative was, first, the amount of music in it—as Leonard Bernstein said, "A tremendously greater amount of music than I expected—ballet music, symphonic music, developmental music"—and second, Jerome Robbins's expanded use of choreography and musical staging.

If Jerome Robbins was stepping into the future of musical theater as he approached the notion of the concept musical, Laurents's script was firmly rooted in conventional musical theater. His was a libretto for a book musical, a play with songs and dances. Perhaps this orthodoxy was because it was his first libretto, but thirty years later the score of *West Side Story* would remain electrifying and the choreography exciting, while the script would seem more old-fashioned than *Romeo and Juliet*, which is nearly four hundred years older. That is because the Laurents play deals with transient social issues, while Shakespeare's drama, youthful work though it may be, is about timeless matters of love and death. It is also a passionate play, romantic and tragic. There is a beautiful arc toward its painful denouement, with exquisite poetry along the way. To be sure there are creaks in young Shakespeare's dramatic machinery, but Laurents's version keeps the creaks while losing the tragedy as well as the poetry.

He made some changes and is particularly proud of how his Tony/Romeo is misinformed ("because of prejudice") that Maria/Juliet is dead. This device, he says, is "better than the original story," which is not only a trifle presumptuous but also untrue. The sleeping potion was the better storytelling device. It is also amazing that Laurents decided to change the devastating end of Shakespeare's story when Juliet, upon awakening, sees Romeo dead and kills herself. In *West Side Story*, Maria does not kill herself. Richard Rodgers, never a

Tony and Maria fantasize their wedding.

risk-taker, had advised the authors that she needn't do that since she is emotionally "dead already." Laurents agreed, feeling that her death "just didn't work in contemporary terms." These sound suspiciously like rationalizations for pandering to conventional audience sensibilities. Jerome Robbins thought that Maria should die as in Shakespeare, and he was right. Such disagreements typified the acrimonious collaboration between Robbins and Laurents.

As for the songs, we think of them as Leonard Bernstein's, even though, as always, there is no song without words, no "Tonight" or "Maria" without their lyrics. Sondheim was not very proud of these lyrics, because he was bending his own taste to suit Bernstein's. Oscar Hammerstein had taught him always to write honestly and to speak from his own heart, trying not to sound like Oscar or anyone else. But "the way I would write," Sondheim says, "wasn't exactly the way Lenny wanted to write so I had to compromise and there was a lot of purple writing." Bernstein was originally supposed to co-write the lyrics, and at the outset he tried. On the left is a set he submitted for what Sondheim would eventually write as "I Have a Love," on the right.

BERNSTEIN	SONDHEIM
Once in your life,	I have a love,
Only once in your life,	And it's all that I have.
Comes a flash	Right or wrong,
Of fire and light.	What else can I do?
And there stands your love,	I love him; I'm his,
The harvest of your years.	And everything he is
	I am, too.

The "purple" in the Bernstein version is self-evident, as is Sondheim's more appropriate, street-conversational style.

West Side Story starts with a dance-mime prologue that establishes the tension between the show's Capulets and Montagues—the Puerto Rican Sharks and the white Jets. After a few lines of opening exposition, the "Jet Song" introduces one of the gangs and the camaraderie that they enjoy as an escape from the harshness of slum life.

Bernstein's musicianly and electric approach to the theater is immediately apparent in the song's nervous rhythms—alternately deliberate and irregular—the jagged and wide-ranging melodic line, startling musical intervals and dissonances. In setting words to this opening number, young Sondheim was challenged by both the relentless notes and the question of what these boys could sing and still sound tough.

> When you're a Jet,
> You're a Jet all the way,
> From your first cigarette
> To your last dyin' day.
> When you're a Jet,
> If the spit hits the fan,
> You got brothers around,
> You're a family man!

Sondheim was holding himself to simplicity of language and rhyme. Like most restrictions, this made the task not easier but more challenging. Hammerstein had advised him that "the first lyric the audience hears, the first song, is what really makes or breaks a show," and while that is not always true, this lyric accomplishes its task of establishing the white gang and getting the show proper started with energy. The words are clear, concise, and singable, although there are certain lapses. For instance the "last" in "last dyin' day" is redundant (Sondheim was coupling it with "first cigarette" and didn't look for a better option). Also "spit" hitting the fan only calls attention to itself as a euphemism for "shit." In 1957 obscen-

A West Side Story dance number. About getting such numbers on stage, Sondheim says, "Some people like rehearsing [but] I want to go right from the first day of rehearsal to opening night. I get neurotic about hearing my own work. If something isn't going right, I get impatient. That's one of the reasons I can't direct. I get tense during rehearsal periods."

ity was forbidden in the theater (as it was in movies and books). Broadway was still reeling from the cataclysmic shock of Burl Ives saying "son of a bitch" in Tennessee Williams's *Cat on a Hot Tin Roof*. To actually say "shit" at the time probably seemed like risking riots in the streets. Likewise Sondheim used "buggin' " to suggest "fuckin' " in the same song ("Every last buggin' gang/On the whole buggin' street!").

Euphemisms only remind the audience of what *isn't* being said. Sondheim should have finessed the issue by forgetting about obscenities if he couldn't use real ones. In the second act's "Gee, Officer Krupke!", he did originally write,

> Gee, Officer Krupke!
> Fuck you!

feeling that by then the audience would be ready for such language ("Why not? We're supposed to be this avant-garde tough show"), but when one of the producers "blanched visibly" upon hearing it, Bernstein suggested "Krup you!", and that was virtually his contribution to the show's lyrics. This number is such a crowd pleaser that probably anything could have been shouted at the end of it. Instead, "Krup you!" concludes the song with another silly, almost-dirty word, this time (worse, still) *precisely* to shock the audience.

Such language, even euphemisms, would have been unthinkable to Oscar Hammerstein (who "never," Dorothy said, "spoke the way, you know, soldiers would speak"). Sondheim was still showing his lyrics to his mentor, but the relationship was changing. "I started to become argumentative when we discussed the songs I was writing. . . . This show changed his attitude toward me. It was like seeing a bird fly for the first time. He was no longer protective."

"Something's Coming" arrives at the end of the next scene, and, as a song is supposed to in a book musical, it links the previous dramatic event with the approaching ones. The wonderful phrase "whistling down the river" was taken directly from Laurents's script. When Sondheim first heard Bernstein's music for the song, with its unusual rhythm in the vamp (introductory rhythmic pattern), he suggested a more *Broadway* feel.

"You know what Larry sings better than anyone in the world?" he asked, referring to Larry Kert, who was playing Tony, the Romeo figure. "A two-four like Vincent Youmans's 'Hallelujah!'"

"You mean a show tune," the composer said.

"Yes!" Sondheim enthused. "Just put fourths in the inner voices." When Bernstein asked for a demonstration, Sondheim played the song in a two-four, adding parallel fourths (upwardly moving octaves in the bass line) which gave it a very Broadway surge. While this wasn't like suggesting a mambo beat to Beethoven for his "Eroica" symphony, it was still a bit audacious, the lyricist being a twenty-seven-year-old novice and the composer being Leonard Bernstein. But young Sondheim was very confident—or else very nervy.

The open-minded composer tried it, adding the throbbing inner voice that would give the number its drive. As a result of that (and to say the least, the rest of the song), "Something's Coming" is one of the best pieces in the show, helped along its way by Sondheim's anticipatory lyric—a lyric that may owe some slight debt to Dorothy Fields's "I Feel a Song Coming On" (whose Jimmy McHugh music has a similar surge).

The next scene, too, concludes with a song, "Maria," which has perhaps the most Oscar Hammerstein–like lyric that Sondheim ever wrote. That may be one reason why Dorothy Hammerstein wept when he played it for her. "He sat down at a piano in our living room and sang 'Maria, I just met a girl named Maria/And suddenly that name/Will never be the same to me.' I stood in the doorway listening and I started to cry. I thought, 'He's grown up. He's growing up.'"

But Sondheim would cringe whenever he heard

> Say it loud and there's music playing.
> Say it soft and it's almost like praying.

The melody is beautiful, romantic and Latin, but Jerome Robbins didn't listen with the same tenderness as Dorothy Hammerstein, particularly when the time came to stage it. Quoting the lyric to Sondheim, he said, "'Maria, I've just met a girl named Maria, and suddenly that name will never be the same to me.' And then there's this bar-and-a-half pause. What am I supposed to do there?"

"Well," replied the tyro to the choreographer with the legendary mean streak, "I mean, he's just standing there on the stage."

"But how am I supposed to direct him?"

"Can't he just stand there?"

That was when the iceman arrived. "You've got to give me something for him to do," Robbins said, "or do *you* want to stage it?"

In time Sondheim would become a dramatist, learning to provide choreographers with some reason for staging a song and some notion about how to do it. He would also be proud of at least the opening words of "Maria," for he knew that the test of a good lyric is in the singing. "It may be embarrassing," he admits, "to say, 'Maria, I just met a girl named Maria,' but it *sings* wonderfully."

Since choreographers will hate love songs as long as they are slow, it is all the more amazing that Jerome Robbins stood still for yet another ballad—and immediately after "Maria" at that. This is the even more beautiful "Tonight."

Set to Bernstein's elegantly constructed melody, the lyrics are unabashedly romantic:

> Tonight, tonight,
> The world is full of light,
> With suns and moons all over the place.
> Tonight, tonight,
> The world is wild and bright,
> Going mad, shooting sparks into space.

Today the world was just an address,
A place for me to live in,
No better than all right.
But here you are,
And what was just a world is a star,
Tonight!

These are clean, image-filled words, youthfully ardent like *Romeo and Juliet* itself. Perhaps some of its things ("wild and bright") are better than others ("going mad, shooting sparks"), but "today" and "tonight" is the kind of sequence that Sondheim would use throughout his career, and the heavenly imagery ("world," "space," "star") is vivid and appropriate for Shakespeare's star-crossed lovers. Sondheim's notion of impatient young love ("tonight!") being able to transform a mere place in which to live ("no better than all right") into astral paradise meets the challenge of adapting *Romeo and Juliet* to street language. It is more like Shakespeare than anything in the libretto and makes Bernstein's melody seem even richer than it is.

The most conventional musical theater songs in *West Side Story* are the comic numbers, "America" and "Gee, Officer Krupke!" The former is a list song:

Automobile in America,
Chromium steel in America,
Wire-spoke wheel in America,
Very big deal in America!

and the other is a musical comedy turn. "America" is based on a fair enough notion (comparing Puerto Rico's drawbacks with ours), but wordiness makes it tough to sing. Sondheim had to write all those words because of Bernstein's profusion of heel-stamping notes, but phrases like "wire-spoke wheel" only ask for trouble, and Sondheim himself points out that "for a small fee" is nearly unintelligible when sung fast.

"Gee, Officer Krupke!" is a comedy turn that he cleverly adapts to the plot, but it is still a comedy turn (set to music Bernstein had cut from *Candide*). It works because it is funny, but it is a reminder of the show's roots in traditional musical theater. The clean-cut and neatly costumed dancers are difficult enough to accept as hoodlums; this song only proves that they are in a musical.

During the writing of the show, Sondheim did not particularly socialize with Bernstein. He describes as "another world" the composer's circle of friends from high culture: Thornton Wilder, Jennie Tourel, Aaron Copland. His own friends were younger and tended to be in show business: Harold Prince (who came in as a producer of *West Side Story*), composer John Kander (destined to write *Cabaret*), writers William and James Goldman, Mary Rodgers, Dominick Dunne, and Burt Shevelove.

He found the collaboration with Bernstein "a generally terrific experience," although not without conflict. "It was very frustrating," he remembers, "having to go over all the lyrics with Lenny; having him pick them apart. I'd have to argue and defend every point before I'd get it. Endless *chazerei*."

Even more than "Maria," the lyric that for him typifies his embarrassing youth is "I Feel Pretty." Tired of writing simple words for the hoodlums and wanting to demonstrate "that I could do inner rhymes too," he put several of them into the mouth of Maria. This young immigrant suddenly can sing, "I feel pretty and witty and bright" and "It's alarming how charming I feel." The song has become a classic and so its rhymes will not go away, but neither, at least, do the royalties.

On the subject of royalties, during the Washington, D.C. tryout Bernstein offered to withdraw as co-lyricist. "Look, the lyrics are yours," he said. "Do you want me to take my name off?"

"That would be wonderful," young Sondheim said.

"And we'll arrange the percentage points too."

"Oh, don't bother," the novice said magnanimously, only to snap at himself years later, "Shut up, Sondheim!" adding, "I can't tell you the money it cost me, that simple conversation." (Some performing editions of *West Side Story* still list Bernstein as co-lyricist.)

Naturally Herbert Sondheim wanted to invest in the show. Stephen tried to talk his father out of that, especially after hearing Herbert's reaction to the script ("Not many laughs, are there?"). When Herbert asked him to play the songs, young Sondheim stalled because he "knew what would happen if I sat down to play it. If he thought *my* music was dissonant . . ."

Pressing the discouragement approach, he told his father, "At best it's a prestige piece," but a probably very proud Herbert Sondheim raised $1,500 among his friends, a fair enough sum at the time (the whole show cost $300,000), and the investment would pay off handsomely. As a bonus, Stephen would give him the house seat order book (each author is entitled to four tickets for every performance.) This relieved the son of a nuisance and gave the father the power and the opportunity to prove, every day, what a success his boy had become.

West Side Story opened in New York on September 26, 1957, at the Winter Garden Theatre and was well enough received, although the critics considered it short of the Second Coming. Remembered as one of the era's major musicals, it was in fact only a modest hit, running 732 performances—less than two years—before beginning its tour (after which there was a brief return engagement). The big success and the songs' real popularity came with the movie version.

Jerome Robbins choreographed virtually every step in West Side Story, *including this knife fight from the Broadway original company. Thinking back to the show's tryouts, Sondheim remembers, "We spent very little time in Washington on the show. We futzed with the opening number . . . and Jerry fiddled with the ballet. But the show was in excellent shape, it was what it was, good, bad or indifferent."*

The reviewers generally enthused about Robbins's choreography and staging but seemed confused by Bernstein's music, so different from the usual show tunes and so harsh on ears that were accustomed to the wholesome melodies of Rodgers or Loewe. The revered Brooks Atkinson of the *New York Times* called it "an astringent score"—an evasive approach comprising his entire discussion of Leonard Bernstein's music. He omitted Sondheim's name completely. In the *Herald-Tribune*, the less revered but more respected Walter Kerr condescended to the book and lyrics in a single sentence: "The evening hurtles past whatever endearing simplicities may be hidden in Arthur Laurents's text or Stephen Sondheim's lyrics."

Small wonder then that, hit or not, young Sondheim was depressed on opening night. He had reluctantly agreed to write these lyrics. To be dismissed or, even worse, ignored only spoiled the joy of debut, and so it was a painful first experience.

The role of the critic is never more important than at the birth of a young artist, when his future may hang in the balance. A perceptive critic can encourage and even inspire a gifted newcomer whose first work is not a masterpiece. A destructive critic can send this self-same artist to flight. Stephen Sondheim was a committed and confident young man, and he had Oscar Hammerstein in his corner. Without all that armor he might well have been disappointed all the way back to television. This debut experience initiated a lifelong wariness of critics, a wariness that is common among theater people, a wariness bordering on hostility.

With *West Side Story* launched, Sondheim had a dependable income. The lyricist, composer, and librettist usually receive royalties of two percent apiece of a musical's total receipts. Even though Sondheim split his share with Bernstein, it was still enough to live on. He was able to return to composing and started work on a unique musical, based on the comedies of the Roman playwright Plautus. There were two librettists, one of whom was Burt Shevelove, a writer-director and friend since college. Shevelove was an elegant, erudite, and very funny man (who insisted that he once began introducing himself to Israel's prime minister Golda Meier, only to realize in midstream that "she" was in fact the movie producer Sam Spiegel).

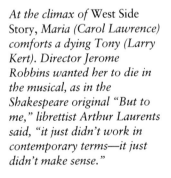

At the climax of West Side Story, *Maria (Carol Lawrence) comforts a dying Tony (Larry Kert). Director Jerome Robbins wanted her to die in the musical, as in the Shakespeare original "But to me," librettist Arthur Laurents said, "it just didn't work in contemporary terms—it just didn't make sense."*

Shevelove's collaborator was the smart, gifted, and unfairly funny writer Larry Gelbart (who would later create the "M*A*S*H" television series and write the musical *City of Angels*). In *Forum* they were exploiting a parallel they'd found between low clowning on the American stage and classic Roman comedies. That was the idea behind this "scenario for vaudevillians," as Shevelove called it.

When they completed a presentable draft, and after Sondheim had written a few songs, the material was shown to Jerome Robbins, who agreed to direct this musical, *A Funny Thing Happened on the Way to the Forum*.

But *West Side Story* had made Robbins the most sought after director on Broadway, and he was simultaneously offered *Gypsy*, which already had its financing and a star, the great Ethel Merman. All it needed—merely—was to be written. Yet it was a time of such theatrical plenty, of so much talent and confidence, that this did not seem absurd.

Ethel Merman was Rose and Sandra Church played Louise in the original company of Gypsy. *Some feel that Angela Lansbury and Tyne Daly later acted with greater depth, but the songs and Merman's singing seem inseparable.*

Gypsy had already been turned down by both Cole Porter and Irving Berlin. The young team of Cy Coleman and Carolyn Leigh was writing four songs "on spec" for it. Robbins, who liked Sondheim's songs for *Forum*, recommended him for the job, but Merman would not have an unknown composer. She insisted on Jule Styne.

Sondheim was appalled by the suggestion that he once again write lyrics for someone else's music, but Oscar Hammerstein suggested that, for a second time, he swallow his disappointment—this time for the experience of writing for a star. The young man consented, but it made him "heartsick."

It is doubtful that Jule Styne could have composed these wonderful songs without Sondheim's influence. He never wrote the likes of them elsewhere, coming close only with *Funny Girl*. It was Sondheim who inspired him to make the most of his gifts. The lyrics (which were usually written first), through shape and construction, rhythmic patterns, and unexpected shifts or gaps, forced the composer away from the traditional structure. The words also gave the music specific theatrical purpose, making these songs not just "good" but part of the show. Indeed, the essential spirit of *Gypsy* is in its songs, and we think of the show as the score.

Following the electrifying overture and some introductory exposition, Momma Rose's kiddie act, "Baby June and Company," makes its first appearance. The lyrics for this number, "Let Me Entertain You," are deliberately written to take on different meanings, changing gradually as the number is performed by a growing June, her sister, Louise, and finally by the woman Louise becomes, the sexy Gypsy Rose Lee.

> Let me entertain you,
> Let me make you smile.
> Let me do a few tricks,
> Some old and then some new tricks,
> I'm very versatile.
> And if you're real good,
> I'll make you feel good,
> I want your spirit to climb.
> So let me entertain you
> And we'll have a real good time, yes sir—
> We'll have a real good time!

The words are simple, the constructions clean, the rhymes are rhythmic and colloquial ("few tricks/new tricks," "real good/feel good"). Moments later, Rose's introductory song, "Some People," establishes her character with trip-hammer affirmation.

> Some people can get a thrill,
> Knitting sweaters and sitting still.
> That's okay for some people,
> Who don't know they're alive.

Like the "funny" in "Small World," the recurring phrase "some people" sets up the song's theme of some people but not her. The rhymes are now assertively masculine ("thrill/still"), softened by rhythmic, internal, feminine rhymes ("knitting/sitting"). As for "alive," it is set to rhyme with "five" at the end of the next chorus and the internal "thrive" along the way:

> Some people can thrive and bloom,
> Living life in a living room—
> That's perfect for some people
> Of one hundred and five.

"Thrive and bloom" is an original phrase that has an idiomatic ring, and so even though poetic, it sounds like Rose. "Living life in a living room" combines common phrases with the device of repetition. It also echoes the soft "i" sound in the first chorus's "knitting sweaters and sitting still." Even so there is room for improvement: "Some people/Of one hundred and five" seems to mean one hundred and five people instead of people who are one hundred and five years old. That is because the pause between the lines makes them sound like separate thoughts.

Just when the song seems over, it turns to a new idea introduced by a melody ("I had a dream") from the upcoming "Everything's Coming Up Roses." These musical cross-references are typical of the Sondheim-induced details that lift *Gypsy* above other Broadway scores.

This is the first lyric mention of Rose's dreams, which are a splendid literary device in Arthur Laurents's libretto. Her dreams will be a recurring theme:

> I had a dream,
> A wonderful dream, Poppa.

Rose is concocting this dream as a ploy to borrow money for her kiddie act. Sondheim's lyrics are dialogue, so well learned from Oscar Hammerstein:

> There I was in Mr. Orpheum's office
> And he was saying to me,
> "Rose!"
> Get yourself some new orchestrations,
> New routines and red velvet curtains.
> Get a feathered hat for the baby,
> Photographs in front of the theater,
> Get an agent—and in jig time
> You'll be being booked in the big time!

The words are meaty enough to chew on, and we can practically hear Mr. Orpheum giving her this show business advice. A big-time booking agent would talk this way, we think, only Rose is writing his dialogue, in her dream. It sounds like her, too—"get" this and "get" that—and Sondheim uses that repeating word for punching out the rhythm in Styne's music. Indeed, he places each "get" on the same note, which is more likely to occur to a composer-lyricist than to a strictly word man.

There are no rhymes in the Orpheum dream, for it is the aggressive Rose, not Mr. Orpheum, who is really talking, and she is trying to stiff-arm her father's resistance until the neat and natural "jig time" rhymes off with "big time," ending the dream with an exclamation point. Unfortunately the spiel doesn't work, as her father tells her, "You ain't getting eighty-eight cents from me, Rose."

A few songs later, she has convinced Herbie, now her kiddie act's manager, to be her beau, and Styne provides Rose with another set of, as he puts it, "big notes." Again, as so well learned from Hammerstein, Sondheim's lyric is conversational even unto its (first-line) title:

> You'll never get away from me.
> You can climb the tallest tree,
> I'll be there somehow.
> True, you could say, "Hey, here's your hat,"
> But a little thing like that
> Couldn't stop me now.

This is flawless work, every syllable landing squarely on its note, each word stress a natural one. Rhymes are tucked into niches where they are heard but not seen—"true/you," "say, 'Hey.' " Outside, too, the rhymes are simple and affirmative: "me/tree," "hat/that," "how/now."

The *Gypsy* parade of assertive and muscular show songs marches vigorously toward the end of the first act. Sondheim's lyrics and Styne's music dovetail consistently to catch a heightened sense of vaudeville. "You'll Never Get Away from Me" is followed by Sondheim's personal favorite in the show, "If Momma Was Married." The idea of a song on this subject was his, and he chose the tune from several that the fertile Styne presented for his approval ("Something like this, Steve? No? You like this? No? Let's tear it up. You like this?").

Why, in this abundance of show tunes, is "If Momma Was Married" Sondheim's favorite? The song is an escape fantasy for June and Louise, who, instead of a forced life on the stage, would prefer a normal home and preoccupied mother.

> If Momma was married we'd live in a house,
> As private as private can be:
> Just Momma, three ducks, five canaries, a mouse,
> Two monkeys, one father, six turtles and me . . .
> If Momma was married.

Does he like it because of the music? He admires a recapitulation of an opening theme in the middle. He likes the "neatness" (high praise from him) of his lyric. He likes the sophisticated musical device of recapitulating "Let Me Entertain You" inside the song.

To end the first act, Styne and Sondheim ignite a rocket, "Everything's Coming Up Roses." It blows the audience into the lobby for intermission. The song starts with two notes that Styne loaded for Merman to launch: "You'll be (swell)." The entire song, delivered after the jolting news that June has gone, is Rose's pep talk to Louise—and to herself. Beginning with the dream motif, it becomes, as Arthur Laurents puts it in his stage direction, "like a gallant, joyous express train."

> I had a dream,
> A dream about you, baby!
> It's gonna come true, baby!
> They think that we're through,
> But,
> Baby,

This is not a verse so much as it is a hold onto your hats.

> You'll be swell, you'll be great,
> Gonna have the whole world on a plate!
> Starting here, starting now,
> Honey, everything's coming up roses!

By now Sondheim has developed a rhyming manner that is strictly Rose's, and it is bone simple:

> Now's your inning—
> Stand the world on its ear!
> Set it spinning,
> That'll be just the beginning!

He has immersed himself in the show and in the character, transcending his own language for the larger purpose of the work. "Everything's Coming Up Roses" is not Sondheim talking; it is Rose. His teachers have had their influence: Oscar Hammerstein on precision, "singability," dialogue; Dorothy Fields on characterization and colloquialism. But as for clarity and simplicity of language, as for the flow of emotion, the poetic imagery within the conversational flow, these are uniquely Sondheim's:

> Curtain up, light the lights,
> We got nothing to hit but the heights!
> I can tell,
> Wait and see!
> There's the bell,
> Follow me,
> And nothing's gonna stop us till we're through!
> Honey, everything's coming up roses and daffodils,
> Everything's coming up sunshine and Santa Claus,
> Everything's gonna be bright lights and lollipops,
> Everything's coming up roses for me and for you!

This is a lyricist on a roll by anyone's definition. Every line lands, each notion says what it has to say the only way it should, and by the time Rose says "Honey," she is a character whose only way to talk is with this song. As for "roses and daffodils," "bright lights and lollipops," by then Sondheim has gone clear into lyric-writing heaven.

As Laurents writes in his stage direction, "Herbie and Louise stand silent, numb as she plows on, singing triumphantly as the curtain falls on the end of Act One." The librettist is plainly in love with the best kind of cheap show business thrills, the kind that made Broadway musicals Broadway musicals.

In traditional musical comedy, the songwriter was allowed second-act reprises of the numbers that he hoped would become hits. Optimism (or greed) usually led to three or four such reprises. The second act of *Gypsy* reprises just one song, "Small World," but elsewise the show's assembly is typical of the period, scene-song-scene-song, ad infinitum.

Perhaps it seems picky to complain about such orthodoxy when, after all, there is such musical theatricality to the show, but a Jerome Robbins free to fulfill his imagination might have raised *Gypsy* to a still higher level of excitement. That is why, after all the dance and music in *West Side Story*, it is so disappointing to find him directing *Gypsy* in the traditional fashion, with static book scenes and almost dance-less staging. And then it is almost shocking to come upon actual cheapness in the second-act comedy turn, "You Gotta Have a Gimmick."

The rationale behind this song is that hardened strippers are giving backstage advice to the tyro, Louise. They are suggesting that she find a new twist for her act. The number's vul-

On the strength of Tyne Daly's performance, Gypsy became the hit of the 1989 Broadway season.

In "You Gotta Have a Gimmick," whose humor is not subtle, the experienced strippers give advice to the novice Louise, who is about to become Gypsy Rose Lee. (Shown here is the 1989 revival.)

garity lies in heavy-handed humor and the awkward, musical comedy way in which the piece is pasted into the show. Given its strident music, the common comedy in its lyrics—

> Once I was a schlepper,
> Now I'm Miss Mazeppa
> With my revolution in dance.
> You gotta have a gimmick,
> If you wanna have a chance!

and its resistance to staging, one is frankly bewildered that it was even created by such men of taste as Robbins, Sondheim, and Laurents.

Its mirror reverse is the legendary "Rose's Turn" that comes near the end of the show. This is an eleven o'clock number, designed to jolt and stagger the audience about ten minutes before the final curtain.

It is Momma Rose's "turn" in two senses, her vaudeville turn (or routine) and her chance to get a load off her chest. Rejected by the daughter she has driven to stardom, she stumbles onto an empty stage in a darkened theater and imagines in madness that the lighting spots her. We, the audience, are the audience that she hallucinates.

(Spoken)

> Hello, everybody! My name is Rose. What's yours? [She does a burlesque "bump"] How d'ya like them egg rolls, Mr. Goldstone?

(Sung)

> Hold your hats
> And Hallelujah,
> Momma's gonna show it to ya!

(Spoken)

> Ready or not, here comes Momma!

What follows are eighteen repeats of "Momma," an astonishing coup of lyricism and a litany of self-pity and fury culminating in a pathetic mutter-mumble of "Momma":

> Momma's talkin' loud,
> Momma's doin' fine,
> Momma's gettin' hot,
> Momma's goin' strong,
> Momma's movin' on,
> Momma's all alone,
> Momma doesn't care,
> Momma's lettin' loose,
> Momma's got the stuff,
> Momma's lettin' go,
> Momma—
> Momma's—
> Momma's got the stuff,
> Momma's got to move,
> Momma's got to go,
> Momma—
> Momma's—
> Momma's gotta let go!

Rose momentarily pulls herself together, although it is ominous. This is an explosive self-pity:

> Why did I do it?
> What did it get me?
> Scrapbooks full of me in the background.
> Give 'em love and what does it get you?
> What does it get you?
> One quick look as each of 'em leaves you.
> All your life and what does it get you?
> Thanks a lot and out with the garbage.

Not only would rhymes have dampened the power by making this a mere *song*; they would have been unnecessary because the music has so headlong a drive that the words are already imbued with the rhythm that rhymes usually provide. Here, Sondheim is tightfisted, doling out only the occasional internal rhyme such as "thousand" and "bows and."

> Well, someone tell me, when is it my turn?
> Don't I get a dream for myself?
> Startin' now, it's gonna be my turn!
> Gangway, world, get off of my runway!
> Startin' now, I bat a thousand—
> This time, boys, I'm takin' the bows and
> Everything's coming up Rose!
> Everything's coming up Roses!
> Everything's coming up Roses
> This time for me!

When Hammerstein saw the show in Philadelphia, he advised Sondheim and Laurents that they had to "give Ethel a hand" after "Rose's Turn"—meaning that they had to put a "button" on the number, an ending to let the audience stand up and cheer. The writers were appalled by the suggestion that with such an ending they make their mad scene a musical comedy turn. Sondheim told Hammerstein, "That seems dishonest to me."

*Angela Lansbury as Rose and
Zan Charisse as Louise in the
1974 revival of* Gypsy.

Above, right:
*Tyne Daly surprised many
theatergoers with her powerful
performance in* Gypsy *in 1989
because she was known
primarily as a television
comedy star. But her
performance was rooted in
extensive stage experience,
much of it classical. Here she
appears with Christa Moore as
Louise.*

"Yes, it's dishonest," Hammerstein replied, "but there's also *theatrical* honesty and an audience out there and if you want them to listen to those last two pages of dialogue [after the song] then you've got to give them their release at the end of that song."

Ultimately, many would question why the curtain wasn't just dropped after "Rose's Turn." Laurents would forever insist that his last two pages of drama were necessary. It does seem as if they are there to keep *Gypsy* a play, rather than letting it go out a musical.

So a high note for Rose—a "big finish"—concludes "Rose's Turn," an otherwise jagged and frightful piece. As Laurents puts it, "She's screaming away and screaming away and suddenly [you're reminded], 'We're in a musical. I forgot.'"

It may be, however, that his two last pages are the real culprits, and that after "Rose's Turn" the curtain is being held up against the show's wishes. This number has a classic inevitability about it, and that is what all creators dream of: a character, a story, an ending, a work that takes on a life of its own. Given the imaginary and ghostly applause that is provided by the real audience, "Rose's Turn" achieves a chilling and overwhelmingly climactic quality. It is not merely a tough act to follow but perhaps an *impossible* act to follow. No matter what Laurents's final scene intends or does, most people remember *Gypsy* as ending with "Rose's Turn."

On opening night Jerome Robbins turned to Arthur Laurents and said, "It isn't my show. It's your show. It's a book show."

Gypsy opened at the Broadway Theatre in New York on May 21, 1959, and ran for 702 performances. The reviews were wonderful, yet this flabbergasting score was treated offhandedly by the critics. In the *New York Times*, Brooks Atkinson wrote that Sondheim "set amusing lyrics to Jule Styne's genuine show business score." Walter Kerr wrote in the *Herald-Tribune* that the lyrics were "just dandy."

The songs for *Gypsy* have long since been given their deserved recognition. They provided Sondheim with a chance to be part of traditional Broadway lore; he leapt onto musical comedy's last car just as it was flying into history. At the same time, *Gypsy* would give him the opportunity to do next what he wanted to do most of all: he would be writing his own words and music at last.

COMPOSER/LYRICIST

Two hits in a row and the phenomenally successful film of *West Side Story* provided Sondheim with a handsome income. The movie also made very popular songs of "Maria" and "Tonight"—which the show had not accomplished—and the soundtrack album became a best-seller. Finally the proceeds from the movie sale of *Gypsy* made him secure enough to buy a town house on the East Side of midtown Manhattan, just next door to Katharine Hepburn's. Sondheim called it "the house that *Gypsy* built."

These shows and their music were to become regularly performed classics, providing continuous royalties. At the age of thirty Sondheim was assured a comfortable income for the rest of his life. Yet that didn't make everything wonderful. He would always seem to find life's dark side. This time it showed up without being sought.

The gloom in the world of show business came from *The Sound of Music* and *Fiorello!* which tied in the season's Tony Awards as best musicals of the season. *Gypsy* lost to both; even its incomparably superior music lost out to theirs. Lyric writing was not considered worthy of a Tony Award until two years later, so Oscar and Stephen were spared the odd pleasure of competing against each other.

However, it was no time for pleasures of any kind. Hammerstein had been sick with stomach cancer since early autumn of 1959, and by the next July a death watch had begun. It was a grim sixty-fifth birthday party that was given for him at his New York town house that summer of 1960; in fact Oscar had already begun his farewells. Summoning the children to the den, he warned each in turn not to go weepy on him. He said there was nothing to grieve about: He'd had a wonderful life doing work that he enjoyed; he'd been married for some thirty years to a woman he adored. He asked them not to let Dorothy do anything "foolish" after he died, by which he meant fall apart. And when he said good-bye to her, he suggested that after the perfection of their marriage it would be greedy to complain that there was to be no more of it.

At a final birthday party he gave everyone a handsome photograph of himself. Sondheim impulsively asked for an inscription, which bewildered Oscar, "this man who had tutored and nurtured and argued with and tolerated me for nineteen years."

Hammerstein scrawled, "For Steve, my friend and teacher."

A week later they went to lunch—Sondheim was not sure why. Later he realized that it was for good-bye. He would dedicate the score of *A Funny Thing Happened on the Way to the Forum* to the memory of Oscar Hammerstein, *his* friend and teacher.

A FUNNY THING HAPPENED ON THE WAY TO THE FORUM

Burt Shevelove and Larry Gelbart wrote nearly a dozen versions of *A Funny Thing Happened on the Way to the Forum*—originally called *Roman Comedy*—before settling on the script that was produced on Broadway by Harold Prince in the spring of 1962. Their libretto is an adaptation of three comedies by the Roman playwright Plautus (251–184 B.C.)—

Zero Mostel serenades the young lovers, Brian Davies and Preshy Marker in A Funny Thing Happened on the Way to the Forum.

Miles Gloriosus, *Pseudolus*, and, of all coincidences, *Mostellaria*, for it was Zero Mostel who would star in the original Broadway company.

Although American musicals were long known as "musical comedies," they were usually musical romances. *A Funny Thing Happened on the Way to the Forum* may not be unique in its ancient setting—Rodgers and Hart alone wrote two toga musicals, *The Boys from Syracuse* and *By Jupiter*—but that may be the only sense in which *Forum* is not unique. Otherwise there is no Broadway musical quite like it. In fact it is so unusual that it does not even seem like a musical—or a play either. *Forum* is one of a kind, and surely the funniest of all Broadway musicals.

Sondheim's songs, while radiant, musicianly, and very cheerful, are not essential to it. Indeed, the authors, including Sondheim, agreed about that. Unlike the integrated musicals by Rodgers and Hammerstein, which used songs to develop character and propel dramatic action, this show leaves the musical numbers to illustrate what has already happened. The songs are rest stops, bracing moments while the farce catches its breath.

Its world is one of laughter. Not only is the lead character a comic role, but so are all the supporting characters—even the empty-headed lovers. The comedy, like Plautus's, ranges from physical to verbal, from clowning and chases to wordplay and one-liners, all within the tight construct of a silly but logical story. What is bracing is that Gelbart and Shevelove play to our intelligence; they make us feel educated even though we don't have to be classical scholars to get the jokes. It is enough that we are familiar with innocent young lovers who want to elope and long-lost children who can be identified by their rings.

A Funny Thing Happened on the Way to the Forum is also one of the most economical of shows, artistically as well as financially. The two acts arrive in less than a hundred pages, and every page counts. There is only one setting and a handful of principal roles, with a total company of sixteen and no singing or dancing ensembles. It starts with the slave Pseudolus leading the company in an announcement song, "Comedy Tonight."

> Something familiar,
> Something peculiar,
> Something for everyone—a comedy tonight!

The characters are clowns in a burlesque landscape and are not meant to be "real": a crafty slave (Pseudolus) and a hypertense one (Hysterium), a dirty old man (Senex), his dominating wife (Domina), a pompous soldier (Miles Gloriosus), a virgin courtesan (Philia), and a lovesick juvenile (Hero). Of these, only Pseudolus and Miles Gloriosus derive from the original material. The rest are invented, but their spirit is faithful to Plautus, and he should only have been so funny.

> No royal curse, no Trojan horse—
> And a happy ending, of course!
> Goodness and badness,
> Man in his madness,
> This time it all turns out all right!
> Tragedy tomorrow,
> Comedy tonight!

Sondheim's lyrics are direct and clear, and before any dialogue has been spoken, he establishes a language, a style that is casual yet elegantly appropriate to this Roman never-never land. And that number, "Comedy Tonight," was what Sondheim calls "the turnaround song"—the one that saved the show during the unnerving Washington, D.C., tryout. The reviews had been terrible (the *Washington Post* notice was headlined, "Close It"), and Jerome Robbins had been called in to help director George Abbott. He asked for a number to give the audience an idea of the evening awaiting them. Sondheim had already written one ("Invocation"), but Abbott had dropped it and reinstating it would have been disrespectful (Abbott was Robbins's mentor). So Sondheim wrote "Comedy Tonight" and, as if magically, the show worked.

The plot is complicated yet simple. Young, brainless Hero has fallen in love at the first sight of young, brainless Philia, a courtesan new to the business. His family slave Pseudolus offers to get this virgin for him in exchange for freedom. The problem is that she has already been bought by Miles Gloriosus, the military hero who is returning to claim her.

Pseudolus manages to extricate Philia from the brothel, The House of Marcus Lycus, and places her as a maid in Hero's house. There, his father, the dirty old man Senex, dallies with her as much as his decrepitude will allow (a fair amount). When Gloriosus returns from battle, Pseudolus convinces the second family slave, Hysterium, to pose as Philia—dead of the plague.

When Gloriosus insists on a funeral pyre for "her," Hysterium panics and flees in his dress. This begins a classic chase, choreographically staged by Robbins. It is the show's eleven o'clock number, musically staged, yet—symbolizing the nonmusical quality of this show—not a song (although Sondheim himself composed its underscoring). In fact, after the funeral dirge for "dead" Philia, there are no more new songs in the show. *Forum* concludes with a series of long-lost fathers, brothers, and sisters being discovered and a recapitulation of:

> Lovers divided
> Get coincided.
> Something for everyone—
> A comedy tonight!

So *A Funny Thing Happened on the Way to the Forum* is neither a musical musical nor a book musical. Rather it is a thing of its own kind.

Something else that is unusual about it, and striking, is that the songs are almost ritualistic—like vaudeville turns in a pillared temple (which they are). Except for "Lovely" and "Everybody Ought to Have a Maid," they certainly are not musical numbers typical of 1962 Broadway (ballad, ensemble, etc.), and for another thing, except for the early part of *Into the Woods*, this is the only time that Sondheim ever wrote merry songs.

They begin with Hero sighing over Philia, having just seen beauty, having just discovered love. He confides to the audience

> Forgive me if I shout . . .
> Forgive me if I crow . . .
> I've only just found out
> And, well . . . I thought you ought to know . . .

Like its singer, "Love I Hear" is sweet and brainless. The melody and lyrics reflect that, touched up with a strain of vulnerability in the harmony. Sondheim's counterpoint—the second melody in the background—is the verse to "Free," which will be the next song. So this is one case where there *is* a musical relationship between one number and another; generally, the *Forum* songs are melodically and harmonically disparate.

When Hero accepts Pseudolus's offer of Philia in exchange for freedom, the slave sings "Free," and Sondheim's musical voice can be heard for the first time. This music is spunkily dissonant. Its melody skips cheerfully across quirky intervals, hardly "pretty" in the conventional sense but interesting and dry yet still in the Broadway vernacular. It is, as Sondheim describes the overall score, "a vaudeville sound transmuted through my own style."

The lyric for "Free" is less interesting than the music, technically correct but without a comic point of view. As a matter of fact, few of this show's lyrics catch the script's dry and offbeat humor. One song that does, though, is "Pretty Little Picture," and it is just ingenious. It has Pseudolus urging Hero to elope with Philia, even suggesting what the elopement might be like, and it demonstrates how a composer and a lyricist can inspire each other to higher levels, even when they are the same person.

Feel the roll of the playful waves!
See the sails as they swell!
Hear the whips on the galley slaves!
Pretty little picture?
Well,

Let it carry your cares away,
Out of sight, out of mind.
Past the buoy and through the bay,
Soon there's nothing but sea and spray.
Night descends and the moon's aglow.
Your arms entwined,
You steal below,
And far behind
At the edge of day,
The bong of the bell of the buoy in the bay,
And the boat and the boy and the bride are away!

This, the song's second chorus, is but the best of three clever ones. The rhymes are straightforward, and each chorus/scenario is set off by a prefatory word––here, "Well," in the first chorus, "Now," while in the final chorus, "Think." Composer Sondheim helps lyricist

Phil Silvers was the authors' first choice for A Funny Thing Happened on the Way to the Forum. *When he turned it down, Milton Berle was announced as the star, but the show opened on Broadway with Zero Mostel and never seemed quite right with any other actor playing Pseudolus.*

The movie version of A Funny Thing Happened on the Way to the Forum *took Zero Mostel and Jack Gilford from the Broadway company and was enriched by the legendary clown, Buster Keaton, and comedian Phil Silvers. But the work was mutilated by director Richard Lester, who dropped almost the entire Sondheim score, and whose speedy cutting blurred the academic zaniness.*

Sondheim by providing rests after the notes for these words. That makes the music feel prefatory too.

Finally, "Pretty Little Picture" may be the only show tune in history to be about a literary device: imagery. For Pseudolus imagines that "The sun gets pale,/The sea gets red," then he imagines ". . . an island waits,/Smooth and sandy and pink,/Filled with lemons and nuts and dates," till finally he pictures "just the shore/Where the lovers lie." Moreover Sondheim chose the title not only because his song is about imagery, but also because it is about alliteration. In the first chorus there is ". . . a blushing bride/Slim and slender and starry-eyed." In the second chorus we hear "The bong of the bell of the buoy in the bay/And the boat and the boy and the bride are away!" Finally there are "The sand and the sea/And the stars and the sky/And the sound of a soft little satisfied sigh." These alliteratives occur on virtually repeating beats and that, too, shows how the composer-lyricist can help himself.

The music for this song is cheerfully dissonant, but Sondheim has mixed feelings about that. He recalls that Leonard Bernstein thought it was self-conscious about its "wrong note harmony [and thought] I was putting in dissonances just for the sake of dissonances. Lenny told me, 'You get afraid of just writing a C-major chord and so you add an F sharp to it just to make it literate. Don't do it just to be different.' "

Sondheim took the advice. He would use dissonance not simply for decoration but functionally. He feels that if any song in *Forum* suggests his music to come, it is "Pretty Little Picture." Ultimately, a heart-catching dissonance would be his musical signature.

When Hero's father, Senex, discovers Philia in their house, he's told she is the maid—a blatant cue for Hysterium and Pseudolus to join the old man in a typical musical comedy number, the vaudevillian "Everybody Ought to Have a Maid." This is the most irrelevant song in the show, but it is a marvelous number with its togaed lechers and it certainly works for *Forum*. It is the only old-fashioned showstopper that Sondheim would ever write.

After the encores dirty old Senex has to be kept from entering his own home because Philia is there with his son Hero, and it is making the second slave, Hysterium, very nervous. The music Sondheim writes for the spot, "I'm Calm," first reflects Hysterium's nervousness by way of a ⅜ time signature that puts a hitch in the song's flow. Then, with a serene waltz rhythm, the music reflects the calmness the slave is striving for. Again the lyrics do not contribute much to the fun, and so the number's effectiveness depends, rather, on the actor's delivery. Perhaps Sondheim was having trouble finding subject matter for lyrics that were not allowed to advance the action.

When Philia's owner, the soldier Miles Gloriosus, returns from battle to claim his bride, everyone panics except the unflappable Pseudolus. And when the pompous Gloriosus makes his entrance, Sondheim's march for the spot—"Bring Me My Bride"—gleefully captures the tone this paragon of vanity might adopt toward his sycophantic soldiers. There is delicious material here—

This Roman bath scene represents the kind of filmic realism that drained the humor from the movie version of A Funny Thing Happened on the Way to the Forum.

> There are lands to conquer,
> Cities to loot
> And people to degrade!

as well as Sondheim's own favorite funny line: "I am a parade!" It is a direct translation from the original Plautus.

By intermission most of the songs (nine out of eleven) have been sung. The two remaining are the show's weakest. First, "That Dirty Old Man" is never as funny as it first promises to be:

> I want him,
> I need him,
> Where is he?
> That dirty old man . . .

This must have seemed a wonderful notion for a song, and it actually relates to a character in the show, a real dirty old man. But there is nowhere for it to go.

> That dirty old man,
> Where can he be?
> Profaning our vows for all to see,
> Complaining how he's misunderstood,
> Abusing me—(If he only would!)

Sondheim might have been able to do more than reiterate that Senex is a dirty old man if he'd been allowed to add to, or steal from, the script. Instead he could only stretch to "abusing me" for his laugh. It is a stretch because the character is a Margaret Dumont type who would never talk about abusive sex.

The last new song in the show is "That'll Show Him" for Philia, the Kewpie doll courtesan. It is a one-joke song.

> When I kiss him,
> I'll be kissing you,
> So I'll kiss him morning and night—
> That'll show him!

The music is inexplicably set to a tango rhythm, which the orchestrators introduced at director George Abbott's suggestion and over Sondheim's protest. This is a formula show tune whose only musical interest is a cut-off chorus that creates a certain tension. The middle part of the song, the release, has nothing to do with the main theme and is about as workaday as anything Sondheim ever wrote.

But this is one lapse in a generally delicious score, original yet still traditional, musicianly without pushing a fistful of notes in an audience's face. Yet the score was not recognized for what it is: fresh, smart Broadway music and an extraordinary debut for a new young composer.

In the *Herald-Tribune* Walter Kerr, who was more intellectual than the average theater critic, saw the point exactly, calling it a "classically funny musical." He even noted the "faint touch of musical sarcasm" in the score, but in general the show got the notices rather than the songs; in fact, while *Forum* won the Tony Award as the best musical of the 1962–1963 season, Sondheim was not even nominated for the music prize.

Nevertheless, it was his first hit. Opening at the Alvin Theatre on May 8, 1962, it played 964 performances on Broadway, ran successfully in London, and became a staple of stock and repertory companies. Some twenty-five years later, Sondheim would consider it "the only really popular show I ever had."

Why didn't he count *West Side Story* and *Gypsy*? Presumably because they were not "his" since he had not written their music. Now, with a hit to his credit, he set out to show the world exactly what he could compose when given free rein.

ANYONE CAN WHISTLE

First called *The Natives Are Restless* and then *Side Show*, *Anyone Can Whistle* was written from 1962 to 1964. It is the failure that tested Sondheim's professional mettle, and with it he proved that he was willing to dare what he believed in—on commercial Broadway; it proved too that he could survive rejection. If what was wrong with *Anyone Can Whistle* made it unacceptable at the box office, what was right about it made Stephen Sondheim the theater's man of hope.

It was also a self-righteous and unfocused social satire, too frequently humorless in its relentless effort to be funny. The libretto is about a fictitious town gone bankrupt. To save it for themselves, the unpopular Mayoress Cora Hooper (Angela Lansbury) and her political cronies fake a miracle: curative waters that spout from a rock in the town square. The hoped-for tourists ("pilgrims") soon come flocking.

Nurse Fay Apple (Lee Remick) of the local mental hospital, the Cookie Jar, is a dedicated realist and arrives with her patients, the Cookies, to test—that is, disprove—the miracle waters. When the alarmed Mayoress orders them arrested, Nurse Apple turns her wards loose. That is when Hapgood (Harry Guardino) arrives, actually a new patient but mistaken for the assistant psychiatrist who was expected to arrive that same day. The Mayoress prevails upon him to separate the sane from the insane. Instead he declares everyone mad.

In the second act, Nurse Apple returns disguised as a sexy "Lady from Lourdes," an authority on miracles, but she personally is so repressed that only in disguise can she be free of "control and order." When she admits that what she really needs is a personal miracle, Hapgood tells her that there is only one miracle, "being alive," and, he adds with similar wisdom, "Either you die slowly or you have the strength to go crazy."

The Mayoress, under threat from the governor, decides to resupply the mental hospital by arresting the first forty-nine people she sees. That is when Nurse Apple agrees to identify her patients—named for history's nonconformists, from Brecht and Freud to John Dillinger and the first transsexual, Christine Jorgensen. Finally she realizes that she has found her own miracle—love—and falls into Hapgood's arms.

Arthur Laurents, who wrote this story, was also the show's director, and that made for an inauspicious beginning. In the first place, he had directed but one musical (*I Can Get It for You Wholesale*), and secondly, the director-author combination rarely works because the temptation for self-indulgence is too great.

Anyone Can Whistle had other handicaps: It was Broadway's riskiest business, a musical with an original book and an unorthodox one in the bargain. The audience for musicals is the most conservative on Broadway; it wants every new show to be like the good old ones.

Sondheim became very close to Lee Remick during the run of Anyone Can Whistle *and even after her death he would speak of her work in the present tense: "Lee, though she has occasional pitch and rhythmic problems, can sing." Here she sings the stirring "There Won't Be Trumpets."*

Above, left and right:
In Anyone Can Whistle, *the rollicking "Cookie Chase," also featured a bearded Don Doherty.*

Finally, escapist theater like musicals is inhospitable to messages, and no theater is hospitable to the scattershot ones this show was delivering. Thus it was going the wrong way in a 1964 season that was parading Broadway musicals at their best (*Fiddler on the Roof*, *Hello, Dolly!*). In fact show business was so healthy that year that even musicals like *Funny Girl*, which weren't so good, weren't so bad.

Broadway is an exciting place. A great adventure like *Anyone Can Whistle* can showcase a fabulous, freshly developed artist like Stephen Sondheim and be a very important event in the evolution of musical theater. But Broadway is also a tough place, and if the show doesn't work, it doesn't work. This show would have succeeded, avant-garde and all, if it had been a good show as well as a brilliant one, but despite its clever production, abundant and inventive choreography, and dazzling score, *it simply did not work*.

The overture comes in the style of a madhouse carnival, a cacophonous and dissonant announcement of the bold Broadway music ahead. Then, as the curtain rises, the Mayoress is carried into a "Pop Art" town square (as the script describes it) by four chorus boys. This was Angela Lansbury, reclining atop a litter in her first musical, relaxed and professional and, of course, destined for stardom.

Sondheim wrote two "town" numbers for her, and both demonstrate his gift for applying musicianship to the Broadway vernacular. The first of them, "Me and My Town," again betrays his weakness for pastiche—writing old types of songs and setting them within quotation marks.

This number can be funny ("I'm so depressed I can hardly talk on the phone") and musically smart as it satirizes the overcomplicated vocal arrangements of some nightclub acts, their tight harmonies and syncopated clapping. Unfortunately, as throughout the show, Sondheim's musical sophistication is blurred by Don Walker's generic orchestrations. Walker, a respected veteran of eighty musicals, tended to give every score a "Broadway" sound, whether it was a Sigmund Romberg operetta or *Fiddler on the Roof*.

Despite the strident brass that often created an ugly statement of Sondheim's harmonies and leveled his dynamics, there could be no mistaking the freshness of this music.

As much could be said for Lansbury's other "town" song, "A Parade in Town." There is a tarnished gaiety to this number, a false bravado. A march beat is always assertive; to it, Sondheim sets an almost patriotic melody before drawing his accompaniment along dissonant lines. That undercuts the bold front and laces it with feelings of rejection and resentment. The lyrics articulate these feelings:

> Did you hear? Did you see?
> Is a parade in town?
> Are there drums without me?
> Is a parade in town?

Well, they're out of step, the flutes are squeaky, the banners are frayed.

Any parade in town without me
Must be a second-class parade!

Depression and fears of unpopularity are sadly familiar symptoms in modern life, but nobody had been writing about such things in the musicals of 1964. In dealing with them, Sondheim was coming closer to real life than the libretto's R. D. Laing-inspired pontifications on insanity as a higher form of individuality.

Angela Lansbury had a good chest voice (lower registers in a natural sound) and a satisfactory head voice (operatic vocalizing), but Lee Remick was on shakier singing ground. Sondheim tried to help by composing her songs within a modest range. He developed lifelong friendships with both of these women, and of course, ultimately, Lansbury was to become a great star of the musical stage and the leading lady in Sondheim's own *Sweeney Todd*.

The unusually intelligent Lee Remick would play a more personal part in his life, becoming as close as possible to a Sondheim who would always regret being unable to settle down with anyone, male or female. As a friend says, "He'd much rather love than be loved. There's something that terrifies him about being loved too much. He really is a loner." Sondheim himself told a magazine interviewer, "One of the reasons I've been in analysis for years is that there are things I miss—like having a permanent relationship, and I don't know how else to work for it."

Even after Lee Remick's tragic early death in 1991, he would speak of her in the present tense.

Remick would finally have three songs. The best of them was the show's title song, a very beautiful piece suggesting the mature Sondheim ahead yet too difficult, in all fairness, for her to sing well. The song that was better suited to her (being faster, lower, and without all those rangy, sustained notes) was "Come Play Wiz Me." It is sung by Nurse Apple disguised as the "Lady from Lourdes," enjoying a romantic interlude with Hapgood. It is a very theatrical song, consistent with these characters and this moment; it is also the show's lightest number as well as being a familiar type of show tune (thus it was the most accessible song, and the reviews tended to mention it). Written as if for Rogers and Astaire, it follows through on Laurents's charming scene, where these characters speak in French clichés that are translated on a title screen above.

We have ze lark—yes? Ze fling—yes?
Ze play is ze—how you say?—is ze thing—yes?

However Sondheim's most impressive work in *Anyone Can Whistle* are two elaborate musical-dramatic sequences: "Simple," a wonderful example of teamwork between a librettist and a composer, and "The Cookie Chase," a comic ballet with dialogue.

"Simple" begins with Hapgood announcing that he is going to separate the sane from the insane "according to the principles of logic." Then, to music written in a dry, nursery-rhyme style, he sings:

Grass is green,
Sky is blue,
False is false and
True is true,
Who is who?
You are you,
I'm me!
Simple? Simple? Simple?
Simple as ABC,
Simple as one-two-three!

Comic actors appearing with Lansbury in this scene from Anyone Can Whistle *are Arnold Soboloff (left) and Henry Lascoe.*

Angela Lansbury as the Mayoress in Anyone Can Whistle, *with henchmen Arnold Soboloff and Henry Lascoe.*

Hapgood has no intention of separating the sane from the insane. He is going to taunt the Mayoress and her political cronies as he "interrogates" the mixed crowd, and here Laurents's dialogue becomes as tart as Sondheim's music. In all of our musical theater, there was as yet no better example of interwoven drama and song. Its roots lie in the "Bench Scene" that Oscar Hammerstein had written to Richard Rodgers's music in *Carousel*.

"Simple" marks an important moment in Sondheim's work, the start of a major line of development. He and Laurents wrote it simultaneously, the librettist at the piano alongside the composer.

HAPGOOD

(Spoken rhythmically) Married?

GEORGE

Yes, sir!

HAPGOOD

Two children?

GEORGE

Yes, sir.

HAPGOOD

Two TV sets?

GEORGE

Yes, sir.

HAPGOOD

Two martinis?

GEORGE

Yes, sir.

HAPGOOD

Do you vote?

With Angela Lansbury, the lead players in Anyone Can Whistle *were Lee Remick and Harry Guardino—actors rather than singers. Lansbury later became a star of musical comedy, but Remick concentrated on dramatic acting. Guardino, Sondheim felt, "had a wonderful voice—a big natural sound—which he ruined by not taking any lessons."*

In Anyone Can Whistle, *Mayoress Angela Lansbury asks Harry Guardino to separate the sane from the insane. Such a number, "Simple," exemplifies why it was so hard to get the show on.*

(Sung) Only for the man who wins.
Only for the man who wins.
Only for the man who—

HAPGOOD

All right. Headaches?

GEORGE

No, sir.

HAPGOOD

Backaches?

GEORGE

No, sir.

HAPGOOD

Heartaches.

GEORGE

No, sir.

HAPGOOD

Thank you . . . Group A. Over there, please.

POLITICIAN

What's Group A?

MAYORESS

Obviously mad as a hatter.

POLITICIAN

Place that Cookie under arrest.

HAPGOOD

Just a moment. George—do you ever wonder whether you're real?

GEORGE

No, sir. I know I'm not.

HAPGOOD

Group One. Over *there,* please.

Considering the dark ingenuity of all this, it may seem small potatoes to note the interior rhyming of "You be you and me to some degree," but it isn't small potatoes. It is only because Sondheim has absolutely digested the fundamentals of the lyric writing craft that he can proceed—*he has earned the right to proceed*—to such ambitious sequences as this.

His music in this number uses dissonance to the powerful advantage of putting a cutting edge beneath strong melodies. There is also knowing and confident use of alternating rhythms to state attitudes—first an assertive march, then a mockingly compliant waltz. But Sondheim, who in general avoids social or political messages in his musicals—and wisely so, now found himself writing a lyric for just such a message:

The opposite of Left is Right,
The opposite of right is wrong,
So anyone who's Left is wrong, right?

It follows the lead of Laurents's dialogue within this *eighteen-minute* sequence, an assault on the entire liberal hate list, from the military to racists, religious fundamentalists, even nuclear stockpilers. No clear connection is made among these or with the sanity-insanity theme, to which "Simple" finally returns with a stunning theatrical coup: The entire ensemble becomes irrational.

After a blackout in which only Hapgood's face is visible—telling the audience, "You are all mad"—the lights go up on a row of theater seats. There the cast is seated, mocking the audience with applause as the curtain falls. At the theatergoer's end of this equation, a certain unease was understandable.

The other elaborate sequence comes in the third act (this is the rare, three-act musical). The show's extensive use of dance culminates in this "Cookie Chase."

Unlike classical ballet, which is choreographed to a finished piece of music, in a Broadway musical the dance steps usually come first: A dance pianist, working with the choreographer, draws upon melodies from the score and improvises with them as the steps are devised. That is why the dance music for most musicals sounds pasted and cut. However, for "The Cookie Chase," Sondheim (mostly) composed original dance music. Herbert Ross, a ballet-trained choreographer, was fully up to matching this score with satiric dancing, and Laurents wrote rhythmic dialogue to slip through peepholes, crannies, and pauses in the dancing and the music. The result is a unique sung-danced-dramatized sequence.

Binding all the activity in "The Cookie Chase" was Sondheim's music—the only extended, unsung music he ever wrote for the theater. These are waltz variations in the style of the Tchaikovsky of "Swan Lake," the Ravel of "La Valse" and "Valses Nobles et Sentimentales," but in Sondheim's own voice—a musical voice that begins to emerge in this show like a butterfly from a cocoon. That voice, thoughtful in its melodic and harmonic character, can also be heard in "Me and My Town," "Come Play wiz Me," "A Parade in Town," and the show's title song. The musical voice is certainly young, strong, and clear in this dance music. Nearly all the waltzes are his own, although some variations were worked out in rehearsal by the gifted dance arranger Betty Walberg.

Not everyone was this impressed with Sondheim. Some years later Herbert Greene, the show's musical director and conductor, said frankly, if not graciously, "The music was grubby and ugly, so I designed an orchestra that was so unusual that it would make the music sound as though there was something really going on. . . . somebody was talking about *Anyone Can Whistle* as being way ahead of its time. And its musical level was such blah, blah, blah, I just *howled*." (He also had the brass to ask Sondheim for work after saying this.)

The critics were only slightly more appreciative of Sondheim's music ("pleasant") when the show opened on April 4, 1964 at the Majestic Theatre. The rest of the show, to say it gently, was not admired, and it closed after nine performances. The score has endured, thanks to an original cast recording made at the insistence of Columbia Records's Goddard Lieberson. His belief in it was visionary: A major composer and lyricist of Broadway musicals had arrived.

It would be six years before he would be welcomed back.

DO I HEAR A WALTZ?

"Humiliating" is probably too strong a word for Sondheim's agreement in the months following to return to writing lyrics for another composer's music. Was it embarrassing? Perhaps the right words are "reluctant" and "mistaken." He was confident enough not to have lost faith in himself following the disastrous fate of *Anyone Can Whistle*. He was not in financial need. He simply allowed himself to be talked into doing something he did not want to do, and it would lead to his one association with mediocrity.

The experience would prove him professional enough, and man enough, to work well under the most difficult conditions. If we are measured by what we survive, *Do I Hear a Waltz?* is Sondheim's yardstick.

It was Arthur Laurents who convinced him to collaborate with Richard Rodgers on a musical version of Laurents's own play *The Time of the Cuckoo*. A minor Broadway success starring Shirley Booth in 1952, the drama is about a repressed American schoolteacher who is psychologically liberated while on vacation in Italy (it had already been made into the movie *Summertime*, starring Katharine Hepburn).

Teaming with Rodgers made for a dramatic personal situation, as Sondheim would be taking his beloved Oscar's place. It was dramatic for Rodgers as well, working with his first new lyricist since the famous partnerships with Lorenz Hart and Hammerstein. But Rodgers and Sondheim was not a heaven-made match; in fact "it was a ghastly combination of people," Mary Rodgers remembered.

The lyrics came to seem modeled here on Hart ("We're Gonna Be All Right," "Moon in My Window") and there on Hammerstein ("Someone Like You," "Do I Hear a Waltz?"). In each of these songs, Rodgers's music also seems to resemble his work with Hart or Hammerstein. Sondheim's unhappiness with the project did not lead to a lowering of standards, but he was confronted with serious problems: Rodgers was writing old-fashioned songs and Laurents was not providing well-defined personalities for the writing of character lyrics.

Worse than that was the atmosphere, with monstrous clashes of personalities. Rodgers was, by all accounts, pitiless in his abuse of Sondheim, and yet the proud and powerful composer was inspired to write some of his best songs in years. He had not yet lost his miraculous gifts (he had once said, "I can pee a melody," and while it might have been more elegantly expressed, it was true). *Do I Hear a Waltz?* is in fact the last good work that he would ever do.

The show, however, was a dispirited affair, an unnecessary and processed musical, safe and predictable and heartless. It was in almost every way the opposite of the audacious *Anyone Can Whistle* and gave Sondheim his one unpleasant theater memory. After opening at the 46th Street Theatre on May 18, 1965, and eking out 220 performances, it closed unmourned the following September.

EVENING PRIMROSE

Less than a year later, Herbert Sondheim died at seventy-one, but if, personally and professionally, this might seem a low point in Sondheim's life, he never stopped working. He did, however, change partners. After having collaborated with Laurents on three of his four musicals, he now chose a librettist—James Goldman—closer to his own age (Laurents was then forty-seven and Sondheim thirty-five). They worked on two projects: an original stage musical about a reunion of Ziegfeld Follies girls called *The Girls Upstairs* and a one-hour television musical play, "Evening Primrose."

While original musicals have been attempted on television, they have met with little success. ABC, for a short-lived series called "Stage 67," commissioned this one, along with other original musicals by Comden, Green, and Styne as well as Burt Bacharach and Hal David. The Sondheim and Goldman show was broadcast on November 16, 1966.

"Evening Primrose" is about a failed poet who has fled the world, hiding away in a Manhattan department store (the old Stern Brothers on West 42d Street, actually). Years later Sondheim would complain about being identified with the subjects of his shows, but after his experiences with *Anyone Can Whistle* and *Do I Hear a Waltz?*, he might well have been telling his critics:

> Good-bye, despoilers of beauty,
> Ruin another career.
> When you wake up
> With one genius less,
> If you can find me
> I'm here.

"I'm Here" is the first song in "Evening Primrose," and like a trumpet fanfare it

With Richard Rodgers at the piano, Arthur Laurents and Sondheim posed for a publicity picture during their Do I Hear a Waltz? *collaboration. Friction between Rodgers and Sondheim poisoned the atmosphere. Mary Rodgers recalled that her father thought Sondheim "was a brilliant lyric writer, but they were utterly incompatible from every point of view."*

Sergio Franchi sings the beautiful "Stay" to Elizabeth Allen in Do I Hear a Waltz? *Although there was a blandness about this show, its score is ingratiating, with melodious music by Richard Rodgers, set by Sondheim to smooth, dextrous and charming lyrics.*

announces the arrival of Sondheim's musical voice. The promise of *Anyone Can Whistle* has been kept. This is a great moment, unmistakable, for the artistic language is simply *there*, bright and shining and proud of itself, as it should be.

Starting with the poet's nervous heartbeat as he hides in the store, Sondheim establishes a jittery vamp (rhythmic motif). This becomes a Broadway rhythm, surging and muscular. The melodic theme is wary but then soars. The harmonies are French, muted, bittersweet. The spaces between tones are widened, building in a theatrical way to a real peak in the middle before concluding with fear and uncertainty in the lyrics as well as the music.

Goldman's script, based on a story by John Collier, is a fanciful but sometimes coy tale about a subculture of dropouts who live in the department store, posing by day as mannequins. This poet falls in love with one of them, a girl who is nearly as naive as Philia in *Forum*. Together they worry about the "dark men" who punish disobedient dropouts by changing them into real mannequins.

The song Sondheim wrote for this girl is called "I Remember," although it might be subtitled "The Simile Song."

> I remember snow,
> Soft as feathers,
> Sharp as thumbtacks,
> Coming down like lint,
> And it made you squint
> When the wind would blow.

Perhaps "Evening Primrose" is about a poet, which would make the song's continuous similes appropriate, but the poet is not singing the song. Coming from the girl, these images seem precious. The music also has ambitions, but achieves them more successfully. It is built from a five-note figure that Sondheim takes through a series of modulations, an almost mathematical and ultimately satisfying exercise. "I Remember" is nearly an art song, and the occasional jazz singer still performs it, but the lyric makes it seem coy.

Sondheim's television experience clearly made him comfortable writing for the medium, and he made rather sophisticated use of its possibilities. Anticipating future movie techniques, he wrote "When?" to be sung as a voice-over, so that the characters could do other things while they were heard singing it. This is a long, sweet, and melancholy duet between the poet and the girl, cannily arranged for its final notes to coincide with a clock chiming the hour.

The best of the show's four songs is the concluding "Take Me to the World." The yearning in its lyric is reflected in the long-lined, wide-ranging music.

While the piece is traditional in structure, it is very sophisticated musically. The middle part relates to the main theme in a harmonic way, rather than as a melodic development, which creates a subtler wholeness. As accompanied by Norman Paris's spare and melancholy woodwind orchestration (the show used a chamber group, mostly reeds), the piece is all the more evocative for its harmonies. An ordinary composer would have made "Take Me to the World" a big, expansive, and affirmative number. These harmonies raise doubts. In a Sondheim song, wishes are hopes for better than the worst.

Finally "Evening Primrose" features a Sondheim rarity, an instrumental piece. This is a charming waltz for two clarinets, evocative of Satie, and it is delightful.

As for the story, it has a trick dramatic ending, a kind that was typical and effective enough at the time: The lovers almost escape the "dark men" of the department store; the show's last scene is of their wedding—in a store window, for they are mannequins.

Neither "Evening Primrose" nor the "Stage 67" series fared well. The American Broadcasting Company was, in those days, the runt of the network litter, and these original musicals—quite a bold notion—did nothing to increase its stature. For Sondheim the broadcast was to be his last public hearing in several years.

THE PRINCE COLLABORATIONS PART ONE

Collaboration is the essential paradox in musical theater. It can be a productive way for creative people to work together, or it can be a euphemism for compromise. When one of the collaborators is a bona fide genius like Jerome Robbins, altering a vision to suit other tastes becomes unbearable. And so, following *Fiddler on the Roof,* he quit the theater for the New York City Ballet. There he would create a body of exquisite dances suggesting the theater works he might have made had Broadway allowed him the autonomy that a visionary deserves and requires.

Stephen Sondheim, on the other hand, likes the teamwork and enjoys sharing in a variety of visions, for he can apply his sophisticated and idiosyncratic musical mind to art or show business with equal relish and finesse.

When he teamed up with Harold Prince, the prospects were bright. They were old friends who understood and respected one another, and each brought an essential quality to the partnership—Sondheim artistry and Prince showmanship. They made a unique team, a composer-lyricist and a producer-director, and their collaboration would become symbiosis as they embarked upon a historic series of musicals. This series would free Sondheim to flourish as a theater composer while establishing Prince as one of the most creative directors of musicals in American stage history. Theirs would be the most important work to come out of Broadway in the 1970s.

COMPANY

Company was their first project, and it cropped up unexpectedly when Prince promised Sondheim he would produce the long-germinating *Girls Upstairs* if this show came first. It had been first conceived as an evening of eleven unrelated dramatic vignettes starring one actress (Kim Stanley). When Prince and Sondheim finished revising it with playwright George Furth, it was a musical about marriage and only three of the original playlets remained. Moreover, instead of being sequential, the vignettes (now five of them) overlapped and all the characters knew each other, watching each other's lives like a Greek chorus of kibitzers. This free-flowing and essentially plotless form was a breakthrough, a kind of play designed specifically for the musical theater.

Company was also mature in content, as it examined questions of love among the intelligent: whether a sophisticated person in the anxious atmosphere of a big city could function happily and productively in a marriage or even feel romantic love and sustain an enduring emotional connection. This combination of adult content and sophisticated form was one that would characterize all the Sondheim-Prince collaborations.

Thus ended the era of book musicals, in which the script minus the songs equals a play. There might be more, there *would* be more—*Annie,* for instance, and *La Cage aux Folles*—

because there is always room for a show that (as they say on Broadway) *works*. But henceforth a traditional musical—one with a realistic story and musical numbers that end every scene—would seem old-fashioned.

Company was characterized by Prince as "Pinteresque," because it takes place in its characters' experiences and is mildly surreal. The show is like a large, revolving sculpture with the characters' lives looked at from every angle: one complete rotation, that is the show's plot.

During the transformation from playlets to a musical, a central character, Robert, was created to link the libretto's five couples and their stories. The only other characters in the show are his three girlfriends; in fact these fourteen characters are the entire cast, or "company." This, then, was a chamber-sized musical on a Broadway accustomed to ensembles of singers and dancers and elaborate costumes and scenery.

The Boris Aronson–designed set was abstract, a sleek scaffold evocative of modern Manhattan, looking like a three-dimensional Mondrian made of chromium and lucite. It was fitted with two elevators to move the actors between levels, and its various areas could serve as apartments or even a nightclub.

The show begins and ends with a surprise party for Robert's thirty-eighth birthday. At the start, as the five couples gather in the dark of his apartment, the dialogue establishes a tone of sophisticated banter ("I am very rich and I am married to him and I'd introduce him but I forgot his name"). Then a busy telephone signal becomes a two-note vamp for the opening number, set to pet names as the friends serenade the hero: "Bobby," "Bobby baby," "angel," "darling," "fella," "sweetie." That evolves into an antiphony of telephone conversations ("Your line was busy," "What have you been up to, kiddo," etc.), finally building to Robert's observation:

> Those good and crazy people, my friends.
> Those good and crazy people, my married friends!
> And that's what it's all about, isn't it?

Except for a rare lapse like stretching the two syllables in "married" over three notes, which Sondheim insists is intended ("a melisma"), the lyrics for the show meet the standard he set in *Gypsy*. Of course this milieu is very different from that, and so while these lyrics, too, are conversational, the characters, being better educated, are more articulate. They are glib, their speaking style is sophisticated, and for the first time Sondheim could justifiably write lyrics that were as clever as he liked.

If exemplary lyrics were by now expected of him, what was unexpected was his music. With *Company* he had quite simply *arrived* as a composer and the arrival was announced by this opening title number, a driving, incantatory piece that has the feel of Broadway yet goes in a fresh musical direction. Jazzy but tense, its melody moving up and then down along close steps with tight and bluesy harmonies, it builds from a hush to a shout—just like a surprise birthday party. There is also a feeling of choreography about this music, a physical impulse even though it is not a dance number.

Finally it does what Jerome Robbins had stipulated any opening number ought to do: It tells the audience what lies ahead, what mood to be in.

The first couple introduced is an amiable enough pair who demonstrate the wife's karate lessons to Robert. This violence reveals the hostility in their marriage, as they taunt each other about assorted shortcomings. It leads to "The Little Things You Do Together," a perfectly evil song of marital discord, for the things done together are not charming:

> It's the little things you share together,
> Swear together,
> Wear together,
> That make perfect relationships.
> The concerts you enjoy together,

> Neighbors you annoy together,
> Children you destroy together,
> That keep marriage intact.

Throughout the score, Sondheim seems stimulated by the subject matter, and at least with this song, he would write more lyrics, each outdoing the previous.

> It's not the profound philosophic discussions
> That get you through desperate nights.
> It's not talk of God and the moon and the Russians,
> It's who gets to turn out the lights.

Sondheim ultimately replaced the above quatrain with:

> It's not talk of God and the decade ahead that
> Allows you to get through the worst.
> It's "I do" and "You don't" and "Nobody said that"
> And "Who brought the subject up first?"

Why replace the earlier version, which is technically flawless and aptly refers to "desperate nights," even providing a specific example of marital hostility in "who gets to turn out the lights?" Perhaps because the later version is *all* fighting.

Small wonder that Robert asks the singing husband whether he is ever sorry he got married, and it isn't a joke. The responding song, "Sorry-Grateful," is so thoughtful and touching that many reviewers cited it as one of the show's best. It is a moving expression of romantic ambivalence.

> You're always sorry,
> You're always grateful,
> You hold her, thinking, "I'm not alone."
> You're still alone.

Popular culture tells us that love is romance: immediate, passionate, and unmistakable. Perhaps that explains our high divorce rate. In "Sorry-Grateful," Sondheim speaks for the intelligent, uncertain romantic who knows that even when profoundly involved with another person, there is no panacea for loneliness—no escaping the self.

In this song the words are more important than the music. The understatement of the waltz rhythm seems deferential to that, and the modesty of the melody (its tightness of range) reflects the careful thinking in the lyric.

A funny scene about another couple smoking marijuana ends sadly when the husband squelches his wife's fun. Marriage in general is definitely not looking good. That is when Robert's three girlfriends are introduced—with the only questionable song in the score, "You Could Drive a Person Crazy."

The problem is its style. All the other songs have a very definite, consistent, and unified style but this is pastiche, a 1940s, Andrews Sisters–kind of song like "Boogie Woogie Bugle Boy." Why? Sondheim says his intention was to have a number "tonelessly done—there is absolutely no emotion whatsoever in their voices as to what they sing." But the point of his lyric,

> Exclusive you,
> Elusive you,
> Will anybody ever get the juice of you?

is that Robert is emotionally unavailable, not the girlfriends. That is what the unattainable "juice of you" means, aside from being a clumsy metaphor.

Another problem is that pastiche does not merely evoke a period but comments on it.

Even when the tone is nostalgic and affectionate, there is mockery in the air and a sense of dissembling, a crooked smile on a covered heart. While the words are the character's, the musical comment is the composer's.

Finally, "You Could Drive a Person Crazy" is a set piece. It seems like an entertainment, and since that is not part of the show's style, it is an interruption.

On the other hand the next song is direct, playfully serious, and layered. The idea is to contrast Robert's thoughtfulness and anxiety about relationships with the locker-room attitude of his male friends. They get to sing first, and the sequence starts with their lustful envy of the single life in "Have I Got a Girl for You."

> Smart!—She's into all those exotic mystiques:
> The Kama Sutra and Chinese techniques—
> I hear she knows more than seventy-five . . .
> Call me tomorrow if you're still alive.

Why get married? the five men ask, kidding-on-the-square.

> Whaddaya like, you like coming home to a kiss?
> Somebody with a smile at the door?
> Whaddaya like, you like indescribable bliss?
> Then whaddaya wanna get married for?

The music for this sequence, which connects with Robert's musings just ahead, is a high-spirited and sophisticated waltz. There is an unexpectedly nice blend here of a musical comedy attitude in the lyric and an elegance in the music (elegiac, perhaps, like the words ahead). "Whaddaya" catches the lilt in this waltz. The words and rhymes are direct, and this seems how these fellows would be talking on such a subject.

When they leave, the waltz winds down to a reverie, as the number becomes Robert's melancholy soliloquy, "Someone Is Waiting."

> Would I know her even if I met her?
> Have I missed her? Did I let her go?

The music for this is heartbreakingly hopeful and hesitant, yet its melody is long-lined. The intervals between notes are tight, as if reflecting his constricted emotions, expanding only toward the end, as he expresses yearning and hope. Then the song comes around most satisfyingly to where it had begun. The lyric's musings on chance and possibility, hope and despair, present a thoughtfulness that had been all but unknown on the musical stage.

This is a man who despairs that all might be lost before he can wrench himself toward a human connection. The words are eloquent and touching in describing an Eve who combines the best traits of Robert's woman friends.

> My blue-eyed Sarah
> Warm Joanne
> Sweet Jenny
> Loving Susan
> Crazy Amy,
> Wait for me,
> I'll hurry, wait for me.

It is an art song, plain and simple, and from this point forward, *Company* will be a succession of musicianly theater songs, some tough, others tender, all with articulate, dramatic, and ingenious lyrics. Sondheim himself describes the score as being "traditional except for some rock treatments in the orchestration and a certain amount of anger and ferocity," but that is a modest assessment. It is a wonderful series of songs.

The next section weaves Robert's girlfriends through a scintillating theater piece, "Another Hundred People." The first of the women, Marta, starts singing it on a park bench as soon as the lights go up on her. The number is a rendering of the single life in New York City, of single people who want to meet other single people. It is propelled by the nervous energy with which Manhattan seems to jolt newcomers, as Sondheim sets a long and rising line of melody against a jangling and relentlessly descending accompaniment.

> Another hundred people just got off of the train
> And came up through the ground
> While another hundred people just got off of the bus
> And are looking around
> At another hundred people who got off of the plane
> And are looking at us
> Who got off of the train
> And the plane and the bus
> Maybe yesterday.

The song describes their depressing search for romance through meeting and courting and dating; the embarrassment, the vulnerability, and the foolishness of it—and the urgency.

> And they find each other in the crowded streets and the guarded parks,
> By the rusty fountains and the dusty trees with the battered barks,
> And they walk together past the postered walls with the crude remarks.
> And they meet at parties through the friends of friends who they never know.
> Will you pick me up or do I meet you there or shall we let it go?
> Did you get my message, 'cause I looked in vain?
> Can we see each other Tuesday if it doesn't rain?
> Look, I'll call you in the morning or my service will explain . . .

The city imagery is ground out in meaty words and the rhymes seem as indigenous to this landscape as parked cars. The details of dating—"pick me up, meet you there"—become ritualistic, and the refrain concludes in a New Yorkism that conveys the heartlessness in this search for romance, "I'll call you in the morning or my service will explain."

These words to "Another Hundred People" are set to a rush of melody, harmony, and rhythm barreling into a second chorus as the accompaniment turns sweeping and booming. Then, as the piece goes on, there are pauses for brief scenes. Robert's girlfriends, who had earlier sung "You Could Drive a Person Crazy," are introduced individually. The first informs him that she is giving up on him and marrying somebody else. The other two talk about themselves, but too sketchily to offer any sense of personality. George Furth's script, although filled with glib and funny dialogue, is not nearly as effective as Sondheim's lyrics in drawing quick strokes of character detail.

Take, for instance, "Getting Married Today," a patter song for one of Robert's friends on the eve of her wedding. These lyrics are written not merely in character but in *gender*. The song is about altar fright, but it trades in female terror, female nerves, female rhythms, female humor, and female irony. It does this with nervous-wreck female music, a mile-a-minute show tune for a panicking "happily soon-to-be bride" (as Sondheim ungrammatically puts it in the verse. He knows better of course and, again, insists that this is intentional. His intention is obscure).

The conceit of the song is to juxtapose the sedate church wedding against her bridal death rattle, a funny, colloquial, smart and slangy, utterly distraught stream of consciousness.

> Listen, everybody, I'm afraid you didn't hear, or do you
> Want to see a crazy lady fall apart in front of you? It
> Isn't only Paul who may be ruining his life, you know, we'll

Both of us be losing our identities—I telephoned my
Analyst about it and he said to see him Monday, and by
Monday I'll be floating in the Hudson with the other garbage.

I'm not well,
So I'm not getting married.
You've been swell,
But I'm not getting married.
Clear the hall
'Cause I'm not getting married.
Thank you all
But I'm not getting married.
And don't tell Paul,
But I'm not getting married today!

It was for Company *that
Sondheim won his first
recognition as a composer. He
later said, "I think it was
rather good for my growth that
I didn't start getting good
reviews until I was 40 years
old. If you had talked to me
about this when I was 35 I
would have been grumpy
about that, but in the long view
it's a good idea not to get used
to popular success."*

Once again, Sondheim uses repetition to convey a heightened emotional state, as the "I'm not getting married" series concludes the agitated litany. The style of dialogue is consistently of Manhattan, with conversational expressions streaming effortlessly (or so it might seem) through the song: "you must have lots of better things to do," "back to the showers," "listen, everybody," "thanks a bunch," "you've been grand," "I'm not well," "you've been swell," and most charmingly, "do you want to see a crazy lady fall apart in front of you?"

In its tongue-twisting speed, "Getting Married Today" is a showstopper, but it is especially effective because the character is real and likable and sympathetic. It rings of truth right until the moment Robert asks her, if she won't marry Paul, will she marry him? This comes across as contrived. There is something vaguely unconvincing about this bachelor.

More convincingly, she will marry Paul after all, as she announces upon catching her own wedding bouquet ("I'm the next bride"). With that the setting returns to Robert's surprise birthday party and the curtain falls on Act One.

It is to the birthday party that the libretto regularly returns; that is the binding element, and that is where the curtain rises on the second act. In moments the entire cast is doing an ensemble number in the style of a Parents Day school show, an inspired idea of the show's choreographer, Michael Bennett. There would, after all, have been no point in trying to make these actors look like the professional dancers they weren't. The number is "Side by Side by Side," and while its music is vaudevillian, unlike the earlier "You Could Drive a Person Crazy," this time the pastiche is endearing. Although evocative of a soft-shoe dance, it still seems musically relative to the rest of the score.

The lyrics address the friendships between this single man and these various couples.

> Isn't it warm,
> Isn't it rosy,
> Side by side . . .
> . . . by side?

The extra "side," of course, is Robert, and the song seems as sweet and cozy as these three-part friendships.

> Year after year,
> Older and older . . .

And then again:

> Sharing a tear,
> Lending a shoulder . . .

But Sondheim slips in the suggestion that these couples might be using Robert for their own purposes.

> One's impossible, two is dreary,
> Three is company, safe and cheery.

The number doesn't stop there. As if two vaudevilles were more fun than one, a new theme erupts: the exuberant, flag-waving, "What Would We Do Without You?" Sondheim ingeniously uses the style of lyrics such a breakaway song would have in order to further explore the role of the single male in a friendship with a couple.

> What would we do without you?
> How would we ever get through?
> Who would I complain to for hours?
> Who'd bring me the flowers
> When I have the flu?

Like his college satire "How Do I Know?", which satirized Irving Berlin's "How Deep

Is the Ocean?", this too is a question song. It is considerably more clever, sometimes almost too clever for words:

> Should there be a marital squabble,
> Available Bob'll
> Be there with the glue.

But most of the time, Sondheim holds his tongue, and his words are neat and clean as the rhetorical questions continue, repeatedly rhyming with "who" and the unspoken "you."

> Who could we open up to,
> Secrets we keep from guess-who?

And then again:

> Who sends anniversary wishes?
> Who helps with the dishes
> And never says boo?
> Who changes subjects on cue?
> Who cheers us up when we're blue?

It is hard to think of another lyricist who would take upon himself the dare of rhyming virtually an entire lyric with a "you" ending only the first and last lines. This is the puzzler in Sondheim, responding to his own challenge, and the lyricist in him is triumphant.

> Who is a flirt but never a threat,
> Reminds us of our birthdays which we always forget?
> How would we ever get through?
> What would we do without you?

Whether helping with the dishes and never saying boo, or being a flirt but never a threat, these words catch the essence of such friendships. The style of the lyrics is perfectly appropriate to the amiably rousing music and the characters who are singing, as well as to the homemade air of the choreography. The irony that laces the number's good cheer is a shadow passing across its sunlight. In all of life there is always a dark side, certainly with Sondheim, but there is always a light side as well, even with Sondheim. As a theater piece made from words, music, and staging, "Side by Side by Side/What Would We Do Without You?" is altogether right.

Immediately following is another aspect of these three-way friendships: the wives' possessiveness and their competitiveness toward Robert's girlfriends. He is bringing a date to his apartment with seduction in mind. Sondheim introduces some (for him) unusually bluesy music. To it, the onlooking wives cluck sympathetically as they sing that "it's such a waste" because "he's all alone" and "there's no one in his life."

> Bobby ought to have a woman.
> Poor baby, sitting there,
> Staring at the walls and playing solitaire,
> Making conversation with the empty air—
> Poor baby.

But if they think he ought to have a woman, they want to be the woman; they want to baby him, to be his mother. This number is their response to the earlier "Have I Got a Girl for You." The girlfriends, like the one presently in his apartment, are never acceptable to them, and as a Greek chorus, they sing in canon form:

> You know, no one
> Wants you to be happy
> More than I do.
> No one, but
> Isn't she—

Their negativism emerges in waspish (sung) comments:

SARAH:	Dumb? Where is she from?
AMY:	Tacky? Neurotic? She seems so dead.
SUSAN:	Vulgar? Aggressive? Peculiar?
JENNY:	Old? And cheap and
JOANNE:	Tall? She's tall enough to be your mother.
SARAH:	She's very weird . . .
JENNY:	Gross and . . .
SUSAN:	Depressing, and . . .
AMY:	And immature . . .
JOANNE:	Goliath.

The lines for Joanne were written especially for actress Elaine Stritch, whose dry delivery made "tall enough to be your mother" the funniest line in the show. As musicalized drama, "Poor Baby" is the show's most ambitious number and is as close as Sondheim gets, in *Company*, to a longer piece.

When he first played this "moderately dissonant" song for Prince, his friend and director asked whether it was supposed to be "pretty." Sondheim replied, "It will be," knowing that "so often it's a matter of just getting used to something that's dissonant."

After a charming scene in which one of the couples decides that, being divorced, they can now live together, the tough, wisecracking Joanne stands up in a nightclub and socks home the show's eleven o'clock number "The Ladies Who Lunch."

Sondheim finished the song late one snowy winter night. Pleased with himself, he sat alone at the downstairs piano in his Manhattan town house and sang it out in his croaky voice. Next door, Katharine Hepburn awoke with a start. Usually asleep by nine o'clock, she saw on her bedside clock that it was three in the morning. She could hear the singing, indeed; that was what had awoken her.

Steaming mad, she opened the French doors and tipped a bare foot gingerly into the snow. Then she stepped across the little garden and planted herself in front of Sondheim's window. "I stood there," she recalled, "and just stared with my nose up against the glass. And he just kept on playing and singing—until he looked up and saw me and I can tell you this— *when he saw me, he stopped playing that piano*." Indeed, Sondheim promptly bought himself an electric piano with headphones for late night composing.

"The Ladies Who Lunch" is a saloon song set to a sultry Latin rhythm. Its structure is a little unusual: a series of choruses repeating the basic theme, each chorus growing in volume and intensity to a climax, like a pop version of Ravel's "Bolero." The overall effect is that of a nightclub turn rather than a character or plot song. It is sung straight to the audience, which violates the show's fiction, but it works and that validates any approach.

The song is a disquisition by and about a kind of woman Sondheim seems to favor, a tough, boozy, wisecracking survivor of life's wars. Although it is the best song in the show, it is also the least relevant to the story. It is a sardonic toast to the New York women who have money and intelligence but no purpose, time to do everything of no consequence. In its ironies it admires these overqualified idlers, these glib and sardonic survivors.

The title is mentioned only at the beginning and the end:

> Here's to the ladies who lunch—
> Everybody laugh.
> Lounging in their caftans and planning a brunch
> On their own behalf.

Each of the choruses is addressed to a different group of idle women—after the ones who lunch, the girls who stay smart:

> Rushing to their classes in optical art,
> Wishing it would pass.

(Wishing *what* would pass? Sondheim's mental connections are not always clear. He means they wish the Op Art fad would pass.) And then the girls who play wife:

> Keeping house but clutching a copy of *Life*
> Just to keep in touch.

The singer finally includes herself among these grim, vulnerably tough women, as Sondheim laces in a dash of vitriol while repeating "another" to peak emotionally:

> And here's to the girls who just watch—
> Aren't they the best?
> When they get depressed, it's a bottle of Scotch
> Plus a little jest.

Another chance to disapprove,
Another brilliant zinger.
Another reason not to move,
Another vodka stinger . . .

Then, the final and brutal chorus:

So here's to the girls on the go—
Everybody tries.
Look into their eyes and you'll see what they know:
Everybody dies.

As composer for his own lyrics he could, and did, set "dies" on a fat high note, to then conclude with a searing repetition:

A toast to that invincible bunch,
The dinosaurs surviving the crunch,
Let's hear it for the ladies who lunch—
Everybody rise! Rise!
Rise! Rise! Rise! Rise! Rise! Rise! Rise!

This could easily be called "Joanne's Turn," and were the story over, now would be as good a time as any to end it. But (a) being circular, the story defies an ending and (b) if there has to be an ending it will have to involve Robert. And who is Robert anyway? If, at the final reprise of his birthday party, he is to go out making his own statement on marriage, solitude, and company, what is his statement? After trying another finale during *Company*'s pre-Broadway tour and being told by Prince that it was overly negative, Sondheim came up with a song that the director approved, "Being Alive."

Somebody need me too much,
Somebody know me too well,
Somebody pull me up short
And put me through hell and give me support
For being alive.
Make me alive . . .

Musically this song is very interesting, very satisfying, and extremely intelligent, because the pattern that begins it and then pulses throughout lends the piece a feeling of self-inquiry verging on a psychological breakthrough. There is an urgency about it, and even though "Being Alive" is basically an "AABA" song, the "B" part (the release) is so intimately developed from the "A" that the music seems almost circular, rather than linear. In that way, it mirrors the construction of the whole show.

The lyrics are another matter.

Somebody hold me too close,
Somebody hurt me too deep,
Somebody sit in my chair
And ruin my sleep and make me aware
Of being alive, being alive.

In addition to offering an incongruously happy ending, the song deals with loving as needing. The lover's purpose is to make the singer alive, to provide the love the singer cannot give (in Sondheim's earlier "Evening Primrose," a character expressed a similar request in "Take Me to the World"). But the singer offers nothing in return; he seems to see love only as something to receive and, at that, something threatening. For these several reasons, at a time in the evening when a show should be conclusive, "Being Alive" is problematic.

Mary Rodgers is convinced that Sondheim wrote some of the lines in "Being Alive" about himself. " 'Someone to sit in my chair,' " she says, "that's really the way he feels." In fact, the other finale, "Happily Ever After," reads:

> Somebody always there
> Sitting in the chair
> Where you want to sit—

Sondheim himself feels that "Happily Ever After" was the honest finale. It certainly was dark.

> No one you have to know well,
> No one you have to show how,
> No one you have to allow
> The things you'd never allow—
> That's happily ever after,
> Ever, ever, ever after,
> Ever, ever, ever, ever, ever after,
> Ever, ever, ever after . . .

Company, a musical of smart originality—modern, sophisticated, and thoughtful—deserved a better ending than the falsely optimistic "Being Alive." Harold Prince admitted, "I'm afraid it imposed a happy ending on a play which should have remained ambiguous." He concedes that "Happily Ever After" was the best finale, but as the producer he felt "it was too dark and I wanted the show to run."

Judging by the bleak ring of "Happily Ever After," Sondheim doesn't seem to have thought the ending should be either happy or ambiguous but, rather, gloomily ambivalent, for alone, while uncrowded, is also *alone*.

Prince would later say that the finale was the show's "major musical problem, one we never solved." He even went so far as to say, "Excepting its final moments, *Company* represents the first time I had worked without conscious compromise." Twenty years later, a perhaps unfair perception of Prince as assuming for himself the martyrdom of compromise continued to rankle Sondheim. "*He* was the one who threw out 'Happily Ever After.' "

Resentment thrives in the spaces between why feelings are expressed, how they are expressed, and how that expression is perceived. Was this where trouble began in the Sondheim-Prince relationship—unnoticed at the time but remembered long after?

The problem with the end of *Company* was not really this song; the problem was the script. After two hours of fudging, the show had to confront and define its ambivalence toward marriage. Sondheim was being asked to do that with a song, asked (he insists, by Prince) to invent an assertive and positive conclusion. That was the compromise, a denial of everything preceding, and Sondheim obviously feels that it was forced upon him.

Another problem lies with Robert: He is less a character than a subject. At the end he struggles to emerge as a character. Everyone wants this to happen—the authors, the director, the audience—because that is the only way to achieve theatrical catharsis. But the character has just spent two hours defying believability. What is his problem? Why can't he fall in love?

The answer is another question, one *Company* never faces: Is there an unspoken or subconscious level of homosexuality to explain him?

Despite this troubling conclusion, *Company* remains a landmark musical. The libretto strides toward a formulation, at last, for a musical's book as a play of its own kind. Sondheim's lyrics, by turns pyrotechnical and tender, set new standards for technique and dramatic aptness, but it was his music that made this day for him. Its extraordinary diversity and depth, its melodic richness and its accessible sophistication, finally won him recognition as a *composer*.

In fact the score earned what he considered his "first set of good reviews." After opening at the Alvin Theatre on April 26, 1970, *Company* enjoyed a healthy run of 706 performances. It even won Tony Awards for the season's best music and lyrics, along with the prize for best musical. All of this had to be tremendously gratifying, for it was a vindication of his self-belief as a composer. He was forty-one years old and he had arrived.

FOLLIES

The Girls Upstairs, which Sondheim and James Goldman had been writing for five years before *Company*, was a murder mystery set at a reunion of Ziegfeld Follies girls. In 1971, however, one year after *Company*, Harold Prince was not about to produce or direct a traditional musical. Inspired by a photograph of the silent movie star Gloria Swanson standing in the sunlit rubble of a razed movie palace, Prince envisioned the Follies musical as a metaphor for age.

Part of a director's job is supervising script revisions. This is especially true in the case of a concept musical, which is as much a stage creature as it is a realization of written materials. In the course of this show's rewriting, so much of it would be told through song and choreography that the final script would run a mere ninety pages, a third of that taken up by lyrics. Sondheim would write twenty-two songs for it, compared to fourteen for *Company*.

Although this was going to be a big show in terms of settings, costumes, and performers, its story has just four characters: the glamorous Ben and Phyllis, the unsophisticated Buddy and Sally. Arriving at the Weismann Follies reunion, these two former stage door Johnnies and the chorus girls they married use the occasion to contemplate what has happened to their lives over the last thirty years. The only thing that seems to have happened is unhappy marriages. Ben and Phyllis are at each other's throats, while Buddy cheats on Sally because she doesn't return his love. She has been in love with Ben ever since a secret dalliance in the old days; she has in fact come to this reunion to revive that romance.

Structurally the script is hardly as sturdy or as sophisticated as *Company*'s. In that show the theme is marriage in New York, and everything relates to it: The songs and the scenes are about marriage, and all the characters except Robert and his girlfriends are married couples. And so the theme (instead of, as in book musicals, the plot) serves as the armature on which the music, lyrics, and staging elements are constructed. The musical numbers do not illustrate or propel a story; they exemplify the theme. Thus, instead of the usual process of a director "staging" (making theater of) a script, the director of a concept musical devises a production concept that will serve as a metaphor for this theme. He is an artist, and his medium is theater.

In *Follies*, as the show came to be called, there is a powerful concept based on age and memory, but while the songs, the dances, and the stagings resonate with ghosts and images of decay, the dramatic scenes are simply about marriages that proved unhappy over the course of time. That is an inadequate approach to the concept's theme. Moreover, there are no subcharacters, subplots, or subtexts, only some old Follies singers who have splendid musical numbers but do not figure as characters. For much of this show, then, the book has little to contribute and seems an addendum that drags along behind the rich music and lyrics, the vividly pictorial direction, the pyrotechnical choreography, and the dramatic musical staging. Ultimately it is this book that keeps the show from being the perfect musical it almost is anyhow.

However, there is one aspect of the script that does share the strengths of the production concept. The leading characters' younger selves materialize. As Prince puts it, they look "as they had existed thirty years earlier. So much ectoplasm, they . . . wander as silent memories across the paths of their present selves."

These alter egos create a surrealism in the drama to match the surrealism in the staging. They allow the audience actually to see the characters' memories, to see the physical fact of age. Scenes involving the young Ben, Phyllis, Buddy, and Sally would come to occupy much of the libretto, and Sondheim understandably gravitated toward these vivid sequences for musicalization.

The show begins not with an overture but with an exquisitely eerie waltz that builds with ironic harmonies and dramatic dissonance through a billowing crescendo to a sweeping climax. The setting is the stage of a gutted theater. A statuesque show girl looms out of the darkness. Her makeup is chalky, her dress black and white, and she is followed by other towering and spectral Follies girls. Then six ghostly chorus girls emerge, their mouths chirping in silent song. Only after this establishment of the past does the present begin to emerge with the start of the reunion party and the entrance of the guests.

They are introduced by a Ziegfeld-like producer, and the reuniting Follies girls enter in promenade to "Beautiful Girls." Modeled on Irving Berlin's "A Pretty Girl Is Like a Melody," it is the first of Sondheim's pastiche songs, which not only re-create period but resurrect it. Like the Prince production, then, the score is composed in past and present tenses, to counterpose past against present and age in apposition to youth.

The alumnae enter wearing sashes that state the years of their shows (1919 to 1941). Like "A Pretty Girl Is Like a Melody," "Beautiful Girls" is simple, singable, and four square. Like stage songs of the period, too, it is set with lyrics that push, slightly, to be smart:

> Faced with these Loreleis,
> What man can moralize?

and often are:

> This is how Samson was shorn:
> Each in her style a
> Delilah
> Reborn,
> Each a gem,
> A beautiful diadem
> Of beautiful—welcome them—
> These beautiful
> Girls!

Among the ex-chorines are Phyllis and Sally, with their husbands. In the flush of seeing Ben again, Sally sings fearfully of her aging ("Don't Look at Me"), and then all four old friends reminisce about their youth. As if memory could materialize, their younger selves appear. The effect is startling and wonderful. Sondheim capitalizes on it with "Waiting for the Girls Upstairs," plumbing again the techniques of sung dialogue and musicalized drama that Oscar Hammerstein had pioneered with the "Bench Scene" in *Carousel*.

> Waiting around for the girls upstairs
> After the curtain came down.
> Money in my pocket to spend,
> "Honey, could you maybe get a friend for my friend?"

Enfolding drama and lyrics, he re-creates the sounds and images of these characters' memories. His music sounds uncannily like walk-out music heard backstage at the end of a show, echoing in the background. We sense Ben and Buddy's excitement, their eagerness as they await Phyllis and Sally at the theater just before show's end. We sense the wings and props and dressing rooms, we see the chorus kids and hear their sounds:

> BEN
> Hearing the sound of the girls above
> Dressing to go on the town,

No Broadway director was more painterly than Harold Prince. His staging of Follies *set a visual standard, opening an era of spectaculars.*

Clicking heels on steel and cement,

Picking up the giggles floating down through the vent.

This is an inspired choice of language and image, the rhythm of activity created through repeating gerunds ("hearing," "dressing," "clicking," "picking"), while onomatopoeia re-creates high heels clicking down the metal backstage stairs and giggles filtering through the air ducts. This is a picture show: what backstage looked like ("That's where the keys hung and/That's where you picked up your mail") and what Ben and Buddy did when they arrived early, to "hang around the wings/Watching things" until the curtain fell.

BUDDY

Then all hell broke:
Girls on the run
And scenery flying,
Doors slamming left and right.

BEN

Girls in their un-
Dies, blushing but trying
Not to duck out of sight.

BEN & BUDDY

Girls by the hun-
Dreds waving and crying,
"See you tomorrow night!"

Sondheim sends the words, this lyric-dialogue, along a breathless and giddy musical course to carry a rush of backstage sounds and images, and there emerges so vivid a pictorialization of that busy, noisy place that we are simply *there*.

The girls recount their own memories of waiting for the boys downstairs:

SALLY

Holding our ground for the boys below,
Fussing around with our hair,

PHYLLIS

Giggling, wriggling out of our tights,

SALLY

Chattering and clattering down all of those flights—

Here are more gerunds—active, colorful, evocative—and again they are onomatopoeic—"giggling" once more, "chattering," and "clattering." The images materialize for us—the girls fussing and wriggling—until the song, its lyrics as seemingly casual as everyday conversation, blossoms into an ensemble for present and past as the young alter egos take a turn:

YOUNG SALLY

Boy, we're beat.

YOUNG BUDDY

You look neat.

YOUNG PHYLLIS

We saw you in the wings.

The youth-age theme of Follies *was personified in the casting of performers who had been famous in their youths. The original Broadway company included Gene Nelson, Alexis Smith, Yvonne De Carlo, Mary McCarty, and Dorothy Collins. Alexis Smith stunned opening nighters with her time-defying beauty. Other productions were cast with Dolores Gray, Eartha Kitt, Juliet Prowse, and Patrice Munsel.*

YOUNG BEN

How are things?

YOUNG PHYLLIS

Did someone pass you in?

YOUNG BUDDY

Slipped a fin
To what-the-hell-is-his-name,
You know, the doorman.

These youthful ghosts are promptly deposited in the presence of age, as some of the alumni sing their Follies numbers—phantom songs in Sondheim's pastiches—"Listen to the Rain on the Roof," "Ah, Paree!", and "Broadway Baby." The last is the best of them, perhaps even more endearing than the songs on which it is modeled. There is a time warp created by these echo songs, but unfortunately the book scenes break such spells, drawing the show back to conventional reality, restraining the haunting theme of time, age, and memory with domestic melodrama.

To Sondheim the meaning of time is deeper and more provocative than that. He writes about life span, about the past being lost, or existing within the present. Ben's soliloquy on the subject, "The Road You Didn't Take," represents a major step in Sondheim's development as an artist. It is about past choices, but where another writer might have conjectured on what could have been, Sondheim takes an existentialist approach: There is no knowing where other choices might have led.

His thoughts are set to a rich and painful melody whose jolting drops and urgent rhythms musicalize a limbo beyond lost youth. Going to the heart of the subject, this song is about making choices and living with the consequences.

You take one road,
You try one door,
There isn't time for any more.
One's life consists of either/or.

Philosophy in a show tune? It is hard to imagine a better, a pithier, or more poetic way to express the finality of past choices than "one's life consists of either/or."

> The road you didn't take
> Hardly comes to mind,
> Does it?
> The door you didn't try,
> Where could it have led?
> The choice you didn't make
> Never was defined,
> Was it?
> Dreams you didn't dare
> Are dead.
> Were they ever there?
> Who said?
> I don't remember,
> I don't remember
> At all.

The rhymes are spare: a simple "dare/there," an understated "led," "dead," and "said." They keep the song coolly painful. Without this underlying technique—the clarity and precision of language—the eloquent aria would not be so expressive or effective. A honking in the musical interior jabs home the jeering doubts. As the piece continues the younger selves again appear, but Ben stops himself from further regret.

> You take your road,
> The decades fly,
> The yearnings fade, the longings die.
> You learn to bid them all goodbye.

The melody is repeated for the last two lines. It is the composer working on behalf of the lyricist, underlining the finality of youthful choices. Then, in a very fancy couple of lines that make a heady mix of past and future tenses, Sondheim has his character conclude:

> The Ben I'll never be,
> Who remembers him?

Had the script been the equal of these lyrics and this music, what a show *Follies* might have been!

The reuniting show girls reminisce about a dance turn and line up as one of them sings it.

> Who's that woman?
> I know I know that woman,
> So clever, but ever so sad.
> Love, she said, was a fad.
> The kind of love that she couldn't make fun of
> She'd have none of.

These lines merit rereading. In his shows Sondheim seems attracted to funny and sardonic women like the mayoress in *Anyone Can Whistle* and Joanne in *Company*—women like the one in this mirror, "so clever, but ever so sad." There is a dark side to their brightness, and it shows in their unwillingness to deal with love except in mockery: "The kind of love that she couldn't make fun of/She'd have none of."

As "Who's That Woman?" continues, the song prepares to become everything that

Follies is about. The old chorines first add a countermelody:

> Mirror, mirror, answer me:
> Who is she who plays the clown?
> Is she out each night till three?
> Does she laugh with too much glee?
> On reflection, she'd agree.

They start to dance and as they do, their Six Memories emerge from the upstage shadows. Within the *Follies* company, "Who's That Woman?" would come to be known as "The Mirror Song." As its halves are sung simultaneously—by the old-timers and their younger selves in the "mirror"—it becomes a union of past and present.

> Young Phyllis, Young Sally and the rest—lined up and dancing. Their scanty costumes are made up of bits of mirrors, which flash and sparkle as they move. The Memories upstage move in mirror image to the "chorus girls" down front. The tempo and excitement rise, the steps and turns grow harder, faster. Then the explosion comes as past and present mingle: the Memories join the "chorus girls" downstage . . . the two tunes mesh and all the girls sing out and dance at once.

This is *Follies* at its most wonderful, and Sondheim himself called it "maybe the most brilliant musical number in terms of the staging I have ever seen in the theater." As the song, like the staging, vacillates between past and present, the eerie effect gives way to the ongoing soap opera of the book (Sally to Buddy: "You've always got a woman someplace," and Phyllis to Ben: "When did you love me last? Was it ten years ago or never?"). Clumsy, too, is a song cue that one of the old Follies girls provides for herself: "I had a Follies number once, a solo, and they cut the goddamn thing in Philadelphia."

The cue may be clumsy, but the song isn't. "I'm Still Here" really had replaced a song ("Can That Boy Foxtrot!") cut on the road. Many Broadway composers have written at their best under an out-of-town deadline, and Sondheim did in this case. "I'm Still Here" is an archetypal Follies song; it also tells a character's history from the Depression:

> I've slept in shanties,
> Guest of the W.P.A.,
> But I'm here.

through the Thirties,

> I've been through Gandhi,
> Windsor and Wally's affair,
> And I'm here.

and the Forties,

> Amos 'n' Andy,
> Mah-jongg and platinum hair,
> And I'm here.

into the Fifties,

> Been called a pinko
> Commie tool,
> Got through it stinko
> By my pool.

surviving through character and grit,

Left to right: Betty Comden, Elaine Stritch, and Phyllis Newman sing "Who's That Woman?" at the 1985 Lincoln Center concert version of Follies—*a concert that was recorded and televised. When "Who's That Woman?" was originally staged by Michael Bennett for* Follies *some of the singing in the tap dancing sequences was prerecorded and lip-synched. "Otherwise," Harold Prince said, "they would have been too winded to achieve any volume."*

I've gotten through "Hey, lady, aren't you whoozis?
Wow! What a looker you were."
Or, better yet, "Sorry, I thought you were whoozis.
Whatever happened to her?"

until the singer is, if not triumphant, at least still breathing:

I've run the gamut,
A to Z.
Three cheers and dammit,
C'est la vie.
I got through all of last year
And I'm here.

Set to a plugging blues, "I'm Still Here" has been sung to a fare-thee-well outside of *Follies*.

In orchestrating the song for the show, Jonathan Tunick fulfilled his intention of making the pit band sound not like a real pit band, but a pit band as we remember it. Thus even the orchestra reflects the theme of age and memory, and here Sondheim's raunchy accompaniment is drenched in whiskey, befitting the kind of saloon song that "I'm Still Here" replicates.

Meantime Goldman's book rehashes the unhappy marriages, as Phyllis tells Ben that she "won't go back to what we've had" and he says, "Just leave me, that's all I want." It is a straightforward cue for one of the most powerful songs in this masterful score, the classic "Could I Leave You?"

In the soliloquy songs of various shows, Sondheim's lyrics are so conversational and dramatic that some singers are tempted to play the scene rather than sing the melody. That was a temptation with the funny "Getting Married Today" in *Company*, and so it is with the vitriolic and painful (pain-giving, pain-felt) "Could I Leave You?" He set these words, for irony's sake, to a beautiful waltz in the musical language he created for the present-tense songs in *Follies*. There is a hint of mockery, perhaps even madness, in the accompaniment, which heightens this waltz's relation to Ravel's "La Valse." Music and lyrics, the piece is vintage Sondheim. The tension between the acid words and the lilting music makes it a savage and intense classic.

Could I leave you
And your shelves of the World's Best Books
And the evenings of martyred looks,
Cryptic sighs,
Sullen glares from those injured eyes?
Leave the quips with a sting, jokes with a sneer,
Passionless love-making once a year?
Leave the lies ill-concealed
And the wounds never healed
And the games not worth winning
And—wait, I'm just beginning!

What, leave you, leave you,
How could I leave you?
What would I do on my own?
Putting thoughts of you aside
In the south of France,
Would I think of suicide?
Darling, shall we dance?

"Could I Leave You" is the only "plot" song in the show, that is, it is the only song that is a speech being sung by one character to another the way it is done in a Rodgers and

Hammerstein musical. The resemblance stops there. The piece is so personal it makes a listener cringe and turn away from invading a character's privacy. That makes for a strong lead into the show's most effective dramatic scene, as the four characters interact with their younger selves. As Prince put it, the younger selves "had intruded more and more into the evening, taking stage, confusing time, confronting the present with the past. [Now] in a sort of collective nervous breakdown, they took over."

Young and old, the eight of them explode, venting their frustrations in simultaneous speeches, and the show itself approaches climax. At this point—page 60—the rehearsal script ended, noting only that "what follows is a capsule Follies—costume parades, comedy routines, specialty acts—traditional and accurate in all ways but one. . . . What's different and unusual about it is the content, what it's all about."

The final third of the show, in fact, did not exist until the last two weeks of the six-week rehearsal period! Harold Prince said, "I wouldn't take that chance with anyone but Steve Sondheim," and it was Sondheim who wrote the rest of the show, some twenty minutes of absolute music theater. Like a skin that a snake has outgrown, the stuff of traditional musicals is now shed. Beyond all else, *Follies* was this new creature.

The eight people rage and the stage opens up like a magic box. "Trumpeters in medieval costumes emerge, heavenly music is heard. . . and [amid] valentine and lace the lights rise to bright gold. Dancers, young and beautiful, all dressed like Dresden dolls and cavaliers appear." Thus starts the nightmare Follies, "Loveland, where everybody lives to love." It is going to be a nervous breakdown in song and dance, and every number in it is going to be about madness of one kind or another. Sondheim has deftly changed the subject from happy/unhappy marriages to a more profound, complex, and abstract subject: love itself.

The towering, lavishly costumed show girls are introduced with traditional effusiveness. The greeting-card mentality of the introductions assume ironic weight in view of the story:

> Two lovers are like lovebirds in devotion.
> If separated, they must swoon and die.

As Young Ben and Young Phyllis enter, the older Ben and Phyllis "stand close to their young selves," according to the stage direction, "watching, listening to what was or never was or might have been." That line is meaningless. Sondheim's lyrics are more salient, meticulously in period, deliciously clever, and related to the characters' truth:

> YOUNG BEN
> I'll have our future suit your whim,
> Blue chip preferred.

> YOUNG PHYLLIS
> Putting it in a synonym,
> Perfect's the word.

But this is only the verse. The song is Sondheim's uncanny inversion of a song cliché, "You're Gonna Love Tomorrow," turning it to the *Follies* subject—to the marriage that Young Ben and Young Phyllis are dreaming of—but also, and more deeply, to time and reality—to the disappointments awaiting youthful optimism.

> You're gonna love tomorrow,
> You're gonna be with me,
> You're gonna love tomorrow,
> I'm giving you my personal guarantee.

The irony is no less relevant to Young Buddy and Young Sally, as Sondheim finds for

*The "Loveland" finale of
Follies is a musical comedy
nervous breakdown.*

*Broadway posters, also called
showcards, have become a
minor art form. The one by
David Edward Byrd for Follies
is a masterpiece of the genre. It
captures a show that is the
apotheosis of the Broadway
musical.*

them another period musical cliché, "Love Will See Us Through," to mock the difference between their love talk and the marriage awaiting them.

YOUNG SALLY

I may burn the toast.

YOUNG BUDDY

Oh, well,
I may make a rotten host.

YOUNG SALLY

Do tell.

YOUNG BUDDY & YOUNG SALLY

But no matter what goes wrong,
Love will see us through
Till something better comes along.

The twin pastiches have been composed in counterpoint, and the two sets of lyrics relate as well. When sung at once the effect is all the more impressive for being *so clear.*

YOUNG BUDDY	YOUNG PHYLLIS
I may vex your folks	Say toodle-oo to sorrow.
YOUNG SALLY	**YOUNG BEN**
Okay.	Mm-hm.
	YOUNG PHYLLIS
I may interrupt your jokes.	And fare-thee-well, ennui.
YOUNG BUDDY	**YOUNG BEN**
You may.	Bye-bye.
YOUNG BUDDY & YOUNG SALLY	**YOUNG BEN & YOUNG PHYLLIS**
But if I come on too strong,	You're gonna love tomorrow,
Love will see us through	As long as your tomorrow is spent
Till something better comes along.	with me.

Every song in "Loveland" will be a Follies-type number whose words relate to the story. Thus "The God-Why-Don't-You-Love-Me Blues" is a baggy pants and slapstick vaudeville about Buddy finding surcease with loving girlfriend Margie when his wife, Sally, tells him he is a "washout." Still, he sings of Sally, "I love her so much, I could die!"

She is tough on him because she is still heartsick over Ben, and as if she were Fanny Brice singing "My Man," she steps through the curtains to torch "Losing My Mind." She really *is* losing her mind.

Phyllis's turn is yet another form of madness, schizophrenia. "The Story of Lucy and Jessie" is about "two unhappy dames": One is Young Phyllis, who was honest and warm but not confident; the other is the woman she grew up to be, sexy but hard, "classy but virtually dead." The point of the song is that each wants to be the other—a variation on the notion of answered prayers.

Finally it is Ben's turn, and with a top hat and cane, he sidles out in front of a chorus line made mythic. (Michael Bennett's subsequent top hat-and-sequins staging of "One" in *A Chorus Line* would appear inspired by this.) In his all-white tails Ben makes an immaculate song-and-dance man. The beat is hushed, the mood is spooky, the song is whispered, a depressive's "top hat, white tie, and tails."

> Learn how to laugh,
> Learn how to love,
> Learn how to live,
> That's my style.

His number is easily elegant—pure Astaire—but not his lyrics:

> Some fellows sweat
> To get to be millionaires,

and then again:

> Some like to be profound
> By reading Proust and Pound.

but not he:

> Me, I like to live,
> Me, I like to laugh,
> Me, I like to love.

and here is the breakdown:

> So when the walls are crumbling,
> Don't give up the ship.

The song-and-dance man suggests laughing, loving, living:

> That's my tip.
> When I hear the rumbling,
> Do I lose my grip?

Losing his grip, he suggests again laughing, loving, living:

> That's my trip.

Ben is indeed falling apart. He forgets his lyrics and has to be cued by the conductor. Behind him the chorus line continues dancing, but the desperate Ben stumbles. He babbles about his own life to the dancers ("I just wanted her, that's all," "The job was there: I took it"). This material is smaller than the stage moment.

The Follies drops begin to disappear . . . through Ben's eyes and inside his mind, a kind of madness. Everything seen and heard previously is going on at once. Ghosts, memories, guests. They stand in groups on platforms which move back and forth. At the center of each little group, a soloist stands singing their number. The singing is eerie and jangled. And through it all, Ben's chorus line continues dancing. The cacophony is terrible.

Incredibly, the songs in the "Loveland" sequence as well as "The Road You Didn't Take" were deleted when *Follies* was finally produced in London in 1987. The excision of these numbers—among the highlights of a superlative score—suggests a continuing compliancy in Sondheim during collaborations.

When the chaos is resolved, the stage becomes quiet, deserted, and eerily sunlit. Sally is perhaps the worse for wear, but she is only depressed, not Depressed. Ben and Phyllis head for the credits with small-talk wisdom (Phyllis: "Hope doesn't grow on trees; we make our own") and a romantic fade-out (Ben: "You see straight through me and I've always thought, 'It isn't possible; it can't be me she loves' "). The only explanation for these catharses is that everyone has gone through the looking glass of the Loveland Follies, surviving breakdown, confronting the nightmare of their lives. But that is not enough of an explanation, at least not in show terms. The ending seems contrived and does not befit a musical that is uncompromising in so many ways; nor did it magically make the show palatable to general theatergoers in search of the saccharine. It was wasted compromise.

Follies opened at the Winter Garden Theatre on April 4, 1971, and received some sensational reviews in the national press, but not in the all-important *New York Times*. The show would run 522 performances, be seen by tens of thousands, and win Sondheim his third Tony for the score, but there is only one kind of hit on Broadway and that is a profitable one. In the language of show business, a succès d'estime is not a success; it is a flop. And *Follies* was, losing most of its $800,000 capitalization (a record at the time). That upset Harold Prince's investors, and placating them was the price that he would have to pay for his own folly—his (as he conceded) self-indulgence. It was time to reestablish his business credit with a show that indulged audiences and repaid investors.

A LITTLE NIGHT MUSIC

A Little Night Music "was about having a hit," Prince would later admit. It was commercial for him, and it would play without conviction. But for Sondheim it would mark a musical turning point. Thus far he had been composing in the Broadway idiom and writing mostly in the song form. That was now at an end. *A Little Night Music* would be replete with soliloquies and extended pieces, and for the first time, a show of his would not sound like a Broadway musical. This is ravishingly romantic music, inspired by Rachmaninoff, Brahms, and Ravel—but only inspired; in no other show would Sondheim's music sing so radiantly in his own voice. It is sad that he so seldom expresses it this way.

Besides beauty there is musical and lyrical counterpoint in *A Little Night Music*, hinting of material ahead in *Sunday in the Park with George* and *Into the Woods*. It is as if Sondheim had listened hard to Ben's soliloquy in *Follies,* "The Road You Didn't Take," and decided to set his career on a path toward unconventionalism and artistic fulfillment, rather than seek out popularity and traditional success. His score for *A Little Night Music* seems inspired—and freed—by such a decision.

Although the show's title comes from the Mozart divertimento "Eine Kleine Nachtmusik," the show comes from Ingmar Bergman's 1955 movie "Smiles of a Summer Night." It is a story of sexual musical chairs played by the upper class in turn-of-the-century Sweden. The material was somewhat alien to Sondheim and Prince, two Jewish gentlemen from New York, and Prince would call it his "gentile musical."

Glynis Johns as Desirée in
A Little Night Music.

Prince aimed for high-minded showmanship. "We wanted to do a Chekhovian musical," he said. "No big opening number, but we hoped, in time, we would draw our audience into it." They succeeded. *A Little Night Music* was destined to be the most financially successful of their collaborations. Sondheim won a record-setting fourth consecutive Tony Award in 1973 for the season's best score, but perhaps a more satisfying reward was a hit song—his first as a composer.

It took two years for "Send in the Clowns" to become popular, thanks to recordings by Frank Sinatra and Judy Collins, but when it happened, Sondheim was as pleased as any Tin Pan Alley tunesmith. Although he hardly respected the sniping from traditionalists and even fellow songwriters that he didn't write any hits, it had hurt his feelings and he surely felt good about proving them wrong.

A Little Night Music begins with a unique overture (*Forum, Anyone Can Whistle,* and *Merrily We Roll Along* are the only Sondheim shows to have traditional overtures). A formally dressed quintet sings in lieder style. They will reappear throughout the show, having character names (Lindquist, Nordstrom, etc.) but no dialogue. They are not part of the story; they are fantastical. Their songs comment on the action, and they are a kind of gemütlich Greek chorus (upon first seeing them, the straightforward Prince asked, "Who are those klutzes?").

Much has been written about the score's being all waltzes, or entirely in 3/4 time. Even Prince describes it that way. Sondheim's comments, which begin with the point that 3/4 time is not always a waltz rhythm, are as usual illuminating as well as pedantic (he prefers to characterize them as "instructive"). "The show wasn't written [entirely] in three," he says. "Many of the songs are in four [4/4 time]. They are just subdivided into three. That's the whole point. 'Every Day a Little Death,' for instance—that's in four. I just said everything's in threes or subdivided into threes. Everyone else went ahead and translated that into 'everything's in waltz time.' "

All right then, it is *mostly* in three, and threes do not *always* sound like waltzes. Although he denies it, Sondheim the puzzler might have indeed been challenged by the notion of writing an entire score relative to a single time signature. In any case, it creates an internal unity that binds the music. On days when he isn't nitpicking about subdivided threes, he simply says that he "wanted to write a waltzy score for a château weekend," and it certainly is a waltzy score.

The story: The fortyish lawyer Fredrik Egerman has an eighteen-year-old bride named Anne who, after almost a year of marriage, is still a virgin. Similarly pure is Fredrik's nineteen-year-old son by a previous marriage, Henrik, a cello-playing divinity student. The father, while a bit stuffy, is worldly and lusty and of course frustrated. Henrik is gloomy and also frustrated, attracted as he is to his young stepmother; they are a bit too obviously destined for each other. As she prattles about her complexion, Sondheim's first piece, "Now," a soliloquy for Fredrik, expresses with lawyerly logic his impatience with this child bride.

> Now, as the sweet imbecilities
> Tumble so lavishly
> Onto her lap . . .

He can only obsess over how to cope with his frustration.

> Now there are two possibilities:
> A, I could ravish her,
> B, I could nap.

Audaciously, the lyric is going to reason through a classical sequence of logical alternatives. If, for instance, Fredrik is to ravish his wife, should that be through

A, the deployment of charm, or B,
The adoption
Of physical force.

Considering the use of force,

Her hair getting tangled,
Her stays getting snapped,

Fredrik discards that option because

Removing her clothing
Would take me all day
And her subsequent loathing
Would turn me away—

Which eliminates B
And which leaves us with A.

With this Sondheim lets his music bubble off and play before the reasoning resumes. Fredrik now considers the charm approach. The alternatives are "the suggestive" or "the direct" ("in the nude"), which

. . . might be effective,
My body's all right—
But not in perspective
And not in the light . . .

And so he considers a suggestive approach:

In view of her penchant
For something romantic,
De Sade is too trenchant
And Dickens too frantic,
And Stendhal would ruin
The plan of attack
As there isn't much blue in
"The Red and the Black."

A stuffed shirt who loses his pants is a staple of comedy. In A Little Night Music, *the stuffed shirt is Count Carl-Magnus (Laurence Guittard), unmasked, so to speak, before his mistress, Desirée (Glynis Johns).*

To complement these clever lyrics, Sondheim composed music to work in the same logical way. Just as the lyrics balance one alternative against the other, likewise are musical alternatives weighed. Melody is minimal; in fact some of the lines are almost monotones, and some of the couplets are note-for-note repetitions, or are simply and sequentially modulated upward. The music, then, which ordinarily comes with the melody, here lies in the harmony. Meantime, the sense that the song is happening in Fredrik's mind is reinforced as Anne prates in the background (long rests are provided so that she can be heard).

Toward the end, Sondheim introduces sudden melody, a coda to, as he says, "allow a lyrical assertion of Fredrik's love and tenderness." (He is using "lyrical" in two senses, rhapsodic as well as put into words.)

When now I still want and/or love you,
Now, as always . . .

The "and/or" is there to remind us that, even when ardent, Fredrik talks like a lawyer. Sondheim doesn't worry about whether an audience can grasp such niceties—and he shouldn't—but he might consider whether an audience can *hear* a sung "and/or."

Aside from this final burst of melody, which is a relief after the repeating sequences of logic, "Now" isn't an easy song to sing. Nor is it "catchy," but like classical reasoning, it can

be quite beautiful. Indeed, were there a picture of the song it might look like a snowflake, a visualization of an elegant, logical musical exercise. When Sondheim's diaphanous, rippling accompaniment is filled out with Jonathan Tunick's voluptuous orchestration, rich with harp and cello, the piece takes on the quality of sensual reason—which is exactly what it is all about.

Such work is unprecedented in our musical theater. "Now" is simply brainy, and it ends with a good show business punch line as Fredrik returns to the first alternative and elects to nap.

The titillation begins in earnest when Fredrik takes Anne to see a play in which Desirée is appearing. From the stage the actress spies Fredrik, which evokes in both a memory of their old affair. Once again, Sondheim spots a song ingeniously. Even if this must be a conventional musical, he will not set the usual assortment of songs in the usual assortment of places. Two of his lieder singers in a stage-side box, watching the play, offer a taste of "Remember," the yearning waltz that was sung in the quintet overture.

The song exploits the sexual spirit of the show, as the entire fantasy quintet recalls romantic encounters. Sondheim creates a full and merry melody for their heartfelt Middle-European waltz, giving the singers juicy chords for their harmonizing.

MR. ERLANSEN

The unexpected knock of the maid—
Remember?

MRS. ANDERSSEN

Remember?
The wine that made us both rather merry
And oh, so very
Frank.

ALL

Ah, how we laughed.
Ah, how we drank.

MR. ERLANSEN

You acquiesced

A weekend in the country figures largely in A Little Night Music. *The show, to director Harold Prince, "suggested a Magritte painting . . . anomalies in a landscape. A gentle greensward on which to play scenes in bedrooms, dressing rooms, dining rooms. I wanted the figures in the landscape out of context, for no more reason than Magritte puts them there."*

MRS. ANDERSSEN

And the rest is a blank.

The bawdiest is saved for last, a sound rule whether in vaudeville or opera.

MR. LINDQUIST

What we did with your perfume—

MR. ERLANSEN

Remember, darling?

MRS. SEGSTROM

The condition of the room
When we were through . . .

MRS. NORDSTROM

Our inventions were unique—
Remember, darling?

MR. LINDQUIST

I was limping for a week,
You caught the flu . . .

ALL (looking uncertainly at each other)

I'm *sure* it was—
You.

Fun as this is to read, it is unlikely that many theatergoers heard all these lines. There are too many words—it is too "lyricky"—to be understood.

When Fredrik visits Desirée at her apartment, their duet, however sophisticated its tone, fits into a traditional musical comedy slot. It is an obvious place for a song and an obvious song for the spot. "You Must Meet My Wife," set to a lovely and appropriately bittersweet waltz, has Fredrik alternately boasting and complaining about his virginal Anne. When Desirée joins in, her humor is tritely bitchy.

FREDRIK

She flutters.

DESIRÉE

How charming.

FREDRIK

She twitters.

DESIRÉE

My word!

FREDRIK

She floats.

DESIRÉE

Isn't that alarming?
What is she, a bird?

"Flutters" may be all right for a start, but "twitters" and "floats" are just repeated setups for the "bird" punch line, which isn't worth the trouble. Sondheim disagrees, feeling that "the kind of laugh" it got (a big one) was worth it. Is a cheap laugh justified by being a big one? Such thinking is the show business in Sondheim.

As if to the rescue the show from this musical comedy, while Fredrik takes Desirée to bed, her mother, Madame Armfeldt, materializes as a one-woman Greek chorus. Hermione Gingold, who played this aging courtesan in the original Broadway production, was a British actress/comedienne with an arch personal style, and Sondheim's song for this moment, "Liaisons," was tailored to her. It is a set piece on the sorry state of modern sexual affairs ("some of them hardly pay their shoddy way"). As a comedy list for a sophisticated courtesan, it is a variation on Rodgers and Hart's "To Keep My Love Alive." Here Mme Armfeldt checks off a list of her conquests and acquisitions: "At the villa of the Baron de Signac . . . ," "In the castle of the King of the Belgians . . . ," and so on.

> At the palace of the Duke of Ferrara,
> Who was prematurely deaf but a dear,
> At the palace of the Duke of Ferrara
> I acquired some position
> Plus a tiny Titian . . .

Although Ms. Gingold had a rusty hinge for a voice, she certainly could *sell* a song in a kind of speak-sing way. With her rasping alto in mind, Sondheim kept his melody to a narrow range in a lower register. His music is made in the lush accompaniment, which has the sultry redolence of Rimsky-Korsakov or some such. The lyrics, though, like Wheeler's endless aphorisms in the dialogue of Mme Armfeldt, seem stilted in their sophistication.

Fredrik and Desirée are surprised in compromising circumstances by Count Carl-Magnus, the blustering military officer who is her lover. He promptly sings about his feelings, as people tend to in book musicals. However this is also a Stephen Sondheim musical, and so instead of merely punctuating the scene, the song seeks out a more ambitious end—namely, to link two scenes. Carl-Magnus first sings of his jealousy in lyrics of unfinished, unrhymed, paranoid sentences.

> She wouldn't . . .
> Therefore they didn't . . .
> So then it wasn't . . .
> Not unless it . . .
> Would she?
> She doesn't . . .
> God knows she needn't . . .
> Therefore it's not.

The music for this is mock-military and reminiscent of "My Bride" from *Forum*, but then is not Carl-Magnus another macho Miles Gloriosus? He is also a scoundrel, for he asks his own wife, Charlotte, to avenge his jealousy of Desirée by telling Fredrik's wife, Anne, about the Desirée–Fredrik affair. The countess complies, and in these brief strokes she emerges as the most telling character in the play. Her depth comes from her situation—being in love with, yet humiliated by, a husband who is her moral and intellectual inferior; from Hugh Wheeler's sharp and pained dialogue for her; and certainly from the exquisite song that Sondheim wrote for her.

> Every day a little death
> In the parlor, in the bed,
> In the curtains, in the silver,
> In the buttons, in the bread.
> Every day a little sting
> In the heart and in the head.
> Every move and every breath,
> And you hardly feel a thing,
> Brings a perfect little death.

Observers have perceived in Sondheim's lyrics a penchant for the words "death," "insane," and "little." There probably is no more to this than their power as words and their appropriateness to his sardonic views. "Little death" is also a euphemism for orgasm. Many gave the ever clever Sondheim credit for a sly inside joke, but in fact he did not know of this phrase when he wrote "Every Day a Little Death."

As Countess Charlotte sings about betrayal, Anne joins in on the same subject, having just learned about her husband's infidelity. They do this in a musical canon.

CHARLOTTE	ANNE
Every day a little death,	Every day a little death,
In the parlor, in the bed,	On the lips and in the eyes,
In the curtains, In the silver, In the buttons, In the bread.	In the murmurs, In the pauses, In the gestures, In the sighs.
	Every day a little dies,
Every day a little sting	In the looks and in The lies.
In the heart And in the head. Every move and	

Every breath,
And you hardly feel a
Thing.
Brings a perfect little
Death.

And you hardly feel a
Thing.
Brings a perfect little
Death.

Len Cariou and Glynis Johns in A Little Night Music.

Hermione Gingold as Mme Armfeldt sings "Liaisons" in A Little Night Music. *Despite Gingold's charm as an actress, her character speaks more in aphorisms than real speech. ("Solitaire is the only thing in life that demands absolute honesty.")*

There is no precedent for such a song on Broadway. Linking love and sex, elegant and elegaic, it is entirely original in the style and mood of the music, in the attitude and structure of the lyrics. There certainly is no precedent for life's painful pinpricks being the subject of a show tune. And this is one song in *A Little Night Music* that is *not* a waltz. As Sondheim points out, "It's just that within it [in the accompaniment] there's that three"—the rhythmic pattern that provides a piquant heartbeat to link this song to the rest of the score.

Once again, however, the show returns to the constrictions of storytelling, of moving from point "A" to point "B." The scene shifts to the country house of Desirée's mother, where the actress is selling her on a weekend party during which Fredrik might be recaptured. The setting up of that weekend will be taken over by Sondheim.

"A Weekend in the Country" is a mini-opera involving all the characters in their various locales and from their various points of view. The boisterous music is vaguely reminiscent of Liszt's "Mephisto Waltz," and the country weekend is appropriately heralded by a hunting horn in the orchestration.

This is Sondheim at a new peak. His lyrics now serve as complete conversations, with the number covering yards of plot. Yet the words never seem like recitative (opera dialogue set to droning, unstructured music); rather, this is a dramatically structured song. It is musical theater and the furthest development yet of Oscar Hammerstein's "Bench Scene" in *Carousel.*

Naturally a weekend in the country starts with an invitation:

ANNE (to Petra, the maid)

"Your presence . . ."
Just think of it, Petra . . .
"Is kindly . . ."
It's at a château!
"Requested . . ."
Et cet'ra, et cet'ra,
". . . Madame Leonora Armf—"
Oh no!

This sequence will last some ten minutes, bringing in Fredrik and his son, Henrik, as well as the jealous Carl-Magnus, who learns about the weekend from his wife.

CHARLOTTE

I've an intriguing little social item.

CARL-MAGNUS

What?

CHARLOTTE

Out at the Armfeldt family manse.

CARL-MAGNUS

Well, what?

CHARLOTTE

Merely a weekend,
Still I thought it might am-
Use you to know who's invited to go,
This time with his pants.

Not only do these lyrics read like dialogue while scanning in meter but the rhymes are ingeniously buried within—for instance, "item" and "might am-"—doing their good works of cadence without calling attention to themselves.

Building from these duets, the piece blends more people into the mix, singing from their various locales and points of view, as characters decide to go, invited or not. Previous conversations are repeated in counterpoint until the number has multiplied:

CARL-MAGNUS	FREDRIK	HENRIK
Charlotte!	We're off!	A weekend in the Country,
CHARLOTTE	PETRA	The bees in their
I'm thinking it out.	We are?	Hives . . .
CARL-MAGNUS	FREDRIK & ANNE	
Charlotte!	We'll take the car.	
CHARLOTTE	FREDRIK, ANNE, & PETRA	MRS. SEGSTROM & MRS. ANDERSSEN
There's no need To shout.	We'll bring Champagne and Caviar!	We're off! We are? We'll take the car.

And so the show rolls to its first-act curtain. All it now has to do is actually play out the cataclysmic weekend in the country.

They all arrive at once, Fredrik, Anne, Henrik, and the maid, Petra, in one car; in another, Carl-Magnus and Charlotte, who adroitly invite themselves into the château. Desirée can only accede, and the infighting has already begun.

Since Carl-Magnus has cut a ridiculous figure from the outset, there is not much suspense about who will win Desirée. It is only a matter of time until she and Fredrik are alone, and when they are the show arrives at its best moment. Sondheim pounces. The song is "Send in the Clowns."

Have Desirée and Fredrik taken so much time making up their minds that they have lost their moment? This comes so close to the question Sondheim dealt with at *Company*'s end that it almost seems as if he is having another go at that troublesome finale.

Glynis Johns, who played Desirée, was a beautiful and luminescent actress but she was not a singer (which was why this was her only complete solo in the show). Although one of her wonderful qualities was her husky voice, when it was raised in song it could not rise very high. Then it croaked, but Sondheim heard something else in it and, as Jonathan Tunick says, "Her strengths and weaknesses are built into the song." Her strengths were the emotion and intelligence that she could contribute as an actress. To allow for her musical weaknesses, Sondheim kept his song's range within a limited span and gave her no extended notes to hold.

It is an exquisite piece, elegantly built upon its four opening notes. Its development from them is academic and formal, almost mathematical, seemingly inevitable, and the "B" section ("Just when I stopped opening doors") is a virtual duplicate of the "A" ("Isn't it rich, are we a pair?") in a higher key and minor mode. The harmonies seem to lead, one to the other, almost as if in reflection of the lyrics' piquancy. As for those lyrics, they are allusive (for Harold Prince, elusive—he never would make sense of them). In dealing with love this time, Sondheim seems to have "Sorry-Grateful" (from *Company*) resolved, concluding that ambivalence is nothing to be ashamed of. ("At least half of my songs deal with ambivalence, feeling two things at once.")

Using the language Desirée knows best, that of the theater, he has her sing of lovers in terms of clowns and farce, making their entrances, knowing their lines. This flamboyant actress who "keeps tearing around" is for once "on the ground," while ironically, the conservative Fredrik "who can't move" is now "in mid-air."

> Isn't it bliss?
> Don't you approve?
> One who keeps tearing around,
> One who can't move?
> Where are the clowns?
> Send in the clowns.

The tempo is extremely slow. In fact it is one of the slowest songs that Sondheim ever wrote, and to make matters worse for staging, between each section there is a very long pause. "Send in the Clowns" would have sent Jerome Robbins through the ceiling.

Up and down the scale it goes, along its tight ladder, the melancholy persisting in melody and lyric. Here is the fear of a rational person that thinking comes at the expense of feeling, the fear that he has lost the lover for whom he now knows he feels.

> Just when I'd stopped
> Opening doors,
> Finally knowing
> The one that I wanted was yours,
> Making my entrance again
> With my usual flair,
> Sure of my lines,
> No one is there.

(Wasn't deciding too late what Robert feared in *Company* in "Someone Is Waiting": "Did I know her,/Have I waited too long?")

It is as if Sondheim is coming close to expressing a sophisticated sense of love, an acceptance of its peril, its insecurity, and the doubts that will always surround it.

> Don't you love farce?
> My fault, I fear.
> I thought that you'd want what I want—
> Sorry, my dear.
> But where are the clowns?
> Quick, send in the clowns.
> Don't bother, they're here.

The show's Chekhovian intentions are thus fulfilled in a song; the foolishness of the human condition is accepted with grace and compassion. The song, of course, is perfect. Perhaps Sondheim had to be perfect to get his hit.

The show opened at the Shubert Theatre on February 25, 1973, and Prince was not terribly proud of it. "I didn't enjoy doing *A Little Night Music*," he would say, "because it was merely entertaining. I suffered no sleepless nights." Like his apologies for the *Company* finale, this statement rankled Sondheim ("He's 'commercial'—then why didn't he enjoy it?"). However *Night Music* accomplished its purpose for Prince; it was a hit. The team wrested its first rave review from the all-powerful *New York Times* ("Great God! An adult musical!"), and the investors received a 125 percent return on every dollar.

Perhaps the price for that return was paid in stress on the Sondheim-Prince partnership; perhaps it was steeper than was realized at the time.

Sondheim first played "Send in the Clowns," for Harold Prince on the eve of the "gypsy runthrough," the last dress rehearsal, performed before an audience of actors. Sondheim asked Prince whether the song sounded too much like a set piece for a nightclub act. The director assured him that it didn't and suggested that Sondheim immediately play it for Ms. Johns, for whom he had written it. Delighted, she asked if she might sing it at the gypsy runthrough, and so it was an audience of actors who first heard "Send in the Clowns."

THE PRINCE COLLABORATIONS PART TWO

The Prince-Sondheim collaborations were the product of a team that included (left to right) choreographer Patricia Birch, who worked on two shows, producer-director Prince, scenic designer Boris Aronson and associate producer Ruth Mitchell.

A black-tie crowd paid charity-event prices to fill the Shubert Theatre on the evening of March 11, 1973, for "Stephen Sondheim: A Musical Tribute." It was a one-performance gala directed by Sondheim's friend, Burt Shevelove, with a company that included Angela Lansbury, Alexis Smith, Glynis Johns, Chita Rivera, Jack Cassidy, Len Cariou, and Larry Blyden. Among the special guests—the nonperformers, the friends—were Harold Prince, Leonard Bernstein, Jule Styne, Anthony Perkins, and Mary Rodgers.

They had assembled to celebrate Sondheim's oeuvre, but some of the songs were youthful work, others were numbers that had been cut from shows, and then there were selections from unproduced musicals. Such trivia made the tribute seem not only padded, but somehow demeaning to the excellence of his more important work—what he had already done, what he was likely to do in the future.

This raised a question that would persist throughout his career: Would he always be "essentially a cult figure," as he would describe himself six years later? He identified Broadway success with the big hit, but only his first show, *Forum*, could be fairly called a big hit. Certainly there was nothing cultish about winning four straight Tony Awards for music and lyrics, but with only five shows to his credit as a composer/lyricist, he was hardly ready for the pantheon. In a Broadway theater that was first of all commercial, he was short on shows that had paid off.

Sondheim himself was mortified by the tribute's atmosphere of eulogy. Was his place in stage history already determined at 43? Was that place a chic oblivion? A five-page cover story in the April 23, 1973, issue of *Newsweek* declared him a "national treasure," the author of "the most brilliant songs being written for the American musical theater today."

It was true, and he had nowhere to go but up or down.

PACIFIC OVERTURES

In 1959 Harold Prince produced the hit musical *Fiorello!*, written by novelist Jerome Weidman. Weidman's son John was a law student who wrote plays; Prince was a producer who enjoyed discovering new writers. When young Weidman submitted one called *Pacific Overtures*, Prince was interested because it was about the gunboat diplomacy of Admiral Perry's 1853 expedition to Japan, and he was inclined to theater that (a) dealt with issues and (b) had visual strength. He perceived the westernization of the "island empire" as a resonant issue, and he could imagine the stage pictures. He convinced the young playwright to rewrite *Pacific Overtures* in the Kabuki style, then as a musical libretto. From Prince's point of view, it was to be the most audacious of the Sondheim collaborations, his most daring directorial conception.

As Prince put it, his notion was to "tell the story as though it were written by a Japanese playwright in the Kabuki style, with the Americans the traditional Kabuki villains." By the time Sondheim and Weidman were finished, style and content had merged.

Ultimately the show itself would symbolize the corruption of Japanese culture: the Kabuki theater made into a Broadway musical. That would be a stunning achievement, but an academic one in a very tough-minded arena.

For 250 years, a shogun's order had forbidden foreigners from touching Japanese soil. *Pacific Overtures* is about the cultural transformation that resulted from Perry's invasive visit. With the coerced signing of the trade treaty, "The Floating Kingdom" is dragged from its "serene and changeless cycle of . . . days" and hurled toward the twentieth century.

The production was constructed like a series of watercolors that dissolve and re-form as giant screens slide and pass each other. From the first sighting of Perry's ships by a fisherman who fears they are "Four Black Dragons," *Pacific Overtures* sweeps Japan toward a technological future it will ultimately dominate. The show ends with a demonstration of the fast-paced, electronically supreme, culturally neutered Japan of today.

Curiously overlooked in this history is the minor matter of the Second World War, along with the atomic bombing of Hiroshima and Nagasaki. If that makes the historical aspect of the show incomplete, *Pacific Overtures* nevertheless remains a unique work of music theater.

In order to cover almost 125 years of cultural history, the script had to be epic in scope and yet spare, like Japanese poetry, painting, or architecture. At the same time, Prince sought to continue the progress made by *Company*, in departing from traditional book structure, and by *Follies*, in a conceptual production. These aims were to be realized, and yet as great an

Sondheim listens to choreographer Patricia Birch at a Pacific Overtures *rehearsal conference as director Harold Prince looks on.*

achievement as the show would be, it would also be an intellectual exercise of little stage potency.

Pacific Overtures, then, is the most troubling of the Sondheim-Prince musicals because it is a brilliant work that failed on entertainment grounds. It not merely ignored, but defied the reasonable expectations of a Broadway audience. Thus was the issue joined: Can art be pursued absolutely in a commercial theater?

Sondheim was not only a less political creature than Prince; he was downright hostile to political theater. Ironically, while Broadway conservatives felt he was too brainy to trust, in fact he had a showman's wariness of arty or intellectual theater. A Kabuki musical seemed a bit much, even to him.

Nor was he the only one with doubts. "It was the strangest situation," orchestrator Jonathan Tunick remembered. "Steve, Boris Aronson [the designer], me, everyone, we were all dragged into this kicking and screaming. We didn't want to do a Japanese musical, we don't know anything about Japanese culture. Who are we to do this? But the challenge was so powerful that it really brought the best out of all of us."

Perhaps that is the ultimate significance of *Pacific Overtures* in an overview of Sondheim's career: It proved that he could write music and lyrics about *anything*.

With *A Little Night Music*, Sondheim had ventured beyond the sound of traditional Broadway music. After that, each show would dictate its own musical language. John Weidman, too, seems to have written *Pacific Overtures* in a style conceived for this particular show. His play script is the dramatic counterpart of Japanese watercolors, "a series of scenes rather than a continuous narrative," as Sondheim says.

As for Harold Prince's production concept, it had the women's roles played by men, like Kabuki. A Reciter sat at stage-side, commenting on the action. Props and costumes were changed in full audience view by stagehands dressed in black. Finally several musicians were seated on the floor beside the Reciter, performing on such exotic instruments as the *shamisen* and the *shakuhachi*.

Sondheim, having settled on the musical language for *Pacific Overtures*, decided on a

Left:
When Sondheim says that he can "personally relate to the gunboat diplomacy in Pacific Overtures*" he means that he cares about it politically. This is an example of word choices that sometimes are overly careful.*

Below:
In being a Kabuki Broadway musical, Pacific Overtures *was itself a metaphor for the westernization of Japan.*

Below, right:
Pacific Overtures. *As in Kabuki theater, all roles were played by men.*

sound based on that of a "prepared" piano—one whose musical quality is changed by attaching objects to the strings and altering the tuning. This approximated the twang of Eastern string music, and with that, he says, "I knew I'd hit the right sound. And once I had the style it was just a matter of writing the score."

When Tunick says, "By the time we got to *Pacific Overtures*, Steve was writing a very spare, very un-Broadway style," that is the least of it. If there is any Sondheim music prior to *Sunday in the Park with George* that is "un-Broadway," it is this. The score seems to capture not only the character of Eastern music but the Eastern *mentality*, renouncing our Western concepts of emotional power and conclusive logic. Technically, Sondheim points out, he approximated the character of Eastern music by basing the first-act music on a five-note pentatonic scale (as opposed to the more familiar seven-note diatonic or eleven-note chromatic scales). To the average listener, this meant subdued—if not minimal—melody set with transparent harmonies. Although the second-act music would become more Western as Japan is westernized, the overall approach did not promise structured or dynamic listening for Western ears. Orchestrator Tunick says, "We all wanted it to be as true as it could be to Japanese sensibilities." Overlooked, perhaps, in the process were American sensibilities.

As a result, if there is any of Sondheim's scores that is impressive but not lovable, it is this one—and it is extremely impressive. It is also so musically remote as to seem like underscoring set with lyrics. Yet, the composer says, "If I had to choose one [score as a favorite], I would choose *Pacific Overtures* because with the exception of two songs ["Welcome to Kanagawa" and "Next"] I don't know how I could improve on it."

There are times when this music does manage to summon up traditional theater power. At the outset, for instance, a whistling Oriental pipe is accompanied by the striking of a woodblock. These spare and alien sounds are jolted by a surging, thumping vamp in the strings. It is a Kabuki-style opening number! It is also very exciting in a Broadway way. The combination is inspired.

In writing the lyrics, Sondheim was faced with a new challenge: doing with words what he had been doing with music—coming up with a language. For unlike all the other shows, here he was not to be simply suiting lyrics to character or period. In turning away from the pidgin English that had traditionally been used for Asian shows, he sought to simulate the Japanese language in English. This would occasionally result in a naive posture, a quality of preciousness. Deprived of one of his greatest assets, colloquial English, the lyrics seem stilted, so stylized as to sound self-conscious.

> The farmer plants the rice.
> The priest exalts the rice.
> The lord collects the rice.
> The merchant buys the rice.
> The craftsman makes the sword
> And sells it to the lord
> And buys at twice the former price
> What he counts on his lord to protect with his sword.

The first act of the show covers the immediate days after Perry's arrival, and "Four Black Dragons," set to four ominously repeating thuds, effectively describes the childlike fright of a fisherman at the sight of the warships.

> And I ran,
> Cursing through the fields,
> Calling the alarm,
> Shouting to the world:
> "Four black dragons,
> Spitting fire!"

As in Kabuki theater, Pacific Overtures employs a reciter (right) to guide the audience through the action of the play.

And the earth trembled,
And the sky cracked.
And I thought it was the end of the world.

Drawn to Japanese poetry, perhaps in reasonable hope of finding a lyrical language, Sondheim first writes a piece called "Poems" and then, in the midst of "Welcome to Kanagawa," suggests traditional Japanese haiku. (Oscar Hammerstein II had done something similar in *Flower Drum Song*, modeling one of his lyrics on a Malaysian form of poetry called *pantoum*.)

Haiku is a severely formal poetry that limits each grouping of three lines to seventeen syllables in a 5–7–5 pattern and places emphasis on allusions to nature. Sondheim did not write actual haiku, although he certainly was capable of it, because he felt it would be rhythmically boring in a show.

"Welcome to Kanagawa" is about a brothel catering to the American sailors. By setting traditional-style Japanese poetry in the midst of such a song, the lyric demonstrates the first cultural violation.

Above, left:
Florence Klotz designed the costumes for Pacific Overtures.

Left:
In Pacific Overtures *a parade of admirals introduce themselves in the song "Please Hello" in their native country's musical styles. (The Englishman, for instance, sings mock Gilbert and Sullivan). But the lyrics are dense and the music seems labored—an instance of Sondheim perhaps being too clever for the show's own good.*

Above:
As the Japanese in Pacific Overtures *become "westernized," so does Sondheim's music.*

Left:
The Pacific Overtures *showcard. Sondheim, anticipating a chilly critical reaction to the unconventional show, suggested that a reviewer might write, "Oh, no! Not another Kabuki musical!"*

The severity of the show's style seems to have limited the ways in which music could be inserted. "Someone in a Tree," for instance, describes the signing of the trade treaty through the memories of two witnesses. One of them was only able to see the event, the other could only hear it, and neither has a good memory. The song nearly lapses into self-parody.

OLD MAN

There was a tree.

RECITER

Which was where?

OLD MAN

Very near.

RECITER

Over here?

OLD MAN

Maybe over there,
But there were trees then, everywhere.
May I show you?

RECITER

If you please.

OLD MAN

There were trees
Then, everywhere.

RECITER

But you were there.

OLD MAN

And I was there!
Let me show you.

A little of this can go a long way, especially when the melody is monotonous to Western ears and the beat repetitive, and there is a lot of this song. Much more effective—indeed, the most effective musical number in the entire show—is "A Bowler Hat," about the transformation of a samurai into a British-style businessman—with the music itself gradually becoming Western. At last Sondheim's own, wonderful musical voice can be heard emerging from behind his research. It is very gratifying.

In the lyric he continues to use the allusions to nature that are so much a part of traditional Japanese poetry. The purpose, of course, is to demonstrate the culture being lost. The recurring image is of birds.

It's called a bowler hat.
I have no wife.
The swallow flying through the sky
Is not as swift as I
Am, flying through my life.

The piece is but a piquant melody, a very French waltz and a very beautiful one. It makes for an abbreviated song, the chorus repeated six times without variation. The effect is cumulative and touching as the samurai dons the hat.

It's called a pocket watch.
I have a wife.

No eagle flies against the sky
As eagerly as I
Have flown against my life.

Sondheim beautifully concludes his bird imagery as the man sings of using a pocket watch, of learning to drink white wine, of reading Spinoza ("*Formidable!*"), of acquiring an eyepiece. The denial of origins is almost complete as the samurai puts on a pair of glasses.

They call them spectacles.
I drink much wine.
I take imported pills.
I have a house up in the hills
I've hired British architects to redesign.
One must accommodate the times
As one lives them.
One must remember that.

After a pause there is a simple one-line coda that finishes the transformation. The former samurai holds up a tailcoat:

It's called a cutaway.

The show opened at the Winter Garden Theatre on January 11, 1976, to thoughtful reviews that did not sell tickets. Perhaps it was as simple as a Kabuki musical being just too esoteric for the average theatergoer.

The musical theater is a hot place, offering emotional transport for the price of admission. This show was as cool as a Japanese watercolor. Perhaps its downfall lay in that very intention and its creators' ingenuity in achieving it. It closed after only 193 performances. The Tony Award for best musical that season was won by *A Chorus Line*, a show that was hardly as brainy as *Pacific Overtures* but, of course, was a wonderful musical with Broadway heat, emotionalism, and showmanship. It had been directed by Michael Bennett, who had learned so much from Sondheim and Prince and had used it all. He did not forget about heat, emotional transport, show business, and the audience.

SWEENEY TODD, THE DEMON BARBER OF FLEET STREET

Three years earlier, while in England for a revival of *Gypsy* starring Angela Lansbury, Sondheim had seen a ripe thriller called *Sweeney Todd, The Demon Barber of Fleet Street*. It was a good-natured adaptation, by an actor named Christopher Bond, of a popular nineteenth-century melodrama, and Sondheim thought it would make for musical theater fun. He urged it on Harold Prince as their next project.

Prince was not a fan of melodrama, and he didn't like the Victorian era ("a man comes out in a stovepipe hat and I fall asleep"). Then again, he was willing to listen. After all, he had not at first appreciated *A Funny Thing Happened on the Way to the Forum* or *West Side Story*. He finally agreed to direct *Sweeney Todd*, but Sondheim would always feel it was "a show he never believed in," and Angela Lansbury, who starred in it, felt much the same way. "Hal," she said, "did it as a favor to Steve," and it would be the only one of their projects to have originated with Sondheim. (Prince has always spoken proudly of the show.)

Sweeney Todd, The Demon Barber of Fleet Street was booked into the biggest theater in New York, the Uris (now the Gershwin). The need to dominate that environment led Prince to a production decision very different from the chamber musical Sondheim had envisioned. "I know what you want, Steve," the director said. "You want antimacassars and curtains

parting. What I'll give you is an epic style. You'll lose on the scary part but you'll gain the size."

Size, for Prince, meant a setting that was not merely a huge factory but a *real* one, transported in its entirety from Rhode Island. Sondheim, in his own words, "just wanted fog and a few street lamps. Then if suddenly beside you up popped an old beggar woman crying, 'Alms, alms,' you'd be scared out of your wits." But he also respected Prince as a director who "has a sense of a whole evening, a sense of an arc, a sense of design, of what an evening of theater is about." And so he decided, "Someday it could be done small . . . why not try it large? Hal is the one I want to do it so let's see how it works his way."

As usual his composing began with thinking and searching for a musical language appropriate to the material. He realized early on that one of the most effective devices in scary movies is continuous music, so he began to think in terms of constant underscoring.

The subject of scary movies brought back the memory of *Hangover Square*, a childhood favorite about a mad composer. Its music was by Bernard Herrmann, celebrated for so many Alfred Hitchcock movies. "I thought, 'Bernard Herrmann,' " Sondheim says, "and out came . . . that kind of music, filled with unresolved dissonances that leave an audience in a state of suspense." (He points out that resolved dissonances—clashes that finally become harmonious—make the listener "comfortable.")

So he had found the musical language, and then it occurred to him that, often in horror movies, a fright-associated theme (as in *Jaws*, for instance) can panic an audience. That was what he wanted next, a motive, a melodic fragment to arouse a shudder even before the creature appears. And what better motive than the "Dies Irae?" This theme originated in a medieval Gregorian chant and was then incorporated into the Roman Catholic Mass for the Dead. Composers from Berlioz to Rachmaninoff have used it to signify Judgment Day. Sondheim decided to use it too.

As if in relief after the rigors of composing *Pacific Overtures* in an Oriental style, he was about to write the most abundant, most assertive, most passionate music of his life. And after laboring within such strict limitations of language, he was to write rich, literary, colorful, and vastly creative lyrics.

For years people had been encouraging him to write not only words and music but librettos as well. It seemed the natural step and not unprecedented. Frank Loesser had written all of *The Most Happy Fella*, and Meredith Willson was the sole author of *The Music Man*. Sondheim certainly had television experience as a script writer, but with continuous underscoring leading to singing everything, was singing everything going to mean singing *everything*, including "I'm going to the grocery" and "What time is it?"

In traditional opera, recitative takes care of that, the minor dialogue sung to a kind of droning, unmelodic music. Sondheim enjoyed a singular advantage: He knew how to heighten everyday conversation, having already spent half his career developing lyricized dialogue for long musical-dramatic sequences. Now he could take that idea to full length and write the ultimate extension of what Hammerstein had begun with his *Carousel* "Bench Scene"—practically a whole show of it. Ultimately there would be a few brief dramatic scenes in *Sweeney Todd* written by Hugh Wheeler, but thirteen years after it opened Sondheim would be musicalizing some of those too.

Does so much singing make it an opera? Opera is not just a matter of everything being sung. There is an operatic kind of music, of singing, of staging. There are opera audiences, and there is an opera sensibility. There are opera *houses*. *Sweeney Todd* has its occasional operatic moments, but its music overall has the chest tones, the harmonic language, the muscularity, and the edge of Broadway theater.

The audience would enter *Sweeney Todd* to sepulchral organ music, because organ music is associated with funeral parlors and scary stories. Startling chords would resound throughout the show. As the house darkens, the morbid tones are jarred by a piercing factory

Harold Prince directed Sweeney Todd *following a smashing success with* Evita—*a show that made Andrew Lloyd Webber the first real rival to Sondheim's musical domination of Broadway. By coincidence, Sondheim and Webber have the same birthday (March 22) although Webber, born in 1948, is 18 years younger.*

whistle. A chorus of working men emerges from the shadows to confront the audience and sing "The Ballad of Sweeney Todd."

In the six shows for which he had written both music and lyrics, Sondheim had tried a variety of opening numbers. There was the chanted cacophony in *Company*, the lieder of *A Little Night Music*, the Reciter's invocation in *Pacific Overtures*. But no matter how unique, each served an opening number's purpose: to set the evening's tone and get things going, for like any inert object, a musical needs a burst of energy to move it from dead weight. Thus although "The Ballad of Sweeney Todd" is called a "prologue" and sounds like a traditional

Sweeney's ingenious setting was by Eugene Lee.

folk ballad, it still "sets the table" and gives the production a shove. Were it sung in its entirety, the plot would be unfolded completely.

> Attend the tale of Sweeney Todd.
> His skin was pale and his eye was odd.
> He shaved the faces of gentlemen
> Who never thereafter were heard of again.
> He trod a path that few have trod,
> Did Sweeney Todd,
> The Demon Barber of Fleet Street.

Now a variation of the "Dies Irae" (Judgment Day) theme comes crashing through.

> Swing your razor wide, Sweeney!
> Hold it to the skies!
> Freely flows the blood of those
> Who moralize!

The tale begins with the entrance of a dinghy carrying two passengers. One of them is a sailor named Anthony Hope, and he sings, "There's no place like London/I feel home again." The other passenger is Sweeney Todd: his flesh chalky, his hair a fright, and his overall appearance Frankenstein-like. Every figure in the show will look extreme like this, a character in a gaslit melodrama.

Todd cynically responds to the sailor, "You are young./Life has been kind to you./You will learn." Arriving in London, they are met by a Beggar Woman, who offers herself with maniacal glee:

> 'Ow would you like a little squiff, dear,
> A little jig jig,
> A little bounce around the bush?
> Wouldn't you like to push me crumpet?
> It looks to me, dear,
> Like you got plenty there to push.

> Alms! . . . Alms! . . .
> For a pitiful woman
> Wot's got wanderin' wits . . .
> Hey, don't I know you, mister?

The music, with its yelping accompaniment, is as demented as its singer. Not a complete song, this is a subsection of "No Place Like London," and the mad, whorish beggar prompts Todd to condemn the city as "a great black pit" inhabited by "the vermin of the world."

> At the top of the hole
> Sit the privileged few,
> Making mock of the vermin
> In the lower zoo,
> Turning beauty into filth and greed.

Why "privileged few?" On the first day of rehearsals Harold Prince addressed the company about the show's relationship to the Industrial Revolution and its social inequities. There would even be a blowup of a famous British poster illustrating this strictly defined "beehive society." Whenever Prince was asked what was made in the show's factory setting (and he was frequently asked because the story had nothing to do with factories), he would reply, "They make Sweeney Todds."

Sondheim went along with this theme and even added social references to his lyrics, but Angela Lansbury remembered Christopher Bond, who wrote the original British adaptation, asking the company, "What's the matter with you people? Why don't you have a laugh? This is supposed to be funny." She felt that Sondheim, although agreeing with Bond, concentrated on his creative role and let Prince do the directing. "Steve," she says, "leaves the business of running the bus to the driver." Sondheim himself says that while Bond felt that his melodrama "is a hiss-the-villain show," the social commentary is there too. "Hal just chose to emphasize it."

As Todd's London tirade subsides, words and music turn yearning, and he recalls a youthful marriage in "The Barber and His Wife." Sondheim's melody for this is lovely but dry, and his accompaniment makes it neither easy nor sweet, but pained and filled with loss.

> There was a barber and his wife,
> And she was beautiful.
> A foolish barber and his wife.
> She was his reason and his life,
> And she was beautiful.

These lyrics convey information but do it gracefully, as Todd sings of a "pious vulture of the law" (Judge Turpin) who had "removed" this barber to get at his wife. With that, Mrs. Nellie Lovett glides onstage in her meat pie shop. Angela Lansbury described her character as "the consummate cockney woman with an eye to the main chance—dishonest, lovable, cheery, typical of the 1850s." And with a leap of rhythm, tempo, and flying notes, Sondheim creates a manic musical personality for this bizarre character. He changes his accompanying lines from the softness of Todd's yearnings to playful clashes as Mrs. Lovett pounces on the man, perhaps already recognizing him ("thought you was a ghost").

> Wait! What's yer rush? What's yer hurry?
> You gave me such a—
> Fright. I thought you was a ghost.
> Half a minute, can'tcher?
> Sit! Sit ye down!
> Sit!

As before, these are not formal lyrics nor are they recitative. This is dialogue enriched with the rhythmic, metric, and poetic qualities of lyrics. To keep the show generally conversational, rhyming is minimized except when there is a set piece. At the same time Sondheim provides music that can help the actor's characterization. In this case the quirky bounce of Mrs. Lovett's music tells us of her impulsive, unthinking, but canny behavior; its odd intervals (the number of tones between one note and the next) suggest her inability to be logical; its jerky rhythms are part of her stage business—swatting flies and bugs—but they also tell of her energy, her vitality, and the unpredictable uses to which it can be put.

The last time Sondheim had written music for Angela Lansbury (*Anyone Can Whistle*), he had given her too wide a range to sing and it strained her voice. This time, with four more scores behind him—and with Lansbury herself a star of musical comedy—they were both more experienced, knowing, and confident. When he demonstrated songs for her in his home, coaching her himself, "he was," she said, "completely explicit—and hard. But he buys what you give to him and he's enormously thankful and pleased when you do well. If something isn't working for the singer, he will do something to make it work."

This song of hers, "The Worst Pies in London," isn't rangy, but it isn't easy either; one note does not immediately suggest the next. It is, however, funny.

> The worst pies in London—
> Even that's polite.

> The worst pies in London—
> If you doubt it, take a bite.
>
> Is that just disgusting?

Todd wonders whether the quarters above the pie shop might be rentable, but Mrs. Lovett says they are undesirable because "years ago, something happened," and she reprises the piquant "Poor Thing"—now using Todd's real name, Benjamin Barker.

> He had this wife, you see,
> Pretty little thing.
> Silly little nit
> Had her chance for the moon on a string—
> Poor thing. Poor thing.

This music is so carefully written within her range that Lansbury was able to act the lyric as if it were a speech. At the same time she felt that "Poor Thing" was the most beautiful song she had ever sung, "the sort of thing you don't get to do in a musical comedy." Its lyrics provide more of the story's background.

> There were these two, you see,
> Wanted her like mad,
> One of 'em a Judge,
> T'other one his Beadle.

Mrs. Lovett sings of how Judge Turpin unjustly sentenced Barker to a faraway prison for fifteen years. Meantime, in mime, the Judge rapes Barker's wife, Lucy, as she is held down by the Beadle (his court assistant). When Todd roars, "Would no one have mercy on her?", Mrs. Lovett realizes he is Benjamin Barker. She tells him that his wife swallowed arsenic and that their daughter, Johanna, has been adopted by the Judge. She then gives him his silver razors—which she had (conveniently) been saving. "See?" she says, "you can be a barber again." In the chilling fashion of an old horror tale, Todd sings "My Friends" to the instruments.

> You've been locked out of sight
> All these years—
> Like me, my friend.

> Well, I've come home
> To find you waiting.
> Home.
> And we're together,
> And we'll do wonders,
> Won't we?

Ordinarily a song lyric develops a notion or a peak moment, generalizing from it. With so much being sung in *Sweeney Todd*, every moment cannot be treated that way or else it would be a concert. By eliminating rhyme and expressing a line of thought, rather than embellishing a single idea, Sondheim creates a conversational song. He sets this lyric to an eerily lyrical melody, suggesting evil doings ahead; he arranges it in duet with Mrs. Lovett so that, while Todd sings of the razors as his friends, she sings of *herself* as his friend.

But her lyrics in the duet are rhymed. They help to create a sexuality even as she becomes part of the evil doings.

> I'm your friend too,
> Mr. Todd.
> If you only knew,
> Mr. Todd.
> Ooh,
> Mr. Todd, you're warm
> In my hand.
> You've come home.

But Todd does not hear, too absorbed, and in love, is he with his razors:

> Till now your shine
> Was merely silver.
> Friends,
> You shall drip rubies,
> You'll soon drip precious rubies . . .

The music now expands to become, like Todd, a perversion of the traditionally heroic. This is very powerful stuff, and orchestrator Tunick does it proud, underlining the chilling crown of the moment when Todd holds his razor aloft and cries, "At last my arm is complete again." With that Sondheim comes triumphantly crashing through in true horror-movie style with his musical motive, the "Dies Irae" theme.

The locale changes to Judge Turpin's house, where Todd's daughter now lives. Johanna is made up to look like a caricature. With her Kewpie doll looks, inability to concentrate, and nonstop babbling, she seems slightly demented. This amused approach to young lovers is familiar in Sondheim shows: girls like Philia in *Forum*, the mannequin heroine of "Evening Primrose," and the stewardess in *Company*, as well as such boys as Hero in *Forum* and the sailor, Anthony Hope, here. Johanna has certainly met her simpleminded match in him. Nevertheless, for these two, in coupled songs, Sondheim now presents his sweetest music to date.

It comes in consecutive serenades, one forlorn and the other adoring. The first introduces Johanna. She has grown up to be a beautiful young woman who is virtually a prisoner in Judge Turpin's home. She identifies with the caged singing birds that are being displayed by a passing vendor:

> Green finch and linnet bird,
> Nightingale, blackbird,
> How is it you sing?

How can you jubilate,
Sitting in cages,
Never taking wing?

Here is a soprano aria of heart-rending beauty, set to a chirping accompaniment that in less careful hands might have been precious. Had anyone ever doubted Sondheim's gift for melody (and detractors have, throughout his career), "Green Finch and Linnet Bird" presents him at his most ariose. It is languid, musically sensual, and very poignant—suggestive perhaps of Canteloube's "Songs of the Auvergne." Yet for all its classical air, there is a throbbing rise in the harmony that bespeaks the Broadway theater.

As in opera, the song's title comes from its first words rather than, as in popular music, from the theme (the paradox of a singing prisoner). Nor does Sondheim repeat his title, as is done in popular music. Some of the lyric phraseology is baroque—for instance, "Whence comes this melody constantly flowing?"—but that is appropriate to the Victorian period, as are the obscure bird names. (The mysterious source of a bird's melody, incidentally, would be fascinating to any composer.) Finally Johanna's identification with these birds is simply touching.

Ringdove and robinet,
Is it for wages,
Singing to be sold?
Have you decided it's
Safer in cages,
Singing when you're told?

As she sings, Todd's young sailor friend enters. There is no reason for him to be walking past Judge Turpin's house, but coincidence is normal in a melodrama. He interrupts Johanna to declare his instant love in a reprise of "I have sailed the world,/Beheld its wonders." Sondheim sets these words too in Victorian locutions, then applies a wonderful device to both music and lyrics to capture youthful ardor: excited repetition.

Lady look at me look at me miss oh
Look at me please oh
Favor me favor me with your glance.
Ah, miss,
What do you what do you see off
There in those trees oh
Won't you give won't you give me a chance?

"Ah, Miss" bubbles with vitality, and it is an original kind of music—original for this moment as the entire score is original to its broader purpose. Sondheim has achieved with this score the ability to invent a complete musical language for a particular stage project. While the music is theater music in a popular vernacular, still it is not musical comedy music. It is *Sweeney Todd* music.

Anthony buys one of the vendor's birds for Johanna, then serenades her. His is as masculine an aria as hers was feminine, "masculine" not only because it is in a lower range but because it is terse, definite, and assertive, as compared to Johanna's more complex, allusive, and subtle "Green Finch and Linnet Bird." This serenade of Anthony's, "Johanna," is an outright love song. As he has only just set eyes on her, it adds to his brainless air.

I feel you,
Johanna,
And one day
I'll steal you.

Sweeney Todd *album producer Thomas Z. Shepard (left) works with Sondheim and Prince on the original cast recording.*

> Till I'm with you then,
> I'm with you there,
> Sweetly buried in your yellow hair.

Not "steal," but "rescue" would seem the right word. Awkward, too, from the usually graceful Sondheim, is "Till I'm with you then/I'm with you there." There is more to be said at a time like this than "I feel you, I'll steal you," but the music is beautiful enough to carry the piece.

When the Judge happens upon the pair, he warns Johanna about "venal young men of the street," while his flunky, the Beadle, plucks Anthony's bird from the cage, strangles it, and warns the young man away. Relief from all this villainy arrives with a grand burst of show business, "Pirelli's Miracle Elixir." If this is not exactly a traditional musical comedy number, it is one in the *Sweeney Todd* style. Sondheim's score now revels in its own language: richly melodic and harmoniously resolved yet spiced with dissonance; solo and ensemble in this one number; earthy and classical, sprawling across a lively canvas; Falstaffian in counterpoint to the elements of revenge melodrama. The only comparable example, on Broadway at least, of music setting a show's character in such a way is Gershwin's *Porgy and Bess*.

"Pirelli's Miracle Elixir" is an exuberant number that begins with a crowd surrounding the decorated wagon of Adolfo Pirelli, a barber who peddles hair-growing tonic. The sequence opens with his assistant, the simpleminded Tobias (a role that the playwright Christopher Bond had written for himself), representing himself as a satisfied customer.

> 'Twas Pirelli's
> Miracle Elixir,
> That's wot did the trick, sir,
> True, sir, true.
> Was it quick, sir?
> Did it in a tick, sir,
> Just like an elixir
> Ought to do!

The number practically chortles with the glee of Sondheim at rhyme, mating "elixir" with "wick, sir," "thick, sir," "sick, sir," "nick, sir," "mixer," "kick, sir," and more. This dizzying verse is framed by exuberant music set to a polka rhythm and styled for street corner band. When he has reason to write such lighthearted music, Sondheim releases melody like a gusher. "Pirelli's Miracle Elixir" is joyous and clangy, like *Forum*'s "Comedy Tonight" and "What Would We Do Without You?" in *Company*.

When Todd happens along with Mrs. Lovett, he examines the tonic and announces that it smells like piss, it looks like piss, and, by God, "This is piss." With that an irate Pirelli makes his entrance, swirling his cape and twirling a mustache that is no more believable than his Italian dialect.

> And I, da so-famous Pirelli,
> I wish-a to know-a
> Who has-a da nerve-a to say
> My elixir is piss!
> Who says this?

The Pirelli sequence is a superlative example of Sondheim's mature technique for blending music, lyrics, and dialogue in long dramatic scenes. It is a scene worth savoring, as Todd offers to wager Pirelli "that I can shave a cheek . . . with ten times more dexterity than any street mountebank!" Pirelli accepts the challenge, and the contest begins. He whips up a lather and sharpens his razor while Todd watches idly. Here is a lot of good fun—tension, suspense, and sham, richly atmospheric with period and place.

Pirelli, disarmed by Todd's inactivity, begins to sing as he shaves, working to the casual bounce of his song.

> To cut-a da hair,
> To trim-a da beard,
> To make-a da bristle
> Clean like a whistle, . . .
> It take-a da pace,
> It take-a da grace—

As Pirelli hits and holds a high note, Todd briskly lathers his man's face, shaves it smooth, and pronounces the job done. He is triumphant—almost. For there have been danger signals: Pirelli has recognized the silver razors as Benjamin Barker's, and the Beadle nearly recognizes Todd himself. Nevertheless the contest establishes Todd's credentials, and Mrs. Lovett announces the opening of "Sweeney Todd's Tonsorial Parlor—above my meat pie shop in Fleet Street." Once again "The Ballad of Sweeney Todd" is chanted by the small chorus, foretelling the story ahead:

> Sweeney pondered and Sweeney planned.
> Like a perfect machine 'e planned.
> Barbing the hook, baiting the trap,
> Setting it out for the Beadle to snap.

Like farce, melodrama requires continuous action, and Judge Turpin abruptly decides to marry Johanna. Normally a wreck, she now becomes hysterical. Sondheim cannot take her very seriously.

Of all Angela Lansbury's triumphs on Broadway, her role in Sweeney Todd *was the most heroic, with the most challenging music and the most complicated character. Mrs. Lovett can seem both a murderer and a victim, but to Sondheim, "while she is womanly and sexual, she is not vulnerable—she is venal. All she cares about is money."*

Below, right:
Tobias (Ken Jennings) and Mrs. Lovett comfort each other singing "Not While I'm Around."

He means to marry me Monday,
What shall I do? I'd rather die.
I'll swallow poison on Sunday,
That's what I'll do, I'll get some lye.

Johanna's music brings her normal babbling over the top. A heroic Anthony tries to calm her with manly offers of security, crying "Kiss me!", and now the music becomes a thrilling love duet for them. Sondheim is not afraid to reach for the big musical line when the situation calls for it. Here, as a young lover cries "Kiss me!", the music soars on a strong countermelody used first as an accompaniment and then, set to words, as the main theme.

For a moment Sondheim brings the passion down with Johanna's nervous theme:

'Tis Friday, virtually Sunday.
What can we do with time so brief?

And then the girl herself sings the rhapsodic "Kiss me!", making these silly lovers real and touching.

They also seem truly endangered when the Judge reappears, talking with the Beadle about his imminent wedding. From this point until the intermission some fifteen minutes ahead, *Sweeney Todd* will be almost entirely musical. Even speeches designed to propel the plot, such as the Beadle's at this moment ("Ladies in Their Sensitivities"), are sung (triple-rhymed, in fact):

Forgive me if I suggest, my lord,
You're looking less than your best, my lord,
There's powder upon your vest, my lord,
And stubble upon your cheek.

As he suggests a visit to a barber, Anthony and Johanna resume their song of elopement. Her prattle, foolish but frightened, once again sets up the dominating theme, the rhapsodic over-melody with which Anthony forces her to stop talking and "Kiss me!"

Judge Turpin and the Beadle make a quartet of it as they sing of going to Sweeney Todd for a shave. The four-part song brings the lush theme to full musical fruition. The only problem is that Anthony sings one lyric, Johanna a second, the Beadle a third, and Judge Turpin a fourth—all simultaneously. The words, inevitably, are unintelligible.

Such simultaneous conversational lyrics will pose problems in subsequent works. Sondheim has now mastered the kind of extended musical-dramatic sequence that he had been exploring throughout his career, and it will soon dominate his work. He will still write the occasional "song-song," but only when the moment calls for it. However a musicalized scene cannot simply be performed like a dramatic scene whose dialogue is replaced by music and lyrics. Spoken dialogue is hard enough to understand when it overlaps; lyrics are almost impossible. They are always hard to grasp on the first hearing, and no matter how long a show runs, virtually everyone in the audience is hearing them for the first time. When more than one set of lyrics is being sung, with an orchestra playing at the same time, they are all the harder to comprehend. Thus in the "Kiss Me" sequence, few in the audience are likely to grasp the ironic contrast between the lovers' ardent music and their inane dialogue:

I loved you
Even as I saw you,
Even as it does not
Matter that I still
Don't know your name . . .

At the pie shop, Mrs. Lovett manages to get over the shock of Pirelli's murder. Her lines always get a laugh after Todd says that the barber had threatened blackmail. "Oh well, that's a different matter! . . . For a moment I thought you'd lost your marbles."

Now Todd's dream materializes as Judge Turpin arrives for a shave. Sondheim provides a cheerful duet for murderer and victim, "Pretty Women." It is a madrigal-like air set with Victorian lyrics and the Judge begins it.

> You see, sir, a man infatuate with love,
> Her ardent and eager slave.
> So fetch the pomade and pumice stone
> And lend me a more seductive tone,
> A sprinkling perhaps of French cologne,
> But first, sir, I think—a shave.

Todd cannot cut Turpin's throat yet; there must first be the almost and the nearly and the close call. Sondheim relishes the moment and has Todd join the Judge in song.

If the opening melody was incongruously sweet, the main body of the piece is still sweeter. Here is an air of real beauty, lovingly harmonized by a masochist and a homicidal maniac. The maniac begins:

> Pretty women . . .
> Fascinating . . .
> Sipping coffee,
> Dancing . . .
>
> Pretty women . . .

The masochist enters.

JUDGE

> Silhouetted . . .

TODD

> Stay within you . . .

JUDGE

> Glancing . . .

The thought is developed as they continue their richly harmonized duet—pretty women "at their mirrors" and "in their gardens" and "letter-writing" and "flower-picking." The two gentlemen agree that pretty women are "proof of heaven," and then, true to the horror genre,

> Todd raises his arm in a huge arc and is about to slice the razor across the
> Judge's throat

when Anthony bursts in singing—not only saving the Judge but, ever brainless, betraying the elopement plan:

> She says she'll marry me Sunday,
> Everything's set, we leave tonight!

Turpin leaps from the chair, vowing to hide Johanna in "some obscure retreat," and Todd is unhinged. His "Epiphany" is the transformation of an unjustly punished and vengeful man into a serial killer.

"I had him!" he screams. "His throat was bare." Mrs. Lovett rushes to calm him with her lullaby, "Hush, love, hush," but he will not be stilled. "Why did I wait? *You* told me to wait!" His mind plunges back to the earlier fury:

Few Broadway stars are as relaxed and self-confident as Angela Lansbury, who permitted photographer Rivka Katvan to snap away in the dressing room.

> There's a hole in the world
> Like a great black pit
> And it's filled with people
> Who are filled with shit . . .

As a chugging "Dies Irae" starts in the orchestra, he slashes at the air, raging, "We all deserve to die!", and the music behind him pounds and clangs like an anvil, very Prokofiev-like in Jonathan Tunick's banging orchestration. Sweeney vows death for not only the wicked but "For the rest of us, death/Will be a relief."

There is a sudden break in the fury, a surge of musical feeling, a long and hurt melodic line.

> And I'll never see Johanna
> No, I'll never hug my girl to me—

And then his mind splinters, as he turns to the audience and vows bloodshed. For this, Sondheim has written crashing lines of real discordance, musical lunacy. It is as if the mind's loss of mooring is being reflected in music that is also without key.

The deadly lyrics for Todd's "Epiphany" are all but unrhymed and ferocious, icy but quite mad and frightening (the lines are delivered directly to the audience).

> You, sir, too, sir—
> Welcome to the grave—
> I will have vengeance,
> I will have salvation!
>
> Who, sir? You, sir?
> No one's in the chair—
> Come on, come on,
> Sweeney's waiting!
> I want you bleeders!
> You, sir—anybody!
> Gentlemen, now don't be shy!

Sondheim traces this piece to Oscar Hammerstein's *Carousel* "Soliloquy," although it has another antecedent in "Rose's Turn" from *Gypsy*. That and the "Epiphany" are nervous breakdowns in song, and both use a shredded musical memory, recapitulating sections of earlier songs as a reflection of a mind breaking down. But there are also differences between them. The "Epiphany" is uncompromising in its fury, unrelenting in its power. Its music is extremely sophisticated, shattered and numbed like a tortured mind. It never gives relief, while "Rose's Turn" offers jazzy rhythms and catchy melodies within its jarring orchestration.

Todd's cries for blood subside with the flowing music of his pain.

> Not one man, no,
> Nor ten men,
> Nor a hundred
> Can assuage me—

And as that theme is repeated, he cries despairingly,

> And my Lucy lies in ashes
> And I'll never see my girl again,
> But the work waits,
> I'm alive at last . . .

This is a strange notion, his being "alive at last" as a murderer. In a way it recalls "Being Alive" in *Company*, where Sondheim also wrote of sucking vitality from outside the self, in that case from another's love. Either these are curious sources of vitality or this is overanalysis.

The "Epiphany" concludes with the perverted "And I'm full of joy!" Todd is elated by the commitment to kill, and yet the outburst endows him with a measure of sympathy and even heroism. He will not seem monstrous to the audience; instead, he will appear a victim, abused and agonized, and this will not be the last time that Sondheim looks into the soul of a killer.

With melodrama having graduated to this harrowing peak, the mood must be relieved. The comic relief is not only cathartic but funnier even than "The Worst Pies in London."

In "A Little Priest," Mrs. Lovett is merely suggesting to Todd that burying the murdered barber

> Seems an awful waste . . .

and, referring to the corpse, she adds with ingenious rhymes:

> Nor it can't be traced.
> Business needs a lift—
> Debts to be erased—
> Think of it as thrift,
> As a gift . . .
> If you get my drift . . .

Sighing, she muses,

> Seems an awful waste.
> I mean,
> With the price of meat what it is,
> When you get it,
> If you get it—

Todd slowly gets it, and the always whimsical Mrs. Lovett is pleased.

> Good, you got it.

The melody ahead is weird and quirky, off center like its singer. It is also catchy and in waltz time, so that Mrs. Lovett can skim and twirl as if she were on the music-hall stage in period London. It is from just such a stage that the piece takes its comic character, and that is what is wonderful and right about it, as they deal with imaginary pies.

MRS. LOVETT

It's priest.
Have a little priest.

TODD

Is it really good?

MRS. LOVETT

Sir, it's too good,
At least.
Then again, they don't commit sins of the flesh,
So it's pretty fresh.

TODD

Awful lot of fat.

MRS. LOVETT

Only where it sat.

TODD

Haven't you got poet
Or something like that?

MRS. LOVETT

No, you see the trouble with poet
Is, how do you know it's
Deceased?
Try the priest.

They sing into the night, cheerfully murderous and quite mad. It is a perfect and perfectly appropriate way to bring down the first-act curtain.

After intermission the grisly cheer grows still cheerier, for the new menu has brought prosperity to Mrs. Lovett's pie shop. The scene is like a stage version of a Breughel painting, overflowing with provincials of exaggerated complexion, shape, and feature, each engaged in a private activity that is part of a boisterous and rousing tapestry. This crowd of high-spirited, ale-swilling, meat-pie eaters is overseen by the very grandly dressed Mrs. Lovett (she is even wearing a hat), reigning in her eatery which has been expanded into an outdoor garden. Tobias, the late Pirelli's assistant, now works for her, waiting tables and innocent of the pies' ingredients. And as he had introduced the number for Pirelli's Miracle Elixir, he now introduces Mrs. Lovett's meat pies:

Are your nostrils aquiver and tingling as well
At that delicate, luscious ambrosial smell?
Yes they are, I can tell.

Well, ladies and gentlemen,
That aroma catching the breeze
Is like nothing compared to its succulent source,
As the gourmets among you will tell you, of course.

This boisterously old-fashioned, but hardly traditional, second-act opening number is actually a rewording of the music for "Pirelli's Miracle Elixir." Tobias continues:

> There you'll sample
> Mrs. Lovett's meat pies,
> Savory and sweet pies,
> As you'll see.
> You who eat pies,
> Mrs. Lovett's meat pies
> Conjure up the treat pies
> Used to be!

So begins a half act of completely musicalized theater. Its dialogue is sung, but the flow is conversational and the rhymes carefully pocketed, never underlining the words as lyrics yet lending them musicality. Although the music will vary and develop, the feeling will not be of musical numbers. Rather, the singing will seem to be the *dialect* of the show.

The sung dialogue of the tavern customers, crying for service and complaining about the prices, evolves into the song "God, That's Good!"

> MRS. LOVETT
> What's your pleasure, dearie? . . .
> No, we don't cut slices . . .
> Cor, me eyes is bleary! . . .
> *(as Tobias is about to pour for a plastered customer)*
> Toby!
> None for the gentlemen! . . .
> I could up me prices—
> I'm a little leery . . .
> Business couldn't be better, though—

With business so good, the stock of meat pies is soon depleted, and customers cry out for more. Sondheim sometimes includes lines for more than one singer *within the same lyric,* for instance:

> God, that's good that is de have you
> Licious ever tasted smell such
> Oh my God what more that's pies good!

That is when Sweeney demonstrates for Mrs. Lovett how they are going to get human meat from his barber chair to her cellar oven. It is the best kind of theater: demonstration.

> TODD
> When I pound the floor,
> It's a signal to show
> That I'm ready to go,
> When I pound the floor!

The customers are calling for "more hot pies!" With a pile of books, Sweeney and Mrs. Lovett test their system. As the stage direction reads, Todd "pounds three times on the floor. Mrs. Lovett responds by knocking three times on the mouth of the chute. Todd pulls a lever in the arm of the barber chair. The chair becomes a slide and the books disappear through a trap . . . reappearing from a hole in the bakehouse wall."

With that a customer arrives for a shave, and Mrs. Lovett takes down the "Sold Out" sign. And while she sings,

God watches over us.
Didn't have an inkling . . .
Positively eerie . . .

Tobias, at the same time, sings,

Is that a pie
Fit for a king,
A wondrous sweet
And most delectable
Thing?

Simultaneously, the customers cry,

Yum!
Yum!
Yum!
Yum! Yum!
Yum!
Yum!

Perhaps all of this could have been as effective with only the spoken word, but that is hard to imagine.

With a shift of stage focus, Anthony wanders the streets of London in search of Johanna, and as he sings of her, Todd does too, while slitting throats in his barber shop. His song, however, is a father's, and so there are *two* "Johanna" songs. (Actually there were three, the other being Judge Turpin's flagellation song, which wisely was cut.) Anthony's is certainly ardent, but Todd's is the more touching because of the pain and longing within it, and because of the loss in it—of Johanna and her mother—signified by a lightly thumping accompaniment.

And are you beautiful and pale,
With yellow hair, like her?
I'd want you beautiful and pale,
The way I've dreamed you were,
Johanna . . .

The vocal demands of Sweeney Todd *made replacements difficult but Dorothy Loudon and George Hearn were good enough to have opened in the show.*

Now, too, Mrs. Lovett's cellar oven belches out its fumes, and in the rhythms of alarm, the Beggar Woman vainly warns,

Smoke! Smoke!
Sign of the devil! Sign of the devil!
City on fire!
Witch! Witch!
Smell it, sir! An evil smell!
Every night at the vespers bell—
Smoke that comes from the mouth of hell—
City on fire!

Todd continues to sing of his daughter, calmly now and serene in his commitment to vengeance. The beat within his "Johanna" grows ominous.

And if I never hear your voice,
My turtledove, my dear,
I still have reason to rejoice:
The way ahead is clear,
Johanna . . .

Anthony continues to sing his own sweet "Johanna," but she now can be seen, ranting in the madhouse where the Judge has hidden her away.

> I'll marry Anthony Sunday . . .
> Anthony Sunday . . .

And still the Beggar Woman cries out in vain.

> Didn't I tell you? Smell that air!
> City on fire!

The entwining melodies have made for a dark dramatic build, and so to lighten things, Sondheim provides Mrs. Lovett with a song with which she can cozy up to Todd. In its theme, "By the Sea" is reminiscent of "Pretty Little Picture" from *Forum*. This song, too, imagines a beach paradise.

> I can see us waking,
> The breakers breaking,
> The seagulls squawking:
> Hoo! Hoo!

"By the Sea" was not Angela Lansbury's favorite song, and she said, "I don't think [Steve] liked it particularly either. [He is a little unhappy with the crowded lyric.] It's like a jingle." But "By the Sea" is too quirky for a jingle. Yet its dramatic intention is to divert Todd and Mrs. Lovett is slightly addled, so it does have a certain brainless quality. When Sondheim first played it for Lansbury, he told her, "I wrote a song for you so crowded there is no place to breathe," and the galloping lyrics probably bothered her as much as anything else.

Beyond all that, she probably disliked the song because it didn't land with the audience.

It is not Mrs. Lovett's song that rouses Sweeney but the appearance of Anthony with the news that Johanna is in the madhouse. A livid Todd tells him that such places sell their inmates' hair and suggests that Anthony rescue her by offering a high price for hair like hers.

Struck with an idea for getting Judge Turpin under his razor, Todd now writes him a note warning that Anthony is abducting Johanna and that she will stay at his shop overnight. As he writes, his note is sung by a quintet, and here *Sweeney Todd* comes closest to sounding like an opera. It is sung prose, not lyrics; as if because of that, "The Letter" is not the most distinguished music in the show. It sounds like generic, modern opera music.

In telling contrast is the following "Not While I'm Around," which a frightened Tobias sings to comfort Mrs. Lovett. After the tremendous amount of music preceding—choral music and arias, spells of musicalized dialogue, snatches of song and connective tissue, boisterous and tragic pieces, reprises and developments—this succinct, formal song does not merely succeed in its dramatic intent as a moment of eerie comfort; it is a song worthy of Franz Schubert.

Sondheim is careful about writing with such tenderness and affirmation. Avowal almost never appears in his work, unless qualified by doubt and uncertainty. Expressions of affection are usually reserved for brainless young lovers like Johanna and Anthony. His most moving songs are bittersweet, about emotional uncertainty or disappointment: "Someone Is Waiting" (*Company*), "Every Day a Little Death," "Send in the Clowns" (both, *A Little Night Music*). There is a shakiness in their underpinnings, a hesitant beat, and they all have pauses to anticipate hurt along the way. They sing of love in terms of hope at best, unlikelihood at worst, and ambivalence at least—in the music as well as in the words.

On the occasions that he does launch a long and rising theme and tops it with a succulent musical resolution to signify such happy feelings, when Sondheim writes *big*—"With So Little to Be Sure Of" (*Anyone Can Whistle*), "Take Me to the World" ("Evening Primrose"), "Being Alive" (*Company*)—it isn't entirely convincing. It is almost as if he were simulating ardor by soaring like Jerome Kern. There is always a darker Sondheim lurking within, with an eyebrow raised in the harmonies, an ambivalence pulsating in the rhythmic underpinnings.

"Not While I'm Around," however, is an honest, open, and vulnerable statement of affection, all-giving in its offer of protection.

> Nothing's gonna harm you,
> Not while I'm around.
> Nothing's gonna harm you,
> No, sir,
> Not while I'm around.

The structure is simple—ABAB—which simply means two brief melodies repeated, the second time with a finishing touch, but in that simplicity, Sondheim achieves complete music. If melody is the musical element that connotes emotion, "Not While I'm Around" is the singular Sondheim song that seems driven not by its harmonies but by its melody (and the powerful accompanying line in the "B" section after "nowadays"). The melody is so stirring that it seems perfectly able to carry on alone, unexplained, unexploited, and unsupported by harmony. And when harmony does arrive it seems almost *demanded* by the turn of melodic phrase. That sense of demand is what is sometimes called "classical inevitability," a quality that some feel is the most an artist can hope to achieve.

The music of this song not only reflects the lyrics but quite the reverse: the lyrics seem to articulate what the composer expresses in the music. They do it with a tentativeness, as if fearing even to speak of the monstrous evil that Tobias senses.

> Demons are prowling
> Everywhere
> Nowadays.
> I'll send 'em howling,
> I don't care—
> I got ways.

Sondheim means for Tobias to be singing specifically of Todd, but that is not clear.

> No one's gonna hurt you,
> No one's gonna dare.
> Others can desert you—
> Not to worry—
> Whistle, I'll be there.

The colloquialisms, "not to worry" and "whistle, I'll be there," are carefully chosen so as not to be anachronistic.

> Demon's'll charm you
> With a smile
> For a while,
> But in time
> Nothing can harm you,
> Not while I'm around.

The song sounds finished, but it isn't. It turns around and heads into what can only be considered a verse, an introduction. Now the words become puzzling. Why does Tobias sing:

> Being close and being clever
> Ain't like being true.
> I don't need to, I won't never
> Hide a thing from you,
> Like some.

Sondheim again means for Tobias to be referring to Todd and Mrs. Lovett, but it isn't clear and certainly sounds too sophisticated for poor Tobias. Nevertheless the song concludes—very, very satisfyingly.

Sweeney Todd roars from the finish of this song until show's end. While Mrs. Lovett sends Tobias into the cellar to learn how to chop the "meat," the Beadle arrives, intent on investigating the stench emanating from the pie shop's chimney. Mrs. Lovett instead sends him upstairs for a shave, where Todd promptly slits his throat and sends him down the chute. The Beadle lands at the feet of a horror-struck Tobias, whose suspicions are now confirmed.

"The Ballad of Sweeney Todd" becomes more urgent now, and the workers who usually sing it are joined by inmates from the asylum. They have escaped with Johanna, who has been rescued by Anthony, and they chant the Beggar Woman's warning:

> City on fire!
> Rats in the grass
> And the lunatics yelling in the streets!
> It's the end of the world! Yes!

The show is building momentum now, heading for a climax with no time for talk. Todd and Mrs. Lovett are afraid of what Tobias knows, but they cannot find him, and meantime the lunatics are roaming the stage with the Beggar Woman. When she has the misfortune to show up in the barbershop just as Judge Turpin is approaching, Todd slashes her throat and sends her down the chute.

Once again, Turpin is in Todd's hands, and this time there will be no escape. The two men sing the barbershop duet they sang earlier, and within its dulcet tones Todd suggests to the judge that "perhaps the face of the barber—the face of a prisoner in the dock—is not particularly memorable." In this last moment of his life, Turpin recognizes the barber Benjamin Barker, and with this final slash the razor can be put away, its mission complete.

> Rest now, my friend,
> Rest now forever.
> Sleep now the untroubled
> Sleep of the angels . . .

Johanna enters the shop, disguised as a sailor as part of her escape. Todd reaches for his razor and, for a horrifying moment—the scariest of the show—it seems as if he is going to cut his own daughter's throat. But she slips free and, quite thrillingly now, the company sings the "Dies Irae" theme again.

> Lift your razor high, Sweeney!
> Hear it singing, "Yes!"
> Sink it in the rosy skin
> Of righteousness!

This climactic scene is a rather unique variation on an old-fashioned eleven o'clock number. To cap it Todd takes a hard look at the body of the Beggar Woman and realizes it is his wife, Lucy.

TODD
You knew she lived. From the moment I came into your shop you knew my Lucy lived!

MRS. LOVETT
I was only thinking of you!

Todd cannot accept Mrs. Lovett's excuse that his wife was "a crazy hag. . . . Would you have wanted to know that?" He waltzes her around the oven. She begs frantically for forgiveness, for marriage, even singing a snatch of

> By the sea, Mr. Todd,
> We'll be comfy-cozy,

In the finale of Sweeney Todd, *Mrs. Lovett and Sweeney rise from the dead.*

but he hurls her into the oven and slams its door shut. Then, cradling Lucy in his arms, he sings longingly and pathetically:

> There was a barber and his wife,
> And she was beautiful.

Tobias emerges from the bake-house gloom, "singing in an eerie voice. His hair has turned completely white." Quite demented he slashes Todd's throat, and with that the company returns to confront the audience with "The Ballad of Sweeney Todd."

TOBIAS
Attend the tale of Sweeney Todd.
His skin was pale and his eye was odd.

JOHANNA & ANTHONY
He shaved the faces of gentlemen
Who never thereafter were heard of again.

The two couples in *Sweeney Todd*, Johanna and Anthony, Mrs. Lovett and Todd, make for a weird variation on an old Broadway custom. Two pairs of lovers are as traditional in musical comedy as overtures and walk-out music. There may be some slight differences between *Sweeney*'s sweethearts and, for instance, the quartet of Sky Masterson, Sarah Brown, Nathan Detroit, and Miss Adelaide in *Guys and Dolls* or Curley, Laurie, Will Parker, and Ado Annie in *Oklahoma!*, but their functions are basically similar: one pair for romance, the other—yes, Todd and Mrs. Lovett—for comic relief.

As "The Ballad of Sweeney Todd" is sung in the epilogue, the dead rise.

TODD & COMPANY
Attend the tale of Sweeney Todd.
He served a dark and a hungry god!

TODD
To seek revenge may lead to hell,

MRS. LOVETT
But everyone does it, and seldom as well

TODD & MRS. LOVETT
As Sweeney,

COMPANY
As Sweeney Todd,
The Demon Barber of Fleet . . .
   (*They start to exit*)
   . . . Street!

Todd and Mrs. Lovett are the last to leave the stage. They look at each other, then exit in opposite directions.

Sweeney Todd, The Demon Barber of Fleet Street opened on March 1, 1979, and received arguably the best reviews of any Prince-Sondheim musical. The two men had become the critics' darlings, regular award-winners, and because of that, the envy of all—or at least some—of Broadway. Sondheim, who'd had to wait until he was forty to get his first good reviews (for *Company*) was now being treated in a class of his own, which did not endear him to his fellow composers. (Lyricists, somehow, are not as jealous—or competitive—as composers and are more generous toward each other.) *Sweeney Todd* won eight Tony Awards including best musical and best score, but was there an audience for a Broadway musical about cannibalism?

There was audience enough for 557 performances, just forty-three fewer than *A Little Night Music*, and while *Sweeney Todd* didn't qualify as a smash hit, the run was certainly respectable (if not profitable). In effect, the run would be much longer. Like *Porgy and Bess*, *Sweeney Todd* would become a repertory item, a staple of opera companies around the world, and an acknowledged classic. Had he composed nothing else, this show would have established Sondheim as a giant of the American stage.

But it did not resolve his melancholy. Just after the premiere Sondheim said, "I'm still essentially a cult figure. My kind of work is just too unexpected for the general public. . . . The only really popular show I've ever had is *A Funny Thing Happened on the Way to the Forum*."

MERRILY WE ROLL ALONG

In a stunning display of versatility, Sondheim followed the ambitious and very serious *Sweeney Todd* with a real Broadway musical. *Merrily We Roll Along* is crammed full of show tunes, sharp and bright and crackling with energy. The rhythms are varied and lively; the harmonies are conclusive and satisfying; and there is an overall "show-biz" quality about it.

But this is no mere assortment of catchy numbers. Sondheim yet again sought out the musical language appropriate to a particular show. In this instance the subject is theater people, instead of Victorian homicidal maniacs and there are some differences. So this is theater music in the smart tempo derived from George Furth's libretto.

Paul Gemignani, who conducted both *Sweeney Todd* and *Merrily*, said, "Part of Steve's ability is this extraordinary versatility." The musical director was awed by the depth of the *Sweeney Todd* score ("It takes so much energy to keep that focus and drive in the show. It's really exhausting."). But like many, he had a weakness for show tunes. *Sweeney Todd* notwithstanding, Gemignani could hardly contain his special enthusiasm for the Broadway sound of *Merrily We Roll Along*.

The musical is based on a play by George S. Kaufman and Moss Hart that was a minor success of the 1934 Broadway season. The subject is artistic corruption, and the conceit is to start at the end and end at the start—that is, to move backward in time. Judy Prince (Harold's wife and Sondheim's closest friend) had suggested a musical about young people and their values. When Sondheim agreed to the idea, and to *Merrily* as the vehicle for it, Prince engaged George Furth (author of *Company*) to turn it into a musical libretto.

Harold Prince feels that one of the most important qualities of any show is its appearance. He believed that the best way to do *Merrily We Roll Along* was without any scenery at all, like *Our Town*. But, he said, "I didn't have the guts—I didn't think you could charge Broadway prices for a show without scenery," and he was probably right. It isn't that audiences are small-minded; it's simply that most people identify Broadway musicals with size and glamour. Even Prince's shows, whether he had been producer and/or director, had been big almost without exception, and the greatest hit of his directorial career was the (then) current *Evita*, a musical with a feeling of epic size.

He never found a successful scenic approach to *Merrily We Roll Along*. The show was ultimately set in a school gymnasium, which was both ugly and awkward. Prince felt that this was the basis for the devastatingly reviewed, sixteen-performance disaster. Sondheim thought, "We never made it clear exactly what it was about." Others believed that the youthful acting company was the reason for the show's fate, or that the libretto was bewildering. Some actually blamed the costumes or malicious gossip during the New York preview period. Sondheim truly believed that "the theater community hated me and Hal," and Prince believed it too.

Merrily We Roll Along did not work, but its score endures. Sondheim had set out to

One of the rare moments of dance in a Sondheim-Prince musical was choreographed for Merrily We Roll Along *by Larry Fuller.*

write traditional songs ("as opposed to the extended things I'd been doing,") and this show even has an overture which, like most overtures, is noisy and motley (put together by the orchestrator, not the composer). But after that there is nothing ordinary about the music.

The plot begins in 1980, working its way back to 1954. The central characters are three high school friends—a male songwriting team and a female author—who come to New York to conquer the theater. They get as far as an off-Broadway revue, a hit song, and a few shows. Along the way the composer is corrupted by ambition, and that undoes the team. The friendships are destroyed while he becomes a rich, famous, and cynical Hollywood producer.

Sondheim provided the original cast recording with a comprehensive note on his approach to the music and lyrics:

> Since *Merrily We Roll Along* is about friendship, the score concentrates attention on the friendship of Mary, Frank and Charley by having all their songs interconnected through chunks of melody, rhythm and accompaniment. And since the story moves backward in time, it presented an opportunity to invent verbal and musical motifs which could be modified over the course of the years, extended and developed, reprised, fragmented and then presented to the audience in reverse: extensions first, reprises first, fragments first. For example, a release in one song would turn up later—later in the show but earlier in time— as a refrain in another, a melody would become an accompaniment, a chorus would be reprised as an interlude.

This is the fancy truth, but *Merrily We Roll Along* also gave Sondheim the chance to write songs in forms and styles he had not dealt with since *Saturday Night*. Even though there was a traditional sound in *Company* and *Follies*, the music was unusual in form, and for Sondheim traditional Broadway music involves form as much as sound. He believes that "content dictates form. Since *Merrily* is a Kaufman and Hart play with their sensibility—a Broadway comedy—it asks for that kind of music," that is, the musical vernacular of Broadway.

To hear him talk about his scores, he seems most personally pleased with this one, and there certainly is a vitality to it, a composer taking his own pleasure. It is as if he were writing the fun songs he had long foresworn so as to become *Stephen Sondheim*; as if this were the debut Broadway musical that *Saturday Night* should have been. There are tender stage ballads ("Good Thing Going," "Not a Day Goes By"), charm songs ("Like It Was," "Old Friends," "Now You Know"), and extroverted ensemble numbers ("Rich and Happy," "Our Time"). There is even a send-up of the Kennedy family in the style of the satiric revues that proliferated in the 1960s.

The centerpiece is "Good Thing Going," because it is the characters' career-making hit. This is a first-rate ballad written to reflect the kind of song popular in 1962 ("A Summer Place," for instance). Constructed on the standard thirty-two measure model, its prime melody is simple and singable, made tart with a light dissonance in the accompaniment. As in "Send in the Clowns," the release (the "B" section) is an ingenious variation on the chorus in a higher and minor key. The original ironic melody concludes with satisfying harmonies plus almost corny drama in the lyric.

> And while it's going along,
> You take for granted some love
> Will wear away.

The "old friends" in Merrily We Roll Along *were played by young actors (from left, Lonny Price, Ann Morrison, Jim Walton, and Sally Klein).*

The original notion for setting Merrily We Roll Along *was that there be no scenery at all. A fear that the audience would resent paying Broadway prices for a bare stage led to the use of simple sets like these bleachers, which somehow only made it look more bare.*

We took for granted a lot,
But still I say:
It could have kept on growing,
Instead of just kept on.
We had a good thing going,
Going,
Gone.

This lyric seems to be intentionally unpolished, with sloppy syntax ("We took for granted a lot") and blatant padding ("still I say"). Sondheim says he simply meant to imitate the style of pop song lyrics circa 1962. That isn't a good enough excuse.

The show's other love song, "Not a Day Goes By," is more complicated, with its tight harmonic modulations and unpredictable melody. Perhaps it might be thought of as Sondheim in an "All the Things You Are" mode, writing an artful popular song. The structure is unusual (ABAA instead of the usual AABA), and the piece is longer than most, with a melody that doesn't care to stop. It is so tightly written, with harmonies so painfully beautiful, that it creates a tension and poignancy most appropriate to the vulnerability in the lyric.

FRANK
Not a day goes by.

MARY
Not a single day—

BOTH
But you're somewhere a part of my life,
And it looks like you'll stay.

As the days go by,
I keep thinking, "When does it end?"

FRANK
That it can't get much better much longer.
But it only gets better and stronger
And deeper and nearer
And simpler and freer
And richer and clearer

BOTH
And no,

MARY
Not a day goes by,
Not a blessed day
But you're still somehow part of my life
And you won't go away.

Sondheim uses repetition in these lyrics to convey intensity of feeling, and the simplicity of language makes the emotional outburst very believable. The expression "not a blessed day" is almost pretentious, but the earnest music brings it through.

The show's rhythmic songs are especially charming. "Like It Was" feels as familiar as an old sweater, with echoing melodic figures that seem appropriate to its theme of loss. "Old Friends" is an eloquent essay on camaraderie sung by the three schoolmates, set to a loping, almost conversational chant so as to highlight lyrics that were written with insight and ingenuity. But it is the fast-paced yet conversational middle section where Sondheim's lyric-writing flashes brightest. Here are lyrics and drama as one.

FRANK

Tell you something:
Good friends point out your lies,
Whereas old friends live and let live.

MARY

Good friends like and advise,
Whereas old friends love and forgive.

FRANK

And old friends let you go your own way—

CHARLEY

Help you find your own way—

MARY

Let you off when you're wrong—

FRANK

If you're wrong—

CHARLEY

When you're wrong—

MARY

Right or wrong, the point is:
Old friends shouldn't care if you're wrong—

FRANK

Should, but not for too long—

Merrily We Roll Along *begins and ends with "The Hills of Tomorrow," the school alma mater, ostensibly written by the leading character, Franklin Shepard. As the audience's knowledge grows, the song makes for musical bookends, sounding first idealistic and then ironic.*

CHARLEY

What's too long?

FRANK

If you're wrong—

CHARLEY

When you're wrong—

This blend of lyrics and dialogue is so deft as to defy separation. Its colloquial tone is reminiscent of *Gypsy*, as is the use of idiomatic phrases for rhythm as well as poetry. Sondheim's use of lyrical dialogue—this is a complete scene, completely sung—is now perfected. The technique seems the ideal way to musicalize drama, whether for the theater or the opera.

It is tempting to read Sondheim into Charley (the lyricist in the story) and to read the Steve–Hal–Judy Prince friendship into Charley, Frank, and Mary. Sondheim complains that people have also accused him of being Robert in *Company* as well as Georges Seurat in *Sunday in the Park with George* (not to mention Sweeney Todd). He says that although his work, like all art, draws on personal experience, it is never literally about himself—with a single exception, and it is in this show. "If there is one number that is really me writing about me, it is 'Opening Doors.' That was my life for a number of years. It is a totally personal number. Luckily it fits into the piece."

"Opening Doors" is about the trio's painful attempts to break into the New York theater, and is based on Sondheim's rejections while auditioning *Anyone Can Whistle*. Written almost entirely in dialogue, it has Charley writing plays, Mary books, and Frank music. When they stop for breath, they sing a chorus of youthful optimism:

> We're opening doors,
> Singing, "Look who's here!"
> Beginning to sail
> On a dime.
> That faraway shore's
> Getting very near!
> We haven't a thing to fear,
> We haven't got time!

They are also working on a show typical of the 1960s—"Not just songs but stories, scenes/Piano pieces, mime—" a topical revue, with subjects from Synanon to the Kennedys. Its lyrics and tone are pressingly clever, as they would be in a such a show.

When Frank and Charley audition for a producer, he complains, "There's not a tune you can hum" (to the tune they have just sung), and asks,

> Why can't you throw 'em a crumb?
> What's wrong with letting 'em tap their toes a bit?
> I'll let you know when Stravinsky has a hit—
> Give me a melody!

This is exactly the treatment young Sondheim had received from philistine producers who advise:

> Write more, work hard—
> Leave your name with the girl.
> Less avant-garde—
> Leave your name with the girl.
> Just write a plain old melody.

He exits humming Richard Rodgers' "Some Enchanted Evening"—wrongly.

The Kennedy satire is yet another gem in the *Merrily We Roll Along* score, summing, mocking, and outdoing the popular political satires of the period. Its music, too, satirizes the kind of music in such revues, but the words are the most fun:

Well, one is good looking and young and rich
While one is good looking and young and rich,
The rest are good looking and young and rich—
There isn't a lot that they lack,
Not Bobby and Jackie and Jack
And Ethel and Ted and Eunice and Pat and
    Joan and Steve and Peter and Jean and Sarge—
There's probably dozens of others at large,
God knows—
And Joe and Rose.

Merrily We Roll Along was not taken out of town but, for economy's sake, played a month of previews in New York. Naturally the Broadway community flocked to see the latest from Prince and Sondheim, and soon there were rumors of a show in trouble and newspaper reports of mass audience walkouts. By the time it opened (November 16, 1981, at the Alvin Theatre), after a great deal of work that included replacing all the sets and costumes, the show was confusing and unsatisfying. Some critics singled out the score for praise, but amid the disastrous reviews, that meant little to Sondheim, who relates to a whole show and not just his own contribution.

He was so devastated that he told some friends he might quit the theater for movies, others that he was going to write mysteries, even video games, instead of musicals. He would later say, "I wanted to find something to satisfy myself that does not involve Broadway and dealing with all those people who hate me and hate Hal."

The most serious casualty of the *Merrily We Roll Along* disaster was the Sondheim-Prince partnership, which was wrecked for ten years at least (the friendship was beyond threat). "Hal said we were just tired of each other," said Sondheim, who didn't think that was true. "We never had a falling out. I just think that in some way Hal was ashamed of *Merrily*."

This interpretation seems borne out by Prince's resentment of the various attempts to revise the show during the 1980s. It was as if he wanted it just to go away. Sondheim believes that "if *Merrily* had been a success we would have continued" and that their professional separation was like a married couple divorcing after a child has died. It is the only way they can deal with the pain.

EVERYBODY'S GOT THE RIGHT TO BE DIFFERENT

For Sunday in the Park with George, *director James Lapine opted for a little show business splash by putting Bernadette Peters on stage "selling a number" for five minutes to put the audience at ease. ("I tend to the arty side," he said.) Later in the act she imagines being in the Folies-Bergère.*

Merrily We Roll Along did not drive Sondheim to quit Broadway for mysteries, movies, or computer games, but it did convince him that there were better places to start a show. Perhaps he was repelled by the hostility—whether real or imagined—that he felt in the theater community; perhaps he was discouraged by the conviction that "with what's going on on Broadway, I have no market . . . no place for me to put my stuff." Perhaps he sought only a safe nest. Although his new shows might end up on Broadway, for ten years at least, they would start elsewhere.

SUNDAY IN THE PARK WITH GEORGE

That began in 1982, when he was asked to meet with off-Broadway playwright James Lapine, who had an idea for a musical. Coincidentally, Sondheim had been so impressed by Lapine's play *Twelve Dreams* that he had thought of making contact himself. He could have simply telephoned, but he responded to his own fame with a wariness of its effect on others ("You can embarrass people. For all I know, he hates me and hates my work").

In fact Lapine had seen only one of Sondheim's shows, *Sweeney Todd*, but he'd admired it so much he saw it four times. Broadway was not his milieu. "I was the arty-farty one," he would say, and his taste did indeed lie with the avant-garde and with visually oriented theater in particular. That was not surprising, given his background in photography and graphic design. On the other hand, Sondheim had not only spent a lifetime in show business but had a positive aversion to artiness. Predictably unpredictable, he met with Lapine to discuss collaboration.

Here was a very special fellow, a playwright who wrote not only poetically but "visually"—a man with intellectual inclinations, unconventional ideas, and not incidentally, a profound interest in psychoanalysis. Sondheim very much shared that interest.

All of this made Lapine very appealing, and then he brought up the subject of the Georges Seurat painting "A Sunday Afternoon on the Island of La Grande Jatte." It was an acknowledged masterpiece, this huge, brilliantly colored portrayal of working-class people relaxing in a park. Its picture-book quality, stylized formality, and magical serenity could well have suggested the imagery of architect-director Robert Wilson, whose slow-motion, painterly theater Lapine especially admired. *Sunday in the Park with George* would ultimately reflect that taste, as would much of Sondheim's score.

Little was known about the private life of Georges Seurat other than that he died at thirty-one. That fascinated Lapine, "the fact that you didn't know a lot about him. That told you a lot. The guy was clearly mysterious."

Talking that way also told a lot about Lapine too.

Seurat's life was his painting, devoted to finding "a kind of painting that was my own." He would call it "chromoluminarism," the roots of which mean "color" and "light." Critics would later call it pointillism, because instead of brush strokes, he painted with dots, thousands of daubs of pure, unmixed colors. The viewer's eye would do the mixing, and because of the daubs, the perceived colors would shimmer and the painting seem to glow.

Seurat was a Post-Impressionist, and Sondheim doted on French Impressionist music. Inevitably—and at times it would seem unfortunately—the composing of this show would be influenced by Debussy's *Pelleas and Melissande*. This is a unique opera, atmospheric rather than melodramatic, with a continuity of diaphanous music instead of the traditional arias and set pieces. "Given the delicacy of [Lapine's] writing," Sondheim felt, "his script was so allusive, and poetic in the sense of resonance . . . the entrance of music would rip at it. I worried that the songs—and in particular, an applause interruption from the audience—would tear the fabric. I wanted to blend the music and the lyrics into the fabric of what he was writing so that it would be a weave."

Sunday in the Park with George would, like *Pelleas and Melissande* have, as Sondheim put it, "an attenuated quality." Much of the music would be spare, almost severe, with duration rather than form and subdued dynamics, rhythms, and colors. At other times it would resemble "minimalist" music, the repetitive, seemingly computer-generated music written by the contemporary composers Philip Glass and Steve Reich (Sondheim particularly admires Reich).

Just as Lapine was trying to "write the way Seurat painted," Sondheim's first impulse ("you know my puzzler's mind") was to imitate musically what the artist had done with paint, putting only related colors next to each other. He quickly realized that if he did so, "the entire score would be made of seconds because you would have to use adjacent notes all the time." Instead he began the show with an arpeggio that sounded like two keys put together. As that particular melody was replayed, he would shift harmonies so that "you would never be quite sure what key that theme is in until the end of the first act." Perhaps that was Seurat-like, but it promised the audience musical disorientation and perhaps tough listening.

Sondheim was also responding to the personal poetry in Lapine's writing. "It's a long way from a certain kind of Broadway. It's about writing what you feel." He was almost quoting Oscar Hammerstein's advice to him as an adolescent, and even now, he compared this show's change in his own music to "exactly the way Rodgers's music changed when he changed from Hart to Hammerstein." That oblique way was the only way he would admit to the dislocation of breaking with Prince. *Sunday in the Park with George* was going to evoke a new emotional commitment from him.

The show begins with Seurat (called George, never Seurat) confronting a white canvas and a blank stage. "White. A blank page or canvas. The challenge," he announces grandly. "Bring order to the whole."

The whole what? A blank page is perfectly ordered already. This demonstrates that it is possible to be pretentious and baffling at the same time.

The first lyrics list some major elements of art, as well as of music—music that, by Sondheim's own description, is "totally unlike anything I'd ever done." Ominously omitted from the list of elements are "tone" and "color."

> Through design,
> Composition.
> Tension.
> Balance.
> Light.
> And harmony.

Tony Straiges's setting, which has begun as a bare white stage, gradually gains color as

pieces drop and slide in, approximating the background of the "Grande Jatte" painting. With George at the easel and his model-mistress (conspicuously named Dot) posing in the summer heat, the opening number expresses her thoughts and his demands with a special charm.

DOT

> There are worse things
> Than staring at the water
> As you're posing for a picture
> After sleeping on the ferry
> After getting up at seven
> To come over to an island
> In the middle of a river
> Half an hour from the city
> On a Sunday.
> On a Sunday in the park with—

GEORGE

Don't move the mouth!!

DOT

—George.

The music is spare but not yet severe, artistic but not arty. It is recognizably an opening number, sprightly enough, if subdued, for Broadway (Lapine was so un-Broadway that, from his point of view, it had a "show bizzy razz-ma-tazz"). The lyrics are funny, and there is a sweet moment as Dot, enumerating what she loves about George (his eyes, his beard, his size) concludes,

> But most, George,
> Of all,
> But most of all,
> I love your painting . . .

Sondheim sets that last line, "I love your painting," upon a vast musical sigh. At such moments he can be so brainily romantic that the head swims, but he will not linger.

Now on its way, *Sunday in the Park with George* seems not only about art and the artist but about itself and the pictures it is making. With George daubing at a great scrim placed between himself and the audience, a theater rarity takes place: An artist can actually be seen at work, and that is a directing coup.

As George paints, Sondheim musically replicates the pointillism. One gets his message in the lyric too ("Red red orange"), but it does go on like Seurat's thousands of daubs.

The mistress-model provides humor and warmth and whatever musical comedy there will be. George, although he is devoted to his work to the point of excluding personal relationships, is not completely disconnected from people; he even offers to take Dot to the Follies, but painting a hat distracts him. "There's only color and light."

In "Color and Light," his song about painting, the words and music do not make for song. This is the strongest example of the musical canvas Sondheim had talked about. It is like a wash of music across a vast scrim. Perhaps it is appropriate to the subject, but there is no definition to it, no stage muscle to grab the spectator. To break up the musical pointillism, the song slows down for Dot to imagine herself more attractive:

> If my hips were flatter.
> If my voice were warm.
> If I could concentrate—

Then, as the rhythms cavort, she is kicking up her legs and being vivacious:

> I'd be in the Follies.
> I'd be in a cabaret.
> Gentlemen in tall silk hats
> And linen spats
> Would wait with flowers.
> I could make them wait for hours.

George, beneath his artistic obsessiveness, is a deeply emotional man, but he does not (cannot?) make any commitment except to his art. Too busy painting Dot's hat to take her to the Follies as he'd promised, he wonders whether she will leave him.

> Too green . . .
> Do I care? . . .
> Too blue . . .
> Yes . . .
> Too soft . . .
> What shall I do?
>
> Well . . .

His answer to himself reveals that work still matters most.

> Red.

Here at last, Sondheim injects this man's suppressed emotion into music and lyrics, to glimmer beneath the technique, the shimmering canvas, the spare and remote music, the "blue blue blue blue" daubing of the lyrics. This emotional subtext puts *Sunday in the Park with George* at its best so far.

The show occurs on a series of Sundays, and George continues to sketch as the characters who will ultimately populate the Seurat painting begin to appear. They all sing about Sunday being everyone else's "Day Off," which isn't much of a subject for a song even if its purpose of introducing the characters is valid. Ideas for spotting songs just do not leap out of a show about a painting. The song's perky dissonances are set to a bright syncopation, but seem a lot of musical fuss with little melodic material. It all has the feel of conversation set to music in a modern chamber opera, high-class recitative with a lot of plinking and plunking in the accompaniment: very *composed*.

Sondheim is show-wise enough to know when comic relief is needed, and the following "Everybody Loves Louis" is a lot catchier. Louis is the baker with whom Dot takes up, mainly to get a rise out of George. He gives her baker jokes, but is she, like Maria in *West Side Story* ("I Feel Pretty"), being more clever than an uneducated young woman has a right to be?

> Everybody loves Louis,
> Louis bakes from the heart . . .
>
> The bread, George.
> I mean the bread, George.
> And then in bed, George . . .
> I mean he kneads me—
> I mean like dough, George . . .
> Hello, George . . .

There is a good emotional basis and therefore a good reason for this song, which may be one reason why it came out so well and is certainly why it works. It is about a painful choice: Dot does not love Louis, she loves George, who seems to care only about "Finishing the Hat" (which the next song is called), only about his work. With its metaphoric title, this song is a sensitive statement by Sondheim on the personal sacrifices an artist must make, the distance he must keep if he is to look at life and then create his vision of it.

> Finishing the hat,
> How you have to finish the hat,
> How you watch the rest of the world
> From a window
> While you finish the hat.

And so when George learns that Dot is leaving him ("as I always knew she would"), he soliloquizes on the personal cost of artistic obsession. This is terribly moving.

In a modern era, stars of Broadway musicals must be expressive actors as well as dynamic singers. Mandy Patinkin and Bernadette Peters of Sunday in the Park with George *were such performers.*

And when the woman that you wanted goes,
You can say to yourself, "Well, I give what I give."
But the woman who won't wait for you knows
That, however you live,
There's a part of you always standing by,
Mapping out the sky.
Finishing a hat . . .
Starting on a hat . . .
Finishing a hat . . .

Then Sondheim explains succinctly and precisely what an artist does,

Look, I made a hat . . .
Where there never was a hat . . .

but George has only a dog to say it to.

At such moments, *Sunday in the Park with George* is not only beautiful to look at but acutely observant and very touching. The strength here is in the lyrics. Musically, "Finishing the Hat" has a potentially rich theme that is stifled by a repeating accompaniment figure, lending it a minimalist musical drone.

George and Dot sing the ensuing "We Do Not Belong Together" as they sing almost everything in the first act, which only emphasizes the feeling of one long song. This particular piece is musically evasive, with brief phrases repeated wholly or in part. There are moments when the music seems poised to expand, but repetition is resumed. Perhaps Sondheim's intention was to express George's repetitive art (a theme that is developed in the second act). Or perhaps this reflects George's inability to express emotion. After all, that is what he is singing about to Dot in the verse.

The poster for Sunday in the Park with George, *designed by Fraver, suggests the two eras represented in the show's two acts.*

What I feel?
You know exactly how I feel.
Why do you insist
You must hear the words,
When you know I cannot give you words?
Not the ones you need.

One of the most wonderful things about musical theater is its use of song for things that are hard to talk about. Deep feelings that cannot be articulated are especially affecting when expressed in song. The music could have been as touching as these words, but at the brink of providing the melody they deserve, he again returns to the repeating of phrases as before. George heartbreakingly concludes,

There's nothing to say.
I cannot be what you want.

Perhaps the script is dealing with two simple stage issues, the making of the painting and a slender love story, but Sondheim's lyrics combine them masterfully to evoke an artist's commitment to work and the emotional price he pays for it. When Dot, pregnant with George's child, announces (hoping to provoke him) that she is going to America with Louis, there is a bitter eloquence in the lyrics.

DOT
What do you want, George?

GEORGE
I needed you and you left.

DOT

There was no room for me.

GEORGE

You will not accept who I am.
I am what I do—
Which you knew,
Which you always knew,
Which I thought you were a part of!

DOT

No,
You are complete, George.
You are your own.

Sondheim is justifiably proud of writing "I am what I do" and says, "I feel that all creative artists reveal themselves more in their work than in their conversations. An artist isn't *only* what he does. He is also a human being but the core of a serious artist is what he does." And he is right.

On yet another Sunday, George again sketches. His painting is almost done. Besides Dot and her baby, many of the figures in Seurat's painting have been assigned characters—the baker Louis, a workman, a pair of loud-mouthed American tourists (a tired joke, all the more tired for their being Southerners), a couple of girls and their soldier beaux, some of George's patrons, and now his mother. He sketches her and they talk. In their song ("Beautiful"), Sondheim defines beauty not as inherent but as the artist's perception—"What the eye arranges/Is what is beautiful"—while shaking the show from its lazy orbit toward a first-act climax. The act's finale, "Sunday," is introduced within this piece, and then the stage is set for the finishing of the painting as well as the love story.

George tells Dot that their daughter, Marie, "is not my child. Louis is her father now. Louis will be a loving and attentive father. I cannot because I cannot look up from my pad." (Lapine's dialogue is simple and formal so as to seem translated from French.) Finally rejected, Dot leaves as George says, "I am sorry." She pauses but does not turn, and it is a very sad moment. The final tableau is at hand.

Once again George intones, "Order. Design. Tension. Balance. Harmony." More to the point, the forces of theater are brought together: Drama. Music. Scenery. Lighting. The figures take their positions in the painting. The orchestra surges, at last bringing a full sound to support the gorgeous climactic song. It is as if Sondheim had been waiting to complete the music along with the painting. Now both are on display, and the company sings in ensemble, melodiously and harmoniously. The orchestra rises, the singing expands, and the painterly lyrics are not important ("Sunday/By the blue/Purple yellow red water"). The music is rich and rewarding, set to a gentle rock beat (call it pointillism). The line keeps rising and so does the volume, as the final props fill in the tableau. When everything and everyone is in position, the stage freezes. The artist beholds his work. A framed copy of the painting drops in front of the stage picture. The first act is ended.

Is another act necessary? Sondheim thinks so. "To me without the second half, the show is a stunt." But *is* there a second act?

It opens as the first one concluded, with the living tableau of "La Grande Jatte." A quirkily syncopated opening number ("It's Hot Up Here") effectively puts the audience in a bouncy mood, and in a brief recapitulation it relates to the first-act opening. There is good fun in the lyrics for the eternally frozen people in the painting ("I am completely out of proportion," "I trust my cigar is not bothering you—unfortunately, it never goes out," "Don't you ever take a bath?", and so on).

The subjects discuss the artist ("his work was not as mechanical as some suggested") and his death ("no one knew he was ill until the very last day"). Then the time and setting change to the Art Institute of Chicago, where "A Sunday Afternoon on the Island of La Grande Jatte" is presently exhibited.

Dot's baby daughter, Marie, is now an old woman whose grandson is a modern-day Seurat, a kinetic sculptor. Also named George, he introduces his latest work, a laser-generating piece that looks like something out of a "Frankenstein" movie and is called a "chromalume" (from Seurat's "chromoluminarism"). Its unveiling is followed by a reception for the artist, museum officers, donors, and critics. For this, Sondheim wrote a long musical/dramatic sequence that suddenly brings *Sunday in the Park with George* to exciting life.

The way for this sequence, its music as well as its words, had been paved in the first act. Now, fully realized and developed, it sets the show on a new course. This is assertive music, no longer dominated by dryness and dissonance but supported by them. The more potent elements of melody, harmony, and rhythm have come to the forefront. The satiric dialogue and lyrics are woven so deftly that there is no sense of this even being a song and the energy is jolting after the vagueness and diffusion of what has come before.

This classic Sondheim sequence is called "Putting It Together." In its expression of an artist's anger about needing to court investors, it reflects his own experiences. "The anger in 'Putting It Together,' " he said, "is the same kind of anger that is in 'Opening Doors' [*Merrily We Roll Along*]. It's about the artist's plight in the contemporary world. And ever since the days when patronage stopped it's just very hard to make a living."

> Say "cheese," George,
> And put them at their ease, George.
> You're up on the trapeze, George.
> Machines don't grow on trees, George.
> Start putting it together . . .

The dialogue that Sondheim sets to music mocks the art scene without becoming heavy-handed.

PATRON #1

This is the third piece of yours I've seen. They are getting so large!

GEORGE

> *(To audience, putting a cutout in his place)*
> Art isn't easy—
> Even when you're hot.

PATRON #2

> *(To the cutout)*
> Are these inventions of yours one of a kind?

GEORGE

> Advancing art is easy—
> *(To patron)*
> Yes.
> *(To audience)*
> Financing it is not.

Small talk winds through the singing, some of it as dialogue and some of it as lyrics: "The board of the foundation is meeting," "You'll come to lunch," "Trying to make connections," "Trying to form collections." There is an inevitable mocking of art talk: "There's nuance, and there's response, there's relevance." Absurd opinions are offhandedly expressed: "Anyway, the painting ["La Grande Jatte"] is overrated."

Through it all, George seethes:

The climactic full stage replica of the Seurat painting provided a stunning visual effect.

Link by link,
Making the connection . . .
Drink by drink,
Fixing and perfecting the design.
Adding just a dab of politician
(Always knowing where to draw the line),
Lining up the funds but in addition
Lining up a prominent commission,
Otherwise your perfect composition
Isn't going to get much exhibition.

This magnificent sequence initiates a second-act score composed in an entirely different musical language from the first, which was set in 1884 and dealt with an avant-garde artist; its music reflected his vision in that period. The second act not only occurs a century later, but it reflects the artist's emotional development. Young George is seeking to relate to people as his great-grandfather could not. He is trying to get past color and light, trying to transcend "painting the hat" (living only for work) to connect with another person. This is expressed in a newly earnest musical voice. Even two shows later, Sondheim thought his last three songs for this second act were "as moving as anything I've done so far."

They start after "Putting It Together" has left George and his grandmother Marie alone with the Seurat painting. Marie looks up at her mother, Dot, in the painting and sings to her about him. It is a jazz-inflected waltz, "Children and Art." It is unfortunate she has to sing it like an old woman because it is an exquisite piece.

> Mama said, "Honey,
> Mustn't be blue.
> It's not so much do what you like
> As it is that you like what you do."
>
> Mama said, "Darling,
> Don't make such a drama,
> A little less thinking,
> A little more feeling—"

Sondheim remembered that "Robert Barrow [his music teacher at college] taught us the principle that is prevalent in *Sunday in the Park*—that art is hard work." Maturing at fifty-three, he seemed to have decided that making art is not the goal; making beauty is, and that requires humanity.

In the next scene, Marie has died and George ponders his great-grandmother Dot's red grammar book. The song is "Lesson #8," and it is very beautiful, very pained. Is being what you do enough? Does the artist, by observing and expressing life, miss it?

"Lesson #8" is like a lesson from Oscar Hammerstein. It is about the need to relate to another person, to love and say so. Sondheim's lyrics are in the language of Dot's reading primer.

> George looks around.
> George is alone.
> No use denying
> George is aground.
> George has outgrown
> What he can do.
> George would have liked to see
> People out strolling on Sunday . . .

In the beautiful "Move On" that follows, Dot materializes, and George talks to her about having nothing to say and not knowing where to go. How is he to stop making endless "chromalumes" (as perhaps Sondheim felt he had made clever Broadway musicals) and "make things that count?"

> GEORGE
> . . . Notice every tree . . .
>
> DOT
> Understand the light—
>
> GEORGE
> . . . Understand the light . . .
>
> DOT
> Concentrate on now—
>
> GEORGE
> I want to move on.
> I want to explore the light.
> I want to know how to get through,
> Through to something new.
> Something of my own—

Mandy Patinkin and Bernadette Peters were well suited to the roles of George and Dot, but Sondheim had written his music with different voices in mind. George's songs were composed for bass-baritone, and Patinkin is a lyric tenor; Dot's music was for lyric soprano and she has the chest voice of a musical comedy singer. Sondheim transposed what he had already written into singable keys and wrote the rest to suit their voices.

In the second act of Sunday in the Park with George, *the painter's great grandson, a sculptor who works with laser light, confronts Seurat's masterpiece.*

These words are so earnest. They are what Seurat had said a century earlier.

DOT

Stop worrying if your vision
Is new.
Let others make that decision—
They usually do.
You keep moving on.

Look at what you've done,

Then at what you want.
Not at where you are,
What you'll be.
Look at all the things
You gave to me.
Let me give to you
Something in return.

GEORGE

. . . Something in the light,
Something in the sky,
In the grass,
Up behind the trees . . .

Things I hadn't looked at
Till now:
Flower in your hat.
And your smile.
And the color of your hair.

Talking about these later songs, Sondheim's musical director and conductor, Paul Gemignani, said, "Steve single-handedly saved *Sunday in the Park with George* by going home and killing himself writing [those] great songs . . . 'Lesson #8' and 'Children and Art'—because the show was going to die."

No question, the songs in the brief and virtually plotless second act are startlingly different from those in the first and are tremendously satisfying. Their melodies are strong with consonant tone combinations that evolve through gratifying harmonies into full resolutions. Michael Starobin's orchestrations fulfill Sondheim's elegant arrangements while dispensing with the first act's severity. At the end of the second act there is no harshness, no glassy sound. This instrumentation is acoustic, the feeling is soft and honest; the strings and brass, even in the small orchestra, make a voluptuous sound.

The show had played a four-week engagement in the tiny (135-seat) Playwrights Horizons theater before being transferred to Broadway and the Booth Theatre for a May 2, 1984 opening. There, Lapine was heartsick about people walking out "in droves" at every preview. Since his background was with more experimental theater, *Sunday in the Park with George* did not seem particularly unorthodox to him, but, he said, "I guess for Broadway it was." His distress amused Sondheim. "I mean, he had never seen anyone walk out of a show! You don't walk out of Joe Papp's theater. You stay there whether it's shit or not. I said, 'James, you ought to come and see more of my shows. This is called 'what they do.' "

Then the *New York Times* critic, Frank Rich, liked it so much that for a time he seemed to be the show's press agent. *Sunday in the Park with George* eventually ran for 604 performances and won the Pulitzer Prize for drama. It didn't make any money, but Sondheim and Lapine had blended the professionalism of the commercial theater with the adventurousness of the avant-garde to make a different kind of musical. That was important.

Sondheim's work has such reach, there is so much emotional resonance, that many observers take it personally and become as fascinated with the artist as with the art; they see him in his work. In the case of *Sunday in the Park with George*, comparisons were made between Sondheim and Seurat, the unrecognized, disengaged loner who, like Robert in *Company*, could not make an emotional connection. James Lapine was bemused by the comparisons. "Steve," he said, "is very much Mr. Social Responsibility, head of the Dramatists Guild and all that. And very social. It seemed to me he was a tremendous success. Seurat was never a success in his time."

Still, the resemblance was striking.

INTO THE WOODS

After a musical that Sondheim himself considered "weird," he couldn't be blamed for wanting to write something that was "fun and entertaining." He wanted to do it with Lapine because he had enjoyed the collaboration; it had stretched him as an artist and as a man. He seemed to be playing a more forceful role in the overall creation than he had with Prince, and the partnership with a poet had evoked a poetic strain in his own work. That would frustrate those who doted on his Broadway stuff. Some would call him a chameleon whose work changed with his collaborators, but that was based on the notion that an artist should have a marked style. Sondheim certainly had a musical identity, and whatever the approach, his voice could be detected; moreover he was perfectly capable of writing catchy music when the subject called for it (as would the movie *Dick Tracy*). More important had been his decision, ever since *Company*, to create a special kind of music to suit each show. That was his rarest and most important musical talent; it was, in fact, unique.

As nothing he had done with Harold Prince had been traditional, so it still was. To be "fun and entertaining" might have been the new show's purpose, but *Into the Woods* would hardly be a musical comedy. It would bring together assorted characters from fairy tales: Cinderella, Little Red Ridinghood, Rapunzel, Jack (of beanstalk renown), and others. Connective tissue would be provided by Lapine's own original fairy tale, the story of a Baker and his Wife who are childless because of a witch's curse. They would be the central characters, and yet because they are not mythical like the others, they would seem like outsiders in this fairyland. They would be the audience's surrogates.

Even a fairy-tale musical by Stephen Sondheim was bound to have its share of twentieth-century angst. The show would involve nervousness and frustration, ambivalence and anxiety. Since Lapine shared Sondheim's interest in psychology, the introspection factor was going to be high.

The show's central notion is that most fairy tales are about a wish and a search to fulfill it. Thus the theme:

> Into the woods
> To get the thing
> That makes it worth
> The journeying.

and,

> Then out of the woods,
> And home before dark!

Sondheim and James Lapine discuss an idea for Into the Woods.

Rejecting the simple fairy tales found in children's books and Walt Disney movies, Sondheim and Lapine went back to the sources. They also considered the interpretations of psychologist Bruno Bettelheim, whose book *The Uses of Enchantment* deals with symbolism in these children's stories.

Lapine took what he called "an anti-Bettelheim approach." Inclined toward the theories of Carl Jung, he felt that fairy tales too often offer false hope, the promise of a happy ending or better (worse), a happily *ever after*. Sondheim felt they encouraged selfishness and social irresponsibility. Being responsible for other people became, for him, the final message of *Into the Woods*.

The show starts, naturally, with "Once upon a time . . ." A nattily dressed narrator says it, but then there is a startling burst from the orchestra. It warns the audience that despite the familiarity of the fairy tales, there are surprises ahead. The burst launches a rhythm in the strings, a steady staccato of quarter notes. It is a vamp to get the evening started.

"I wanted it to be jaunty," Sondheim says of that vamp, for these characters are regularly walking through the woods. The steady beat, or variations of it, will thread the show together and keep its pace.

The narrator continues, ". . . in a far-off kingdom lived a fair maiden, a sad young lad and a childless Baker with his Wife." And there they are, in adjacent cottages on a set that looks like a children's pop-up picture book. With that the introduction to the title number starts, as they all sing of their wishes. Cinderella wants to go to the King's three-day Festival, the Baker and his Wife want a child, and Jack wants his cow to give some milk.

CINDERELLA	BAKER & WIFE	JACK
The King is giving a Festival.	More than life . . .	I wish . . .
I wish to go to the Festival . . .	More than riches . . .	
	BAKER'S WIFE	I wish my
	More than anything . . .	cow would
		give us
		some milk.
	BAKER	
More than anything . . .	I wish we had a child.	
	BAKER'S WIFE	
	I want a child . . .	(to his cow)
I wish to go to the Festival.		Please, pal.

Thus the show is launched and with it, the song "Into the Woods." This piece will provide a musical continuity heard on and off throughout the evening. It is inspired by such children's songs as "The Farmer in the Dell," "Here We Go 'Round the Mulberry Bush," and perhaps most consciously, "Heigh-Ho, Heigh-Ho (It's Off to Work We Go)" from the Disney movie *Snow White*. These all have steady, jaunty, strollable staccato beats, and "Into the Woods" definitely establishes that same rhythm.

There has been a trend toward making opening numbers as long as possible, so as to establish fully the musical convention. The opening number of *Into the Woods* was to date Sondheim's longest and most ambitious sequence of interwoven music, lyrics, and dialogue. In it, many of the other characters are introduced: Little Red Ridinghood, Cinderella's Stepsisters, a Witch, even characters some may have forgotten from the fairy tales—Jack's Mother, for instance, and Cinderella's Father. Still to come are Rapunzel, Little Red Ridinghood's Grandmother, the Big Bad Wolf, and *two* Prince Charmings. Even without them, the number covers a tremendous amount of exposition, continuing for some thirteen minutes. That is a theater eternity, so if the audience is to be held for all that time, the number must seem to play in a trice. Otherwise the show will be lost along with the audience's attention.

The story is told within it as Little Red Ridinghood goes to the Baker, singing,

> I wish . . .

> It's not for me,
> It's for my Granny in the woods.
> A loaf of bread, please—

while Cinderella's nasty Stepmother throws a pot of lentils into the fireplace and snarls,

> I have emptied a pot of lentils into the ashes for you.
> If you have picked them out again in two hours' time,
> you shall go to the ball with us.

The Witch tells the Baker that his parents stole from her garden.

> I said, "Fair is fair:
> You can let me have the baby
> That your wife will bear.

> And we'll call it square."

That baby, the Baker's sister, is (though he doesn't learn it till later) none other than Rapunzel of the long golden tresses, locked high in a tower. Warming to this sense of coincidental humor, Sondheim and Lapine add that the Baker's father took something else from the Witch's garden:

The special beans!

I let him go,
I didn't know
He'd stolen my beans!
I was watching him crawl
Back over the wall—!

And then bang! Crash!
And the lightning flash!
And—well, that's another story,
Never mind—

But the Witch is not yet finished, for angrily,

I laid a little spell on them—
You, too, son—
That your family tree
Would always be
A barren one . . .

Next door, the Witch continues, now explaining to the Baker and his Wife how they can reverse the curse and have children. Sondheim deftly sets this detailed exposition into lyrics:

You wish to have
The curse reversed?
I'll need a certain
Potion first.

Go to the wood and bring me back
One: the cow as white as milk,
Two: the cape as red as blood,
Three: the hair as yellow as corn,
Four: the slipper as pure as gold.

Bring me these
Before the chime
Of midnight
In three days' time,
And you shall have,
I guarantee,
A child as perfect
As child can be.

Go to the wood!

Cross-cutting yet again, the focus returns to Cinderella's Stepmother and Stepsisters, who are leaving for the palace. By now, there has been such an accumulation of urgency, such goals, such purposes, such nervousness, and such anticipation that when the ongoing vamp—that pulsating, walking rhythm—propels the opening sequence toward its conclusion, a real head of steam has been built up.

ALL (variously)

To see—
To sell—
To get—

To bring—
To make—
To lift—
To go to the Festival—!

Into the woods!
Into the woods!
Into the woods!
Then out of the woods
And home before dark!

In writing the music for *Into the Woods*, Sondheim broke with his practice of finding a composer to serve as inspiration. As a result there is a certain disparity of musical styles in this show. He says, "I wanted it to have a dry sound so it wouldn't get like the wet Walt Disney," but his own sound *is* dry. "I wanted it to be very simple in the sense of *diatonic* [based on the do-re-mi scale] and 'up'—bouncy, bubbly."

He feels that with its light dissonances, its occasionally sharp but not jarring harmonies, and its "crisp" lyrics, the score is not unlike *Forum*, *Company*, or *Merrily We Roll Along*. It does share a Broadway flavor with those shows, except that *Into the Woods* is a small-scaled work and doesn't flex their show business muscles; it is a chamber musical with a chamber music feel to it.

The first of the characters to go into the woods is Red Ridinghood on the way to her grandmother's house. She is confronted by the Wolf, whose approach is amorous and whose intentions are gustatory. "Hello, Little Girl" reflects his duplicity—first the leer in a bluesy beginning, with lots of sinister dissonance and a deep bass accompaniment, almost like Sportin' Life's songs in *Porgy and Bess*; then the number becomes a soft-shoe glide, smooth and sly as vaudeville, complete with brush strokes on the snare drums. Throbbing beneath it is the show's opening vamp, the steady, pulsating beat. The number is fun and funny, always getting a hand.

Next the Baker fulfills the first of the Witch's demands, finding a cow as white as milk. He pays Jack for it with five of the six beans he finds in his coat pocket. As he counts them out, a xylophone strikes a tone for each, stating a beans melody—B flat, E flat, F, D, C—that Sondheim will cash in on later. Meantime Jack bids a forlorn farewell to Milky-White. His song ("I Guess This Is Goodbye") is nearly maudlin, although Sondheim considers it a real love song (if one with a comic ending). At least it's short.

On the other hand, the ensuing "Maybe They're Magic" provides the Baker and his Wife with a real husband-and-wife dialogue. Here is a compelling, even enthralling melody accompanied by harmonies that all but pay homage to the Ravel string quartet. This piece deals with a fairy-tale couple in contemporary terms—a marriage in which the wife, stronger than the husband, intimidates him into behaving against his principles. He feels guilty for having given Jack only beans in exchange for the cow. His Wife has no qualms about that, for she believes that the end—in this case, having a child—justifies the means, or as Sondheim puts it punningly,

No, what matters is that
Everyone tells tiny lies—
What's important, really, is the size.

Only three more tries
And we'll have our prize.
When the end's in sight,
You'll realize:
If the end is right,
It justifies
The beans!

Into the Woods is very much about morality. As Lapine says, "The notion of lying and what these characters have to do to get what they want is an important theme." Morality also plays an important part in Sondheim's life. It would be difficult to lie to him twice.

By now the woods are like Grand Central Station. Red Ridinghood has momentarily escaped the Wolf, while Cinderella runs into the Baker's Wife, who is fascinated with the ball and the Prince ("Is he charming?/They say he's charming"). Her duet with Cinderella ("A Very Nice Prince") is a musical interlude, rather than a formal song, but its lyrics are the thing. They define the Wife's dishonorableness; they dramatize Cinderella's uncertainty about the Prince; they continue the Wife's search for the Witch's requirements (golden shoes now); and they reveal that a stalk is growing from Jack's beans. Sondheim's lyrics deliver all of this information while humorously setting colloquial expressions in a storybook context.

BAKER'S WIFE

Is he everything you've ever wanted?

CINDERELLA

Would I know?

BAKER'S WIFE

Well, I know.

CINDERELLA

But how can you know what you want
Till you get what you want
And you see if you like it?

Now they are all moving quickly through the woods, not only the Baker's Wife and Cinderella but also her father, Stepmother, and Stepsisters, the Baker, Little Red Ridinghood, Rapunzel, Jack, his Mother and the Witch. The first midnight strikes; the Witch has given the Baker and his Wife just three days to satisfy her demands, the same three days as the Prince's three-day Festival. Jack, meantime, has climbed the beanstalk and stolen some of the Giant's gold despite the hospitality of the Giant's wife. He returns terrified and sings of what he's seen to a rather catchy, loping melody not unlike a Harold Arlen show tune.

> A big tall terrible giant at the door,
> A big tall terrible lady giant sweeping the floor.
> And she gives you food
> And she gives you rest
> And she draws you close
> To her giant breast,
> And you know things now that you never knew before,
> Not till the sky.

There are two distinct strains in this wonderful song. The main theme is a sly and original variation of traditional theater music. It alternates with an anxious theme set to a jittery rhythm when Jack sings of what happened up there:

> And your heart is lead
> And your stomach stone
> And you're really scared
> Being all alone . . .

Composer Sondheim helps lyricist Sondheim by putting a painfully extended dissonance on "alone," giving the word the anxiety that is its due. The song, which is quite affecting, trades in an emotional quality similar to *Sweeney Todd*'s "Not While I'm Around." Different musically, they are both sung by a simpleminded lad frightened by a powerful force.

Right:
Danielle Ferland played Red Ridinghood to Robert Westenberg's Wolf in Into the Woods. *The score for this show displays everything Sondheim has to offer, from the catchy to the esoteric.*

Far right:
Familiar fairy-tale characters were reinterpreted in Into the Woods: *Jack the Giant Killer became a simple-minded murderer and Red Ridinghood was a street-smart kid with a penchant for cracking wise.*

Costumes for the show were designed by Ann Hould-Ward; the Baker and the Baker's Wife are shown here.

In this more complicated case, however, the Giant is not the evil one; the evil one is Jack, who stole the gold. ("What interested Steve and me," Lapine said, "is that the nicer people would be less honest.") Like the Baker's Wife, he will pay for his immorality.

Of all the characters, as Lapine points out, "the Witch [for all her bluster] is in some ways the most honest of all. I think that theme is evident throughout the show—that you can't always equate nice with good."

Meantime a comic moment is at hand, as two obnoxious Prince Charmings run into each other, and they are brothers. Sondheim has always been good with such braggarts, from Miles Gloriosus in *Forum* to Count Carl-Magnus in *A Little Night Music*. In "Agony," a barcarole-like operetta piece arranged for a richly harmonized duet, each dares the other to match his suffering. One is in love with Rapunzel, locked high in a doorless tower and dementedly babbling a wordless obbligato; the other has lost Cinderella, as she fled his ball at midnight. Their self-centered suffering always gets healthy laughter.

If Sondheim is influenced in any area by his collaborators, it is in the area of humor. James Lapine has the kind of quirky humor that hearkens back to *Forum*, and it is reflected in Sondheim's lyrics.

RAPUNZEL'S PRINCE
You are everything maidens could wish for!

CINDERELLA'S PRINCE
Then why no—?

RAPUNZEL'S PRINCE
Do I know?

The girl must be mad!

You know nothing of madness
Till you're climbing her hair
And you see her up there
As you're nearing her,
All the while hearing her
"Ah-ah-ah-ah-ah-ah-ah-ah—"

BOTH

Agony!

CINDERELLA'S PRINCE

Misery!

RAPUNZEL'S PRINCE

Woe!

BOTH

Though it's different for each.

That dry last line may be the funniest. Sondheim usually writes songs in the order they are performed, unless he is stuck for an idea, and he is not stuck here. The music for these songs is rich and darling, one number laughing its way out, another charming its way in. The Baker and Wife follow with a duet that has all the wit and catchiness of old-fashioned musical comedy—except that it deals with psychological material.

They are doing well in their quest for the Witch's demands. They have the white cow, the hood from Little Red, and some yellow hair, which the Baker's Wife yanked from Rapunzel's head. All that is lacking is the golden slipper. The Wife encourages the Baker ("You've changed, /You're daring. /You're different in the woods"). Her music is lyrical and comforting. She makes him feel good about their marriage, and the music is cheerfully responsive to that. In the spirit of Rodgers and Hart, "It Takes Two" is a lilting and entirely engaging musical comedy number.

Its lyrics are wise, witty, and technically precise. The notion is for Baker and Wife to compliment each other, she praising his manliness, he acknowledging her help after first insisting on going it alone. Sondheim works his way through enough plays on numbers and tenses, colloquialisms and rhymes, to make the overriding wisdom almost unnoticeable, when in fact it is unmistakable.

BAKER

It takes one
To begin, but then once
You've begun,
It takes two of you.
It's no fun,
But what needs to be done
You can do
When there's two of you.

If I dare,
It's because I'm becoming
Aware of us,

As a pair of us,
Each accepting a share
Of what's there.

That was only a quintuple rhyme in the last chorus. Then the song is resolved with conclusive harmonies and a blizzard of word games about numbers, as the couple looks forward to a baby at last. Sondheim starts toward the end with the "walking" rhythm that has been running through the show. By the time he gets to the finish line, he has taken this delightful song through the kind of harmonic changes that bring smiles to everyone but the musically dead.

Beyond woods,
Beyond witches and slippers and hoods,
Just the two of us—
Beyond lies,
Safe at home with our beautiful prize,
Just the few of us.

It takes trust.
It takes just
A bit more
And we're done.
We want four,
We had none.
We've got three.
We need one.
It takes two.

In the thick of such delightful work, Sondheim does not forget the larger purpose. Planted in the lyric is the corrupt seed, the trouble ahead—"Beyond lies/Safe at home with our beautiful prize." For this Wife is insidiously encouraging her husband to act immorally. Meantime the second midnight passes, leaving only one day for the Baker, his Wife, and Cinderella to get what they wish.

The atmosphere is now turning ominous. The Witch dotes on Rapunzel, having had her since infancy, and panics when she learns that a prince has been visiting the girl at the tower. Her song is needy, "Stay with Me," and her words are maternal—"Children must listen"—but they are also threatening, for this is a fearsome mother. Now Sondheim's beat becomes a frightening version of the show's signature jaunt. Indeed, the song starts with Rapunzel's shriek of fright.

She wants to leave the tower, which sends the Witch first to raging ("Why could you not obey?/Children should listen"), then imploring ("I am ugly/I embarrass you"). Although "Stay with Me" is more of a sung scenelet than a song, it does transmit one of the authors' messages: "Stay a child while you can be a child."

Frustrated, the Witch flies into a fury, cuts off Rapunzel's long yellow hair, and exiles the girl, while her pursuing prince falls into a patch of thorns and is blinded. Red Ridinghood has turned bloodthirsty, replacing the cape she gave to the Baker with a new one made from the skin of the Wolf. Jack, obsessed with his mother's poverty, has made a second climb up the beanstalk, this time stealing the Giant's golden eggs and the hen that laid them. Fairyland seems imbued with immorality.

Then Cinderella enters on one shoe, having intentionally left the other on the steps of the palace. She is the character that Sondheim and Lapine discussed at greatest length, and perhaps taking all of this too seriously, they decided she had a self-worth problem. In "On the Steps of the Palace," Sondheim even provides her with a self-questioning song to serve this

identity crisis. In it she reviews her thoughts as she stood with one shoe stuck in the pitch that the Prince had spread in anticipation of her flight. This becomes so complex, and the music is so muted to support the complicated lyric, that after a while the song becomes a run of words. From moment to moment, funny lines pop out ("Why not stay and be caught?/You think, well, it's a thought"), and Sondheim plants the shoe clue in the thick of nine straight rhymes to emphasize that Cinderella intentionally left it behind on the steps.

> You know what your decision is,
> Which is not to decide.
> You'll just leave him a clue:
> For example, a shoe.
> And then see what he'll do.

Now it's he and not you
Who is stuck with a shoe,
In a stew,
In the goo,
And you've learned something too,
Something you never knew,
On the steps of the palace.

What she learned, Sondheim says, is the power of flirtation and the value, sometimes, of letting someone else make a difficult decision for you. Not everyone would agree with that; indeed, not everyone would be so interested in Cinderella's psychology—or be able to follow all of this.

When she trades her remaining golden slipper to the Baker's Wife for a good pair of running shoes, the couple has everything the Witch has asked for, and that is the beginning of everyone getting their wishes. But one of the good signs is actually a bad one: The Giant is killed falling when Jack cuts the beanstalk behind him as he flees. Everyone is too satisfied to worry. Theirs is not mere happiness, but fairy-tale happiness—happiness "Ever After."

For this first-act finale, Sondheim provides some of his most spirited music ever and a rare example of choral writing. Its style is mock-operetta, and as such the piece holds its own in company as heady as Bernstein's *Candide* overture. "Ever After" sets out at a dizzy pace, the show's most breathless yet. It erupts into dazzling counterpoint, with jubilant inner voices and exhilarating syncopation. Short as it is, before the piece is over, one's breath and heart are won away. For sheer joy in show music, only a Gershwin overture can compare.

Though it's fearful,
Though it's deep, though it's dark,
And though you may lose the path,
Though you may encounter wolves,
You mustn't stop,
You mustn't swerve,
You mustn't ponder,
You have to act!
When you know your wish,
If you want your wish,
You can have your wish,
But you can't just wish—
No, to get your wish—

Here the music, the orchestra, and the ensemble plow right back into the main theme. Sondheim brilliantly recapitulates, in one brief lyric, all the wishes, all the journeys, first for the good, then the bad—everything that has happened.

Into the woods to lift the spell,
Into the woods to lose the longing.
Into the woods to have the child,
To wed the Prince,
To get the money,
To save the house,
To kill the wolf,
To find the father,
To conquer the kingdom,
To have, to wed,

To get, to save,
To kill, to keep,
To go to the Festival!

Into the woods,
Into the woods,
Into the woods,
Then out of the woods—
And happy ever after!

With the start of the second act, everyone has more wishes. Cinderella wants another ball, Jack misses the Giant's kingdom in the sky, and the Baker needs another room in his cottage for the baby. Still they feel "happy ever after"—until the roof falls in, quite literally, with a great crash. The Baker's cottage has caved in; the Witch's garden, next door, is destroyed and so is Red Ridinghood's cottage.

So, once more, it is "into the woods," this time to find the Giant they all realize is responsible for the destruction. Although the melody is the same, Sondheim's harmonies lend an eeriness and a wariness to what had at first been a theme for adventure. It is into the woods to slay, to flee, to fix, to battle, to, as Cinderella sings, "see what the trouble is."

Meantime the two Prince Charmings sing a reprise of "Agony" that is even funnier than the first time, for one of these newlyweds has now fallen in love with the Sleeping Beauty, while the other has discovered Snow White. Perhaps in studying Sondheim's growth as a composer and artist, his wizardry with lyrics has been taken for granted. That talent is as gaudy as ever:

RAPUNZEL'S PRINCE

I found a casket
Entirely of glass—
   (as Cinderella's Prince starts to shrug)
No, it's unbreakable.
Inside—don't ask it—
A maiden, alas,
Just as unwakable—

BOTH

What unmistakable agony!
Is the way always barred?

RAPUNZEL'S PRINCE

She has skin white as snow—

CINDERELLA'S PRINCE

Did you learn her name?

RAPUNZEL'S PRINCE

No,
There's a dwarf standing guard.

With everyone combing the woods, the ground shakes and a female Giant looms above—the enraged widow—and she demands Jack. Slaying the Giant may have been heroic in the fairy tale, but it is murder to Lapine, and he uses that insight to start an epidemic of misfortune among the fairy-tale folk.

That is the start of the second act, but Lapine, like many writers, is going to depend on death when at a loss for story invention. The first to go is the narrator, who is sacrificed to the Giant almost for a laugh. Then Jack's Mother is accidentally killed, and Rapunzel is trampled to death by the Giant. The grief-struck Witch swears to hand Jack over to the Giant because of that. Her "Lament" is a powerful song, overflowing with a mother's pain. Its theme is the five notes Sondheim had designated for the beans—B flat, E flat, F, D, C. Is that because all the trouble began with the beans? It isn't really clear, but as she sings the music cries out with lunging tones for the lyric's open, sobbing vowels.

> How could I, who loved you as you were?
> How could I have shielded you from her
> *(looking up the Giant's home)*
> Or them . . .
> *(looking at the group)*

This is the most emotional song in the show, and its feeling is reflected in the bass line serving as a foundation for this mournful and elegiac melody. The words express Sondheim's lifelong concern with teaching and his sensitivity to parenthood, despite never having had a child of his own. He agrees with Lapine that, most of all, the show is about parents and children.

> No matter what you say,
> Children won't listen.
> No matter what you know,
> Children refuse
> To learn.
>
> Guide them along the way,
> Still they won't listen.
> Children can only grow
> From something you love
> To something you lose . . .

Sondheim declines to see this wonderfully pained melody to its conclusion, instead cutting it short to stress the sense of loss. As relief, he provides a song for Cinderella's cheating husband, a lecherous Prince Charming. It is as funny as "Agony." Like Leonard Bernstein, when he is writing a funny song, Sondheim seems to write prettier and catchier music, as if he is (a) enjoying the laughs and (b) musically relaxed because he knows everyone is paying attention to the words. "Any Moment" is a delightful stretch of waltz, even danceable (but, like all of Sondheim's shows except *Follies*, there is virtually no dancing in *Into the Woods*). To "Any Moment," Cinderella's Prince seduces the Baker's Wife, beginning with the suggestion,

> Any moment, big or small,
> Is a moment, after all.
> Seize the moment, skies may fall
> Any moment.

He continues to kiss her and then carries her into the woods, after which she asks whether they will see each other again. His response is a cad's:

> This was just a moment in the woods.
> Our moment.

And she is left to ask, "What was that?"

Then she reflects on such "Moments in the Woods." It is submitted that Stephen Sondheim is the only figure in Broadway musical history who would write a charm song about moral compromise. The song begins with a romantic verse ("Did a Prince really kiss me?") set to one of the composer's patented French waltzes. Wondering "Was it wrong?", the Wife reminds herself to be realistic and "Stop dreaming . . . Back to child, back to husband," because there is right and wrong, "shouldn'ts and shoulds."

But, she ponders, is a choice necessary? The music becomes appropriately assertive and beguiling, as the lyric slyly offers a solution to a choice between righteous duty and wrongful pleasure:

> Why not both instead?
> There's the answer if you're clever:
> Have a child for warmth,
> And a Baker for bread,
> And a Prince for whatever—

Drawing a moral for herself, if not a moral one, she concludes,

> Let the moment go . . .
> Don't forget it for a moment, though.
> Just remembering you've had an "and,"
> When you're back to "or,"
> Make the "or" mean more
> Than it did before.
> Now I understand—

Amusing as this number is, it is incidental to the action and it does not carry much force. In fact the second act has already begun to loosen, if not unravel entirely, and in virtually the same place as in *Sunday in the Park with George*—when the show seems naturally ended because the main story (there, of the painting; here, the fairy tales) is over. In the first show, there was virtually no plot after the intermission; in this one, there is too much.

In the second act, the idea is for the atmosphere to darken as the characters, having gotten their wishes, deal with the consequences. That starts when the Baker's Wife is crushed to death by a tree that the Giant knocks over. The Baker, Cinderella, Little Red Ridinghood, and Jack all blame each other for this second Giant, singing a patter song, "Your Fault." The Witch shuts them up with her "Last Midnight," which begins with a good and spooky theme and evolves into a mocking waltz, which is familiar territory for Sondheim. As with the last few songs, though, he seems to be struggling to find substance or purpose for his musical numbers. In this case, what begins as a warning veers into moralizing and concludes with the Witch leaving them alone to cope by themselves.

It is interesting how Sondheim the composer and Sondheim the lyricist affect each other. When there is a real dramatic purpose for a song, something substantial to be said, the music seems to take energy and heart from the words, inspired by the mood and the ideas ("Lament" is a good example). But when, as with these last two songs, there is no real reason for the song, the music seems more like good work and less like good art.

When a play runs out of plot ideas, of deaths, of steam, the last resort is moralizing. Badly needing to end, *Into the Woods* heads for the final curtain trading its surprises, good humor, and originality for moral platitudes and shorthand wisdom. The Baker throws his hands up and asks for "No More"—for respite, for surcease, for no more questions, and:

> No more riddles.
> No more jests.
> No more curses you can't undo,
> Left by fathers you never knew.
> No more quests.
> No more feelings.
> Time to shut the door.
> Just—no more.

But the tragedies that have befallen him have not been convincing enough for us to identify with his spiritual exhaustion. As "No More" goes on (and it does), its overwrought decency is replaced by something even worse, a cry for utopian simplicity.

> No more giants,
> Waging war.
> Can't we just pursue our lives
> With our children and our wives?

Reminiscent of the finale of *Candide* ("Make Our Garden Grow," by Leonard Bernstein and Richard Wilbur), this is just too falsely naive after the sophisticated taste preceding. Affirmation may be traditional for finales, but it didn't hang comfortably on *Company* and it doesn't hang comfortably here. It just isn't *Sondheim*, and that goes back to his not writing like Oscar Hammerstein. Nice isn't always good. Moreover, although "No More" sounds like a finale it isn't the finale. It sets one up by asking,

> How do you ignore
> All the witches,
> All the curses,
> All the wolves, all the lies,
> The false hopes, the goodbyes,
> The reverses—

That cues the similarly inspirational "No One Is Alone," which has been criticized for being trite and sentimental. Sondheim is rankled by that, but his defense is not strong. "It means," he says, "everything you do affects everyone else." There is no reason to doubt his sincerity, but as Cinderella says to Red Ridinghood,

> Mother cannot guide you.
> Now you're on your own.
> Only me beside you.
> Still, you're not alone.
> No one is alone, truly.
> No one is alone.

She certainly sounds like the greeting-card platitude Sondheim is disavowing. It is only later in the song that she sings of communal responsibility.

There is yet another finale, "Children Will Listen," to tell the audience that besides communal responsibility, the show is also about parents and children. This is simply too many finales and messages, and if a show has to announce its moral, it would be better off dropping the subject. There is almost a sigh of relief from the show itself when *Into the Woods* finally slides into the final reprise of the title song. There are still more morals—this musical simply does not tire of giving advice—but at least they come at the end of the story, where morals belong.

> Into the woods,
> But not too fast,
> Or what you wish
> You lose at last.

However, the show scores so many points in its first hour and a half that the goodwill carries it along, even when things fizzle toward the end.

Into the Woods was first staged at the Old Globe Theatre in San Diego and, with revisions, was brought to Broadway's Martin Beck Theatre on November 5, 1987, playing a healthy 764 performances and ultimately turning a profit. That made it the first profitable Sondheim show in the eight years since *Sweeney Todd*. That was a fact of Sondheim's commercial life.

ASSASSINS

Four years later, at an age (sixty-one) when most Broadway composers were retired or had used up the enthusiasm of youth, Sondheim not only wrote the most youthful and audacious show of his career; he wrote the *defining* show of his career.

Assassins is a musical about people who tried to kill American presidents. At first glance seemingly reckless in subject matter, at final examination it displays Sondheim at a peak of professional and artistic assurance. It is also a work of unimpeachable craftsmanship and integrity. If, as a whole, it was not in all ways successful, there is an electricity about it, a muscle, and vast power.

A dark vaudeville about the nature of our country and the American spirit, *Assassins* is an examination of the richness of our myths and the dangers in depending on them for personal fulfillment.

Did *Anyone Can Whistle* startle anyone, an absurdist musical about madness? Was it risky to write a Kabuki musical, *Pacific Overtures*? Was *Sweeney Todd* off the beaten track, a Victorian melodrama about cannibalism? What about the arty, musically daunting *Sunday in the Park with George*? Sondheim does not consider these works radical but understands that Broadway audiences are drawn to the familiar. "I write the unexpected," he says.

In such company, *Assassins* would seem the most "unexpected." Its cast of characters includes successful assassins—John Wilkes Booth, Charles Guiteau (Garfield), Leon Czolgosz (McKinley), and Lee Harvey Oswald—and failed ones—John Hinckley (Reagan), Squeaky Fromme and Sara Jane Moore (Ford), and Samuel Byck, who hijacked an airplane with the intention of crashing it into President Nixon's White House. Some of these people were deranged, some were hapless, some were seriously dedicated to their beliefs.

Sondheim insists, not disingenuously, that he and librettist John Weidman were surprised by the reaction to their idea as offensive. Certainly, had it been a *play* about assassins, there would have been no quarrel with the subject matter. But for many people, a musical—even a serious one like *West Side Story*, *The King and I*, or the Sondheim-Prince collaborations—is still a *musical*.

"People thought that we were going to trivialize the subject," Sondheim said, but he believes that music adds a powerful emotional element to theater, and that some of the most serious subjects might be more seriously treated with that added element. No artistic medium is in itself profound or trivial—only the mentality that uses it.

On the other hand, musical theater is generally perceived as light entertainment. That is a fact of life, and Sondheim's shows must prove otherwise every time. In this instance, he and Weidman underestimated the continuing trauma of John F. Kennedy's murder. What was bothersome about *Assassins* was not a musical treatment of assassins generally, but of Kennedy's murder in particular. Stephen Sondheim might have made even that work, but did anyone care to see him try? (In fact, he made certain there was no song involving Oswald.)

His and Weidman's notion was to examine our history of assassination and to portray it as perhaps a perverse tradition, but an American one nonetheless. Instead of viewing the assassins as freaks and misfits outside the American experience, the authors saw them as products of it, victims of it, people who misread the guarantee of the right to the pursuit of happiness as the right to be happy.

The opening number of Assassins, "Everybody's Got the Right," is set in a carnival shooting gallery.

BOOTH

Free country—!

SHOOTING GALLERY PROPRIETOR

—Means your dreams can come true:

BOOTH

Be a scholar—

PROPRIETOR

Make a dollar—

BOTH

Free country—!

BOOTH

Means they listen to *you*.

PROPRIETOR

Scream and holler—

BOOTH

Grab 'em by the collar!

BOTH

Free country—!

BOOTH

Means you don't have to sit—

PROPRIETOR

That's it!

BOOTH

—And put up with the shit.

This, the opening number, presents Sondheim at the peak of his genius as a composer and lyricist. Setting a litany of "Free country!" to an angry counterpoint ("scream and holler") and swathing it in pained dissonances, he has musicalized John Weidman's script into something beyond lyrics, music, and dialogue. At the same time the needs of an opening number are served. The show business style of the music tells the audience they will be entertained, even though the characters are frustrated, paranoid assassins.

Sondheim agrees with music director Paul Gemignani's contention that his score for *Assassins* "reacted to Weidman's energy and push and anger," but he had his own moral urgency. No longer a child of show business—the wolf boy who was brought up in a world of overtures and showstoppers—he had developed a sense of responsibility and perspective.

Inspired by the despair of the pained, frustrated, and self-righteous assassins, he harnessed the power of their disenfranchisement. His lyrics are frightening because they so accurately and simply replicate the ideas we are taught as children—and then twist them. This is the American promise that can so easily be taken as a guarantee by the forlorn—the promise broken.

The music offers the candy of that promise, a catchy melody for sweet and simple ideas, laced with clashes that betray the lie. This first number is based on Broadway show tunes; the score is generally based on America's music. The sources range from mountain folk songs to the music of Stephen Foster. In some cases, following the example of Charles Ives, Sondheim quotes or paraphrases—for instance, John Philip Sousa's "Stars and Stripes Forever." Elsewhere he is inspired by barbershop quartets or the classical music of Aaron Copland.

Weidman's script is written in revue form, with each assassin explained by a skit or musical number. From the opening sketch (a carnival shooting gallery—"C'mere and kill a president!") to a visit by John Wilkes Booth inspiring Lee Harvey Oswald, the writing maintains a tone of savage simplicity. By the end, with the assassins singing as a group, Sondheim sums up, in music and words, "all the lamentations that have existed for 130 years over the deaths of these presidents." That summation is "Another National Anthem" for these confused and tragic people who are profoundly convinced that they are abused heroes, patriots

In the London production of Assassins, *Lee Harvey Oswald leads a chorus of his fellow-killers.*

who have been wronged and unfairly denied the American rewards. It is set to harsh, marching snare drums.

SAMUEL BYCK

Listen . . .
There's another national anthem playing,
Not the one you cheer
At the ball park.

SARA JANE MOORE

Where's my prize? . . .

BYCK

It's the other national anthem, saying,
If you want to hear—
It says, "Bullshit!"

LEON CZOLGOSZ

It says, "Never!"—

CHARLES GUITEAU

It says, "Sorry!"

ASSASSINS

It says: Listen
To the tune that keeps sounding
In the distance, on the outside,
Coming through the ground,
To the hearts that go on pounding
To the sound
Getting louder every year—

Listen to the sound . . .
Take a look around . . .

We're the other national anthem, folks.
The ones that can't get in-
To the ball park.

Spread the word . . .

There's another national anthem, folks.
For those who never win,
For the suckers, for the pikers,
For the ones who might have been . . .

Only Stephen Sondheim could have written *Assassins*. The originality of its subject matter is his territory and so is the artistic sophistication, the nobility of commitment.

Assassins was presented for two months at the tiny off-Broadway Playwrights Horizons theater early in 1991. It was not moved to Broadway, and perhaps that was just as well, considering the many outraged reactions as well as a certain overall lack of cohesiveness. That would have meant, in the past, that it had failed, but Sondheim has transcended such rules. He writes on a stage greater than Broadway's, and this show has since been recorded and produced in theaters around the country and in London.

The show reflects his politicization. In 1992 he rejected the National Medal of Arts Award presented by the National Endowment for the Arts. His reason, he wrote to its officers, was that the endowment had been "transformed into a conduit, and a symbol, of censorship and repression rather than encouragement and support."

Stephen Sondheim once described Oscar Hammerstein II as "a moral man," a brief and awesome description. These are not moral times, and "morality" itself has become a watchcry for the narrow-minded, a code word for ultraconservatism.

Ethics and decency are out of fashion, but "moral" is a significant word in Sondheim's vocabulary. As an adolescent under Hammerstein's guidance, his most important lesson was not about writing lyrics or structuring a musical; it was about the responsibility of having intelligence and applying it to all things in life—and that includes morality first of all.

His career has been a triumph of artistic morality as a factor of intelligence and personal character. His pursuit of the best in his work has been uncompromising. Hammerstein, toward the end of his life, expressed an interest in leaving show business to do more important work for society, perhaps in government. It is hardly surprising that the career of his best student, in summation and at last, was likewise dedicated not only to artistry but to expressing what is intelligently right.

INDEX

CREDITS